KURT VONNEGUT

**Recent Titles in Contributions to the
Study of Science Fiction and Fantasy**

Folklore and the Fantastic in Twelve Modern Irish Novels
Marguerite Quintelli-Neary

A Century of Welsh Myth in Children's Literature
Donna R. White

Strange Constellations: A History of Australian Science Fiction
Russell Blackford

Immortal Monster: The Mythological Evolution of the Fantastic Beast in Modern Fiction
and Film
Joseph D. Andriano

Young Adult Science Fiction
C. W. Sullivan III, editor

Spiritual Exploration in the Works of Doris Lessing
Phyllis Sternberg Perrakis, editor

The Road to Castle Mount: The Science Fiction of Robert Silverberg
Edgar L. Chapman

Back in the Spaceship Again: Juvenile Science Fiction Series Since 1945
Karen Sands and Marietta Frank

Tolkien's Legendarium: Essays on *The History of Middle-earth*
Verlyn Flieger and Carl F. Hostetter, editors

Space and Beyond: The Frontier Theme in Science Fiction
Gary Westfahl, editor

Transrealist Fiction: Writing in the Slipstream of Science
Damien Broderick

Science Fiction, Children's Literature, and Popular Culture: Coming of Age in Fantasyland
Gary Westfahl

KURT VONNEGUT

Images and
Representations

Edited by
Marc Leeds and Peter J. Reed
Foreword by Kurt Vonnegut

Contributions to the Study of Science Fiction and Fantasy,
Number 83

GREENWOOD PRESS
Westport, Connecticut • London

Library of Congress Cataloging-in-Publication Data

Kurt Vonnegut : images and representations / edited by Marc Leeds and Peter J. Reed ;
foreword by Kurt Vonnegut.
      p. cm.—(Contributions to the study of science fiction and fantasy, ISSN 0193–6875 ;
  no. 83)
    Includes bibliographical references and index.
    ISBN 0–313–30975–2 (alk. paper)
    1. Vonnegut, Kurt—Criticism and interpretation. 2. Science fiction, American—History
and criticism. I. Leeds, Marc. II. Reed, Peter J. III. Series.
PS3572.O5Z754   2000
813′.54—dc21   99–016096

British Library Cataloguing in Publication Data is available.

Library of Congress Catalog Card Number: 99–016096
ISBN: 0–313–30975–2
ISSN: 0193–6875

First published in 2000

Greenwood Press, 88 Post Road West, Westport, CT 06881
An imprint of Greenwood Publishing Group, Inc.
www.greenwood.com

Printed in the United States of America

The paper used in this book complies with the
Permanent Paper Standard issued by the National
Information Standards Organization (Z39.48–1984).

10 9 8 7 6 5 4 3 2 1

Contents

Foreword

Kurt Vonnegut

"Everything was beautiful, and nothing hurt." When I was middle-aged, as six of my seven children have since become, I said I wanted that for my epitaph. Now, in September of 1999, I am nearly seventy-seven, having so far lived five years longer than my architect father and twenty-five years longer than my mother, a failed fiction writer. And I still want that for my epitaph: "Everything was beautiful, and nothing hurt." A reporter this past summer asked me how come?

"Because I got off so *light*," I said.

Would you look at this book? It is a collection of cordial essays about words it was my destiny to put on paper in any case. I could not help myself. Five are by close friends of many years (Reed, Weide, Leeds, Rackstraw, Klinkowitz), and the rest by total strangers. That I should have a champagne success like this book, and be completely in print in my sunset years, is a surprise. I was completely out of print when I went to work at the Writers' Workshop at the University of Iowa in 1965, thirty-four years ago.

If this isn't nice, what *is*?

Everything was beautiful, and nothing hurt.

Acknowledgments

The editors wish to thank, yet again, Kurt Vonnegut for his friendship, generosity, and appreciation of our work. We have individually written and collaborated on a total of five volumes about Kurt Vonnegut, and none of those texts would have been possible without his cooperation. We particularly wish to thank Kurt and Joe Petro III for permitting reproduction of their artwork in this book. This is the second time they have granted us such kind permission. The first opportunity was when we published *The Vonnegut Chronicles* (Greenwood Press, 1996).

We also wish to thank the contributors to this volume who have entrusted us with the material efforts of their hard work. It is a trust we take seriously and respectfully. We also extend our thanks to Catherine Lyons and Elizabeth Meagher, our editors at Greenwood, for their encouragement, dedication, and good humor.

Leslie A. Fiedler deserves special recognition for granting the editors the privilege of reprinting for the first time his seminal essay, "The Divine Stupidity of Kurt Vonnegut." Though much has been written about Vonnegut over the last twenty-five years, perhaps no single work about him is better known among hardcore Vonnegut critics than Fiedler's. However, the essay was in danger of becoming little more than a rumor because it is regularly torn from the crumpled 1970 pages of *Esquire* housed in libraries across the nation.

Once again, our spouses deserve much of the thanks and credit for the appearance of this work. Maggie Reed and Saralyn Gold are truly forgiving souls. The best we can say in defense of our occasional inattention to them is that our little hobby keeps us at home. Now that this book is finished, we will once again train our energies on ministering to them as they have so unselfishly done for us.

KURT VONNEGUT

Introduction

Peter J. Reed and Marc Leeds

Almost thirty years ago, Leslie Fiedler, the widely acclaimed critic of his time concerning contemporary literature and culture, published his seminal essay "The Divine Stupidity of Kurt Vonnegut." Appearing in the September 1970 issue of *Esquire*, it followed closely upon the publication of Vonnegut's *Slaughterhouse-Five*. At that point Vonnegut had achieved much popular acclaim after twenty years of largely overlooked publication. But Fiedler's essay nevertheless was seminal in giving academic respectability to Vonnegut's recently won accolades. Vonnegut has often lamented that critics put his work in a drawer labeled science fiction, then proceed to use the drawer as a urinal. Taking a view not then widely shared, Fiedler delighted in Vonnegut precisely because he had written science fiction, putting him squarely in the historical mainstream of American popular fiction.

Today, when popular culture has largely displaced the study of literature in American universities, and when Vonnegut may be viewed more as sage than radical, Fiedler's essay hardly appears a departure in its espousal of the American tradition of the Pop Fiction novel over the High Art novel, and of Vonnegut in particular. This collection of essays, one more book among the scores that have been written about Vonnegut since "The Divine Stupidity," amply demonstrates how far-sighted Fiedler's judgment was and how widely his notions have been accepted.

Fiedler's essay, restored here to general access from the fading pages of a vintage *Esquire* by his kind permission, anchors a collection that reaches from Vonnegut's beginnings to the comments of some younger readers and critics among his current audience. One of Fiedler's more prescient remarks is his recognition of Vonnegut's impulse away from words toward visual images. That observation was borne out in his enthusiasm for theater during the production of his play *Happy Birthday, Wanda June*. More recently there have been other film and theater adaptations of the novels, and this collection acknowledges that growing activity. Over the last decade, much as Fiedler suggests, Vonnegut himself has devoted more and more of his time and energy to graphic art, producing paintings that are then silk screened by Joe Petro III of Lexington, Kentucky. We include a sampling of that work. Hence our subtitle, *Images and Representations*, for this book records not just the images and representations created by Vonnegut the literary artist, but examines the images and representations of his thought that increasingly are being brought to life in other media.

For Fiedler, the epitome of Vonnegut's genius was *The Sirens of Titan*, the marvelous science fiction novel that he applauds because "in it he dares not only to ask the ultimate question about the meaning of human life, but to answer it." Science fiction and the other modes of pop fiction contrast with the High Art novel in being "'thin' books—all fantasy and plot, and characters in two dimensions." Such novels "possess our imaginations," he says, because they capture not the High Art novel's "exclusive fantasies of alienation and choseness, but dreams he shares with everyone else." Vonnegut has "—as writers of, rather than *about*, mythology must—written books that are thin and wide, rather than deep and narrow, books which open out into fantasy and magic by means of linear narration rather than deep analysis; and so happen on wisdom, fall into it through grace."

Yet Fiedler sees Vonnegut as a transitional figure in whom something "has always yearned to be a serious writer, to win respect from those professors whom he affects to despise." That tendency "is betrayed in his habit—untypical in Pop fiction—of putting writers and artists at the center of his books." Collections such as this one, and the many critical texts now published on Vonnegut, certainly confirm professorial approval, sought or not. The habit of centering his novels on writers and artists has become emphatically more evident in the novels written since Fiedler's essay.

While Fiedler is unquestionably right in describing Vonnegut as a writer "of, rather than [like the modernists] *about*, mythology," what of his assessment that Vonnegut, as a transitional figure, may be moving increasingly from fantasy to analysis? Certainly *Breakfast of Champions*, the first novel after Fiedler's essay, pointed in this direction. At the time Vonnegut suggested in an interview that he suspected that his writing would become increasingly didactic. The later novels certainly appear more analytical in their currency, their attention to social commentary, and their moral observation. Yet they retain the breadth of mythology through their artistic visions, as in *Deadeye Dick* and *Bluebeard*, or the sweep of fantasy through the perspective afforded by science fiction, as in *Galápagos* and *Timequake*.

Vonnegut's later novels might also be seen as moving in the direction of deeper, more complex characterizations than the "characters in two dimensions" that typify science fiction. One wonders whether some of the early characterizations were really quite that flat; Howard Campbell's self-deceptive confession adds to his complexity, for example. But the later Eugene Debs Hartke of *Hocus Pocus* and Rabo Karabekian of *Bluebeard* are both characters revealed with considerable complexity and depth through their probing first-person narrations. Their portrayals may remain too focused on surrounding events to equal the introspection and psychological minutia of a Joyce or Woolf, but they certainly transcend in depth the level of characterization typically found in science fiction.

In the same way, it is difficult today to think of Vonnegut in terms of science fiction in the way that Fiedler could in 1970. Science fiction has continued to have a place in Vonnegut's writing, but primarily as a source of parables and plot devices, rather than as dominant mode. Of course, Vonnegut quite early disclaimed this categorization of his work and suggested he was simply writing out of his experience in an increasingly technological world and his training in the sciences. He has often used science fiction, in novels such as *God Bless You, Mr. Rosewater*, or *Slaughterhouse-Five*, to add a dimension to events otherwise set in the mundane world. He thus diminishes the distinction between the fantastic and the "real," and can more easily mythologize events. Essentially, then, the uses of science fiction help Vonnegut establish his postmodern vision of existence.

All of which would seem to confirm Fiedler's view of Vonnegut as transitional. He has given depth to Pop Art, but clearly remains in a different camp from High Art. Perhaps this explains the tendency for Vonnegut to no longer quite satisfy his earlier fans who liked the fantasy and science fiction of *The Sirens of Titan* or *Cat's Cradle*, or those who have always trivialized him for not conforming to the expectations of High Art. His being in this sense transitional, however, might be exactly what makes him the man for the season, the appropriate voice for an age of flux and transformation. That is what the following essays will explore.

The Divine Stupidity of Kurt Vonnegut

Portrait of the Novelist as Bridge over Troubled Water

Leslie A. Fiedler

I first read Kurt Vonnegut, Jr., as I now know was proper, in paper, and at the urging of a fourteen-year-old son. He came to me, that is to say, not off the shelves of a library, but from the same world of disreputable entertainment to which comic books and beloved bad movies belong: the world of the pleasure rather than the reality principle, the world of the young rather than the old.

I grew up, for better or worse, in a generation and a class for which literature seemed more a duty than a self-indulgence. And I was a father before I was prepared to admit that books, even the very best of them, can, maybe should, be used to subvert the world of duty and work and success. I don't mean that I did not in fact make such uses of some of them when I was myself still a son and an adolescent, merely that I insisted they be kosher, which is to say, checked out as classics and/or avant-garde masterpieces by accepted critics.

At any rate, I began, at the behest of my son, with Vonnegut's *Player Piano* (then called, as I remember, *Utopia 14*), which moved me oddly, though I still managed to avoid having to come to terms with it by tucking it away in the category of "Science Fiction." And I continued to read his books as science fiction whenever they came to hand on supermarket bookstalls. I am, like everyone else I know, an inveterate impulse buyer and commodity consumer.

Then, just three or four years ago, I was reminded that for some almost as young at this moment as my son was when he first introduced me to Vonnegut, his books seemed more scriptures than commodities. I had been asked for the first time to a university not under the auspices of the English department, but on the invitation of the students themselves; and at the end of my three-week stay was given two books which, to my hosts, represented the kind of writing that compelled their deepest assent: Claude Levi-Strauss' *La Pensee Sauvage* and Vonnegut's *The Sirens of Titan*. It was still the point before student aspiration had been fully

---

By kind permission of the author, this is the first reprint of "The Divine Stupidity of Kurt Vonnegut," which originally appeared in the September 1970 issue of *Esquire*.

politicalized; and I suspect that now such secret scriptures are more likely to be Maoist or Trotskyist than structuralist and fantastic. Still, in this area one nail does not necessarily drive out another; and only last year a group of English students (who would supply me, before the official release date, with lyrics of new Bob Dylan songs) were asking that two books be added to a reading list of post–World War II novels: Ken Kesey's *One Flew Over the Cuckoo's Nest* and Kurt Vonnegut's *Cat's Cradle*.

But Vonnegut seems an odd choice really, being not only immune to Left politics, but neither a pothead like Allen Ginsberg, or an acidhead like, say, Ken Kesey—or even a reformed heroin addict, like William Burroughs. He is—or so he claims in autobiographical asides—only an old-fashioned juicehead, a moderate boozer, now a couple of years past forty-five; and given—when liquored up—to remembering *his* war, which is to say, World War II, rather than World War III which didn't happen, or those smaller ones which did, in Korea or Vietnam. But it is those other wars which possess the imaginations of the young, especially the last, which may, indeed, be the first ever fought by Americans on marijuana rather than whiskey. What, then, has made Kurt Vonnegut an underground favorite of the young?

It is partly, I suppose, the fact that structurally, archetypally speaking, the space-odyssey is the same thing as the "trip"; and that having chosen the mode of Science Fiction, Vonnegut has subscribed to a mythology otherwise sustained by smoking grass or dropping LSD, or, for that matter, simply sitting half-stunned before the late, late show on TV. In a certain sense, it can be said that the taking of drugs is a technological substitute for a special kind of literature, for fantasy—an attempt to substitute chemistry for words; and it can thus be understood as a kind of midterm between science fiction and actual manned flights into outer space, those trips to the moon or Mars, which can be read as the final expression of technology imitating art. And, of course, becoming art once more as television records them.

Not Proust-Mann-and-Joyce, those "thick" books dense with realistic detail, symbol and psychological analysis, but the Western, Science Fiction and Porn, "thin" books all fantasy and plot and characters in two dimensions, possess our imaginations now; or at least so certain writers whom young readers prefer have come recently to believe. Novelists nurtured on the tradition of High Art and avant-garde, and therefore initially committed to a dream of surviving on library shelves and in classroom analyses, learn now that only the ephemeral lives the real life of literature these days, in living hearts and heads; and they begin, therefore, to emulate the Pop forms, which means begin to aspire to making it in paperback.

The long-predicted death of the Novel turns out to be the death of the Art Novel, the "poetic" novel read by an elite audience to whom high literature represents chiefly the opportunity of verifying their own special status in a world of slobs committed to the consumption of "mass culture." Quite "serious" writers, writers who kid neither themselves nor their readers, register their awareness of this in ways many of their most ardent readers seem not yet quite to understand. But only in this context is it possible to see clearly what John Barth was up to either in

The Sot-Weed Factor, where in re-creating Pocahontas he created the Dirty Western, or in *Giles Goat-Boy*, where he married Rabelais to Science Fiction. So, too, the more recent work of William Burroughs, *The Ticket That Exploded*, for instance, only makes real sense to one who realizes how much in it comes from releasing the standard images of run-of-the-mill science fiction in a haze of junk. And he, too, begins now to move toward the classical form of the Western, first and most authentic variety of American Pop—that tale of the male companions, red and white, in flight from women and in quest of the absolute wilderness, which has recently been reborn in books as various as Ken Kesey's *One Flew Over the Cuckoo's Nest*, Truman Capote's *In Cold Blood* and Norman Mailer's *Why Are We in Vietnam?* It was all there in James Fenimore Cooper to begin with, has remained there in the Pop underground ever since, and rises to the surface whenever an American writer wants to indulge not his own exclusive fantasies of alienation and chosenness, but the dreams he shares with everyone else.

Some American writers, John Updike, for instance, and Philip Roth, have been too inhibited by their own parochial commitments to the provinces of High Art as defined by *The New Yorker* or *Partisan Review* to make it back into the world of the Western or up and out into the world of Science Fiction, They, too, have felt the pressure to move toward the world of Pop and have responded by creating—in *Couples* and *Portnoy's Complaint*—fantasies of sex rather than of the Virgin Forest or Outer Space, turning to what Alberto Moravia once described as the last place where urban men (and who more urban than Roth, more suburban than Updike) live in nature. "I am not a Jewish sage," Roth has said recently, talking of his newest book, "I am a Jew Freak like Tiny Tim!" It is his instinct for survival which is speaking; and how splendidly he has survived the death of the Jewish Art Novel the record of sales for *Portnoy's Complaint* sufficiently indicates. But woe to writers, Jew and Gentile alike, who do not respond as he does, since the Novel must cease taking itself seriously or perish.

Vonnegut has had what we now realize to be an advantage in this regard, since he began as a Pop writer, the author of "slick" fiction, written to earn money, which is to say, to fit formulas which are often genuine myths, frozen and waiting to be released. Fortunately, though he has sometimes written to suit the tastes of middle-aged ladies who constitute the readership of the *Ladies' Home Journal*, he has tended more to exploit the mythology of the future. But he has, in any case—as writers of, rather than *about*, mythology must—written books that are thin and wide, rather than deep and narrow, books which open out into fantasy and magic by means of linear narration rather than deep analysis; and so happen on wisdom, fall into it through grace, rather than pursue it doggedly or seek to earn it by hard work. Moreover, like all literature which tries to close the gap between the elite and the popular audiences rather than to confirm it, Vonnegut's books tend to temper irony with sentimentality and to dissolve both in wonder.

Inevitably, however, critical approval has overtaken him; and he appears now elegantly produced between boards—misrepresented, as it were. And who could wish it otherwise, for criticism's sake at least, since he is a test case for the critics. When I was young, literary critics thought they knew for sure that it was their function to educate taste: to rescue a mass audience, largely middle-aged, from an addiction to outworn sentimentality and escapism, to prepare them to read what was newest and most difficult. Suddenly, however, it is the mass audience which leads the critics, educating them, for now it is the critics who are middle-aged, the big audience that is young; rescuing them from an addiction to outworn irony, and teaching them to read for the sake of a joy deeper than that of mere culture-climbing. Understandably enough, many survivors of the old critical regime find it difficult to persuade themselves that if, recently, they have come to esteem Vonnegut, it is not because they have been converted to the side of Pop, but because—though they did not at first realize it—he has all along belonged to the other side of High Art.

Confusion in this regard extends even to Vonnegut's publishers, or at least to the writers of his jacket copy, who assure us that "Once mistakenly typed as a science-fiction writer, he is now recognized as a mainstream storyteller." But all is presumably set straight; for we are also informed he has taught at the University of Iowa Writers Workshop. It is true, of course—however belatedly the universities and copywriters have come to acknowledge it—that Vonnegut *does* belong to what we know again to be the mainstream of fiction; it is not the mainstream of High Art, however, but of myth and entertainment: a stream which was forced to flow underground over the past several decades but has now surfaced once more.

To be, for a while, thus invisible is, in any case, not necessarily bad; art renews itself precisely in the dialectical process of disappearing, reappearing, disappearing. And just as the invisibility of the avant-garde, its unavailability to contemporary criticism at the beginning of the twentieth century, was a source of health and strength for an elitist, neoclassic tradition; so the invisibility of Pop, its immunity to fashionable judgment, seems in mid-twentieth century to have been a source of health and strength to what we now recognize as the New Romanticism: an art which prefers sentimentality to irony, passion to reason, vulgarity to subtlety. But sentimentality and passion and vulgarity had long been consigned to the outer darkness by such reigning critics as T. S. Eliot and Cleanth Brooks. And, as always when seeking renewal, art had to descend into that darkness which exists on the blind side of the critics' heads.

Moreover, for young readers the invisibility of Pop in general, Science Fiction in particular, has seemed a warrant of its relevance, a sign that by virtue of being unavailable to their elders, it belonged especially to them, to *their* "underground." And yet they could not forebear bringing the buried treasure they had discovered to the surface, bugging their presumed betters, urging their parents and teachers to share the pleasures of Pop—in Vonnegut, or, for that matter, Andy Warhol and [Roy] Lichtenstein, or vintage comic books or movies starring John Wayne. To do so, however, is to make the invisible visible, the hidden manifest, to translate certain artists from the paperback shelves or pornographic bookstores to the classroom and the required reading list, which creates confusion for all concerned.

And yet finally who can regret the whole ironic process; since to writers like Vonnegut, on the border between New Pop and Old High Art, their initial invisibility is a torment which leaves scars, if not disabling traumas. To check through the *Book Review Index*, for instance, and discover that from 1952 to 1963 no book of Vonnegut's is recorded as having appeared or been reviewed is to understand the persistent defensiveness which underlies his playful-bitter references to his status as "a writer of science fiction." Even in his latest collection of short stories and articles, which appeared in 1968 under the title of *Welcome to the Monkey House*, he is still fighting it out, saying ironically, "Here one finds the fruits of Free Enterprise"; then going on to explain, "I used to be a public-relations man for General Electric, and then I became a free-lance writer of so-called slick fiction. . . . Whether I improved myself morally by making the change I am not prepared to say. That is one of the questions I mean to ask God on Judgment Day. . . . I have already put the question to a college professor who . . . assured me that public-relations men and slick writers were equally vile, in that they both buggered truth for money." The self-doubt in this latest comment is undercut by the irony. But Vonnegut was not always even this secure about what he was doing; since a writer, however much a pro, lives only days by what his stories earn him, must get through his nights on remembering what the critics say.

Perhaps Vonnegut's initial difficulty on this score, which turns out to be a final advantage, is that he is a transitional figure in a time of transition, a period in which we are rapidly leaving behind the values of Modernism: the notion propagated by such Modernist high priests as T. S. Eliot that "Culture" belongs to an elite, a tiny remnant saved by being able to appreciate an abstruse, hermetic, highly allusive and symbolic form of art. To the Modernist, Pop is a vice of the weak-minded majority, or alternatively, a sop thrown to the exploited by the Madison Avenue lackeys of their exploiters; to the Post-Modernist it is the storehouse of fantasy in which the present Future we now live was prefigured, the twenty-first century pre-invented.

Vonnegut is of two minds on the subject, alternatively, simultaneously. On the one hand, he has lived from the beginning by appealing to the great Pop audience on its own grounds, and yet something in him has always yearned to be a "serious writer," to win the respect of those professors whom he affects to despise, but whose colleague he has recently become all the same. And that something is betrayed in his habit—untypical in Pop fiction—of putting writers and artists at the center of his books. But this habit belongs essentially to the kind of Modernist book whose subject is art, whose hero the artist; and whose classic instance is Joyce's *Portrait of the Artist as a Young Man*.

Vonnegut has never, consequently, seemed to the first generation of hard-core science fiction fans a major figure in the genre, even Kingsley Amis in *New Maps of Hell*, the one broadly inclusive survey of the genre, dismissing him with a single friendly sentence. The older aficionados—weary scientists and hardworking technicians, for instance, to whom Science Fiction seemed a device for escaping rather than expanding their own sense of reality—have always preferred figures like Robert Heinlein, in whose earlier books the familiar conventions of the thriller and the detective story were transferred without fundamental change to interplanetary regions. But Heinlein ever since *Stranger in a Strange Land* has been remaking his own work on the model of Vonnegut's—using images of pursuit and discovery in Outer Space to indicate the possibilities of creating in Inner Space new values, a new language, in short, just such a New World as the New Romantics dream.

Meanwhile, Vonnegut himself, however, has been moving uneasily away from his Science-Fiction beginnings; in books like *God Bless You, Mr. Rosewater* and *Slaughterhouse-Five*, ironically playing with the form he once quite simply practiced. But disengaging from science fiction, Vonnegut seems on the point of disengaging entirely from words, and perhaps it is a weariness with the craft of fiction itself, with, at any rate, telling stories, i.e., making plots or myths, that impels him; as if he suspects the Pop Novel may be as dead as the Art Novel. More and more, he is impelled toward abstraction, the making of constellations or patterns, which may explain his recent statement that "I would enjoy becoming a painter for a while."

To understand how Vonnegut has moved, however, it is necessary to look more closely at his work to date, in particular at the six novels he has written since 1952. His short stories, collected in two volumes, *Canary in a Cat House* (1961) and *Welcome to the Monkey House* (1968), I shall refer to only in passing, since they seem to have been written with his left hand (he himself described them as "samples of work I sold in order to finance the writing of the novels") and he has no special talent for short fiction in any case.

Vonnegut's first novel, *Player Piano*, appeared in 1952, when he had just turned thirty, and was widely (if not always favorably) reviewed as a "serious" book; since, despite its projection into the future and its Science-Fiction gimmicks, it represented quite obviously the kind of earnest social criticism which suggests comparisons with quite respectable writers like Aldous Huxley and George Orwell. In its earlier pages especially, it seems now, in fact, *too* bent on suggesting such comparisons, more committed to morality than play, more concerned with editorial than invention; grimly intent on proving (once more!) that machines deball and dehumanize men—and that the huge corporation, called the Ilium Works but evidently modeled on the General Electric plant in Schenectady, for which Vonnegut once did P.R., corrupts those it nominates as an elite even as it strips of all dignity those it finds unworthy to program its computers. But before *Player Piano* is through, Vonnegut's sense of humor has mitigated his indignation, and he is pursuing (quite like those younger contemporaries, Jules Feiffer or Joseph Heller, for instance) any possibility of a joke, no matter how poor or in the midst of no matter what horror: anticipating, in fact, the mode later called, ineptly enough, "Black Humor."

What *Player Piano* conspicuously lacks, however, is a writer-spokesman at the center. Its point-of-view protagonist is a skeptical technocrat, an engineer who has lost faith in a world fashioned exclusively by those who share his skills; and among his enemies are included the kind of Pop writers who, in a world controlled by machines, provide ready-made dreams of man in a state of nature, whether bare-chested bargemen on the Erie Canal or Tarzan swinging homeward toward Jane in the treetops. Yet Vonnegut is at his best in the book when he himself indulges in Pop fantasy—anticipating what he can do best, as he invents the Ghost Shirt

Society: that association of rebels against the white man's technology, who assume the bulletproof magic garb of those desperate Indians who fought vainly to stem the tide of European immigration in the late nineteenth century, and who, like their Indian counterparts, go down to defeat, destroyed by the technology of men too stupid to know the truth of magic.

Yet he seems not to have known how to deal with what he had begun to guess; for *Player Piano* is followed by seven years of silence—seven years in which he published no novels at all, only stories for the slicks. But he emerges from that silence with a pair of books which between them constitute his main achievement: *The Sirens of Titan*, which appeared in 1959, and *Cat's Cradle*, which was published in 1963. In these two fictions, at any rate, he seems at ease—in a way he was not earlier and would not be later—with Science Fiction; finding in its conventions not a kind of restriction, but a way of releasing his own sentimental-ironic view of a meaningless universe redeemed by love; his own unrecognized need to write a New Gospel or at least to rewrite the Old; his distrusted longing to indulge his fantasy without providing the unimaginative one more occasion for idle masturbation; his unconfessed desire to escape both the stifling inwardness of the traditional Art Novel and the empty virtuosity of avant-garde experiment.

The Sirens of Titan appeared as a paperback original, perhaps because hard-cover publishers would have nothing to do with him. And yet, in a sense they did not intend, the publishers are right; what he begins in *Sirens of Titan*, confirms in *Cat's Cradle*, does not belong in hard-covers at all—being admirably suited to the not-quite-book snatched on the run in airports or picked up to allay boredom in bus terminals. Acquiring them so we are not tempted to hoard them, but to lose them as good things should cheerfully be lost (sitting down to write this article, I discovered that *all* of my Vonnegut books had been mislaid or borrowed and not returned); and reading them, we are not tempted to believe ourselves set apart by the rareness of our pleasure or the subtlety of our understanding. Like all Pop Art, they confirm our solidarity with everyone who can read at all, or merely dream over pages devoted to evoking the mystery of space and time, or to prophesying the end of man.

Mother Night, however, which appeared two years after *Sirens*, in 1961, temporarily interrupts Vonnegut's continuing exploration of the potentialities of Science Fiction—representing perhaps a desire to be more immediately topical, more directly political, more "serious" in short. It is not unsuccessful in its own terms, but finally irrelevant to Vonnegut's special vocation, though deeply concerned with Germany and World War II, which is Vonnegut's other obsessive subject matter: the past he remembers, rather than the future he extrapolates or invents. *Mother Night* does not quite manage to deal with the American fire-bombing of Dresden, through which Vonnegut actually lived as a prisoner of war—but it flirts with it throughout. This past year, he has come closer in *Slaughterhouse-Five*; but even that novel is less about Dresden than about Vonnegut's failure to come to terms with it—one of those beautifully frustrating works about their own impossibility, like Fellini's *Eight and a Half.* And it is inevitable, perhaps, that Howard W. Campbell, Jr., the protagonist of *Mother*

Night, appears in the later book as well, quoted one more (final?) time in the tale Vonnegut could not make him tell first time around.

Eschewing Science Fiction in *Mother Night,* however, Vonnegut turns to another, more established Pop form, the spy novel. It is, in fact, dedicated to Mata Hari, the evocation of whose name introduces a disturbing note of irony; since she has become not merely a byword, but a comic one. The story itself is, however, serious enough; the tale of a double agent, unable to prove for a long time that he was really in the pay of the U.S. Government and unwilling, finally, to save himself from hanging when that proof is unexpectedly offered. Self-condemned and self-executed, Howard W. Campbell leaves behind a book intended to testify that one is always—hopelessly, irrecoverably—what he pretends to be, pretends to himself he is *only* pretending to be.

Campbell is, in fact, the first major author-protagonist in Vonnegut; and, like his own author, a Pop artist before history makes him an autobiographer. He has become for the large German public a successful playwright; and for the smaller public of two, constituted by himself and his wife, a private pornographer. Once the war is over, however, and he has fled back to his native America, his works fall into the hands of a Soviet writer who achieves a second round of best-sellerdom, claiming the translated versions as his own. And why not, since such fables are anonymous, international—pass not only from hand to hand, but from country to country as well. This Campbell does not really understand—but it does not deeply trouble him. What really does is the fact that his Russian counterpart has published (with illustrations) a large edition of his own private porn—titillating the great public with what was intended for the tiniest of elites.

And if Campbell responds so extravagantly to having become, inadvertently, a pornographer, this is surely because his author is especially hung up on the subject of porn, the sole Pop form which, in fact, evades him—despite a theoretical dedication to freeing men to lead full sexual lives. Vonnegut cannot ever quite manage to talk dirty enough to be explicit about sex; though (because?) he is haunted throughout his work by a vision of his own books ending up in the display windows of pornographic bookshops, confused by owners and customers alike with hard-core pornography. He is aware really that the confusion is, on the deepest level, somehow valid; that the best of Science Fiction has in common with the shabbiest sort of erotica, not sex but "fantasies of an impossibly hospitable world."

But he is not really at ease with the fact; and throughout his work, especially as it grows more and more unguardedly confessional, there appears over and over the image of that first of all pornographic photos, in which a girl is vainly trying to screw a Shetland pony: produced, he tells us, by the favorite student of Daguerre, and therefore an apt symbol of revolutionary art becoming (quickly, quickly) a Pop commodity, to be peddled to the unwary on street corners. Yet what bugs Vonnegut even more is the awareness that in his own time pornography is practiced, and accepted, as revolutionary Art itself, a special way of telling the truth about the society we live in; and he parodies mercilessly, in *God Bless You, Mr. Rosewater,* a novelist presumably dedicated to absolute candor who ends up writing: "I twisted her arm until she opened her legs, and she gave a little scream, half joy, half pain (how do you figure a woman?) as I rammed the old avenger home"—which one suspects is intended as a put-down of Norman Mailer.

In the end, however, the spy novel proved for Vonnegut almost as unsympathetic as pornography itself—more unsympathetic, in fact, since the story of espionage posits a world of total alienation rather than one of impossible hospitality. He could not find room in it, moreover, for magic and wonder, the religious dimension so necessary to his view of man. Campbell is a writer, a popular artist, but he is not a guru, and Vonnegut could scarcely imagine him writing a new bible. What religious leaders appear in *Mother Night* are presented as comic nuts gathered together in a tiny American neo-Nazi Party: a defrocked priest and a dentist-minister, convinced that a man's teeth are the key to his character, and founder of the Western Hemisphere University of the Bible, by which, it turns out later, the witch doctor in *Cat's Cradle* has been ordained.

That shadowy figure of Dr. Vox Humana represents, in fact, the sole link between *Mother Night* and the book which follows it, in which Vonnegut returns again to the kind of Science Fiction he had already so successfully exploited in *The Sirens of Titan*, his best book, I think—most totally achieved, most nearly dreamed rather than contrived. In it, he evokes all the themes, along with their sustaining images, for which we remember him with special affection and amusement: the unreality of time and the consequent possibility of traveling therein; the illusory nature of free will and the consequent possibility of heroism and sacrifice; the impossibility of really choosing one's mate and the consequent necessity to love whomever, whatever happens to come to hand. It is, moreover, his most *chutzpahdik*, his most outrageously and attractively arrogant book; for in it he dares not only to ask the ultimate question about the meaning of human life, but to *answer* it.

But what sets *The Sirens of Titan* apart is that, inventing it, Vonnegut has escaped from the limitations of an imagination narrower and more provincial than it is ever possible quite to remember. Despite his dedication to a form predicated on space-travel, Vonnegut is oddly earthbound, American-bound really; there are, in fact, only three localities in which his invention is at home: Ilium, New York, the country around Indianapolis, and Cape Cod—not, one notices uneasily, any of those mythological metropolises so congenial to the minds of most writers of Science Fiction. In *The Sirens of Titan*, however, he imagined for the first time Tralfamadore, the transgalactic world he is to evoke again and again, but to which none of his space-travelers ever actually go; until, perhaps, the Billy Pilgrim of his last book [*Slaughterhouse-Five*], and which we are free, therefore, to understand for the absolute Elsewhere, more easily reached by art of madness than by mere technology. And he has also described in its pages Mars and a Moon of Saturn called Titan, to and from which his protagonist, Malachi Constant, shuttles, returning at last to Indianapolis, where he dies waiting for a bus.

More central, though, to Vonnegut's own development is the antagonist, who is whirled at the book's close quite out of our solar system and our ken; that Winston Niles Rumfoord, who is both author and guru, as articulate and omnipotent as Prospero on his Island, and who seemingly wants to rule the world but turns out only to have longed to create a religion. He manages in fact to launch from Mars a doomed expedition of brainwashed mercenaries, whose intended defeat causes all men on Earth to recoil from conflict and self-delusion, and to live together in peace, worshiping according to the tenets of the Church of God the Utterly Indifferent, whose messiah-scapegoat is Malachi Constant himself. But in the end Rumfoord proves as little in charge of his own destiny as Constant; since not only his two books, but all of his complex maneuvering of men—and, indeed, the whole course of human history which made his actions possible—are revealed as having been plotted, by almost immortal Tralfamadorians, intent only on getting a spare part to one of their messengers, stranded on Titan with a trivial communication to another planet far across the universe. This is not, however, the work's final word, Vonnegut's final position; for that very messenger, it turns out, though an intricate machine, has learned somehow to love in the aeons he has spent as a castaway; and he provides—like a kindly Pop artist—a vision of Paradise to sustain Malachi's dying moments; a false vision sustained by posthypnotic suggestion, but sufficient to make dying more palatable than living. It is as much of a Happy Ending as Kurt Vonnegut could imagine at this point in his career, as much of a Happy Ending—he tries to persuade us—as we need or can use.

But in *Cat's Cradle*, his next work of Science Fiction, he does not even offer us this token Happy Ending, for that book begins and ends with a vision of the total destruction of mankind, to which only an eternal gesture of contempt is an adequate response. It is a book which has nothing to do with Heaven except insofar as it is not there ("No cat! No cradle!"), though it takes place largely on an island paradise in the Caribbean, which stirs in us once more memories of that Master of Illusion, Prospero. This time, however, the Prospero who regulates the actions of everyone else is dead before the fiction begins; a certain Dr. Felix Hoenikker, referred to throughout as "the father of the Atomic Bomb." He is a more equivocal figure even than Rumfoord, the hero-villain of *The Sirens of Titan*.

The name Rumfoord appears over and over in Vonnegut's stories and novels, always signifying the kind of Groton-Harvard-educated WASP, before whom—as a Midwestern German American—he feels that fascinated repulsion all of us Americans experience confronted by some absolute alien who happens to have got here before us. The Hoenikkers, father and children, like Vonnegut bear a name which memorializes their connection with a European people who made soap of dead Jews and were themselves roasted, boiled, turned to tinder by bombs from American planes. And before those Germans he feels the fascinated repulsion all of us Americans experience confronting the particular people abroad from whose midst our ancestors fled, but who persist still in our flesh, our dreams; and with whom therefore we die a little, when we come to bomb them.

Cat's Cradle is presented as if told by an almost anonymous narrator (we learn his first name John-Jonah, are left to guess his last—Vonnegut, perhaps?), who begins by trying to write the history of total destruction (called in his case, *The Day the World Ended*), with which Vonnegut himself was still wrestling in vain. For John-Jonah, however, it was to be a book about Hiroshima rather than Dresden, and in the end he does not even manage that—his imagination (and Vonnegut's) pre-empted not by the Atomic Bomb, which did not quite end the world, but by Hoenikker's next, posthumous invention, which did: not by the final fire, but the final ice—a kind of super-ice, called *Ice-Nine*, which melts at 114 degrees Fahrenheit, and with which Hoenikker was playing like a child at the moment of his death.

John-Jonah moves among the heirs who share the invention—old Hoenikker's children, along with their lovers and friends—learning slowly, painfully how to become yet one more Vonnegut sacrificial victim: the patsy and reluctant messiah of yet one more true, i.e., false, religion. At the book's close, he lies frozen for all eternity, his thumb to his nose and a history of the world clasped to his side. He has learned this sacred gesture of contempt for the God or not-God behind the universe from Bokonon, a Black Prophet who is Vonnegut's most impressive rebel-guru; and who, just before his own suicide, composed the final sentence of his Scriptures, as if for John-Jonah's special benefit: "If I were a younger man, I would write a history of human stupidity; and I would climb to the top of Mount McCabe . . . and I would make a statue of myself, lying on my back, and thumbing my nose at You Know Who."

Indeed, the not-quite nihilism of the book's close is a product of the tension between the religion of Bokononism, which advocates formulating and believing sacred lies, and the vision granted to the dwarfed son of the Father of the Bomb of the emptiness behind all lies, however sacred. The voice of the White Dwarf and the Black Prophet are both Vonnegut's, and they answer each other inconclusively throughout; creating an ambiguity quite like that produced by the opposite claims of High Art (the Dwarf, an avant-garde painter, renders his view in monochrome abstraction) and Pop Art (Bokonon, an entertainer, sings his creed in calypso form).

But, as ever in Vonnegut, something more is presented than the unresolvable conflict of mutually exclusive theories; namely, the possibility of actual joy. John, at any rate, is revealed as having experienced two great joys before his tale is told: one slow and long-continued, as he learns who are the other members of his *karass*, the handful of others in the world with whom, willy-nilly, he must work out the pattern of his destiny: one intense and momentary, as he plays footsie with the blonde Negress, Mona, whom he, and everyone else, loves: their naked soles touching in the ecstatic union called by Bokononists *"Boko-maru." Cat's Cradle* is then a book about loving; but it is even more, as my own language has been teaching me, the words that suggest themselves to me as I describe it, a book about learning, which means, inevitably about learning a new language. It is Vonnegut's great good fortune to know this, and to be able to invent such new languages: to create terms like *karass* and *Boko-maru*, which seem to survive, in the heads of his readers, his plots and even his jokes.

Since *Cat's Cradle*, Vonnegut has written a pair of books, *God Bless You, Mr. Rosewater* (1965) and *Slaughterhouse-Five* (1969), which constitute, in fact, a single work, with common characters, common themes, common obsessions and a common whimsy—and which together rifle his earlier books for other characters, themes, obsessions and whimsical asides; as if he is being driven to make his total work seem in retrospect a latter-day Human Comedy or Yoknapatawpha series. But the last novels are quite different in their tone and effect, being essentially autobiographical rather than mythic: quasi-novels really, in which the author returns to his early material reflectively rather than obsessively—and so ends writing *about* it, rather than simply writing it; and thus falls, for better or worse, quite out of the world of Pop art. It is, perhaps, because of this fall that Vonnegut has become more available to established literary critics; or maybe his acceptance is only the inevitable triumph of time. Any writer who has lived so long (and he *has*) tends to seem at last respectable, even admirable—particularly if he is the sort of writer on whose behalf children tirelessly propagandize their parents.

Yet it is wrong finally to learn to love the late Vonnegut first, and to come to his earlier books backwards through the ones which followed. Ideally, a reader should learn his territory as he revealed it: be introduced to Ilium, New York, in *Player Piano*; to Indianapolis and Cape Cod and Tralfamadore in *The Sirens of Titan*. Vonnegut has, to be sure, returned in his last two novels to his three favorite American provinces and the single transgalactic dream world in which he feels at home; but those worlds are oddly transmogrified. Tralfamadore, especially, has been distanced and ironized into the place "where the flying saucers come from," and serves no longer to release Vonnegut into the world of Science Fiction, but only as an occasion to make rueful jokes about it.

God Bless You, Mr. Rosewater is not Science Fiction at all—not even like *Mother Night* a spy story—but a work of "mainstream literature," in which Vonnegut has transposed from the Future and Elsewhere to the Present and Right Here the themes which he once mythologized in popular, fantastic modes: the compelling need to love the unlovable, whose ranks industrialization has disconcertingly swelled; the magical power of money and the holy folly of renouncing it; the uses and abuses of fantasy itself. But the profoundest and most central concern of *Rosewater* is new for Vonnegut; seems in fact more closely related to Norman O. Brown or Michel Foucault or R. D. Laing than what he himself had dealt with earlier. We remember the novel chiefly as a book about madness, or more particularly, as one about the relationship between madness and holiness; since Eliot Rosewater—a millionaire who becomes a Volunteer Fireman and one-man Counseling Service—is the first of Vonnegut's gurus who lives *in* madness rather than *by* lies. He does not, that is to say, choose deliberately to deceive for the sake of the salvation of mankind, but is hopelessly self-deceived; insane enough to accept as truth what Rumfoord was forced to justify as useful fictions, or Bokonon to preach as *foma*, "harmless untruths."

But if *God Bless You, Mr. Rosewater* is not Science Fiction, it is compulsively *about* science fiction; and this time the writer nearest to its center (Eliot Rosewater himself has only the unfinished scraps of a fantasy novel in his desk) is Kilgore Trout, the author of scores of neglected and despised Science Fiction novels. As the name itself betrays, however (it contains precisely the same number of letters as "Kurt Vonnegut," and, indeed, the four letters of "Kurt" insist on detaching themselves from the rest), Trout is a comic, self-depreciatory portrait of his author—or rather of what his author might have been, in some sense *was*, up to the moment he wrote the book in which Trout appears. As inappropriate to one on the verge of ambiguous success, Vonnegut portrays his alter ego as an absurd failure, driven to earn his living by supervising paper boys or redeeming Green Stamps, and obsessed by the fact that his books are only available in shops that peddle porn.

Yet it is given to Trout to play an equivocal St. Paul to Eliot Rosewater's absurd Christ: to rationalize Eliot's madness in terms acceptable even to his tycoon father; and yet to prepare Eliot himself for lapsing back into insanity, alcoholism and obesity, after he has been cured of all three by a regime of tennis and tranquilizers in a madhouse. And in *Slaughterhouse-Five*, Trout returns to play a similar role for a similar sub-messiah, this time an optometrist called Billy Pilgrim, who had, as a matter of fact, been introduced to the work of Trout by Eliot himself in the psycho-ward of a military hospital during World War II.

But Billy, unlike Eliot, travels in space and time, actually reaching Tralfamadore itself (invented first by Vonnegut in *The Sirens of Titan*, then reinvented by Trout in *God Bless You, Mr. Rosewater*), where he is displayed naked in a zoo, at work, at play, on the john, and in the arms of Montana Wildhack, a Hollywood starlet imported for mating purposes. Oddly enough, however—as Vonnegut pointedly informs us—Trout had already imagined the zoo episode in fiction, and Billy had read it before living it, or dreaming it, or falling through time and space into it. Vonnegut will not, to be sure, let us side with the cynics and realists who would, by psychiatric means, cure Billy of his belief that he has been and is forever on Tralfamadore, but he leaves suspended, not quite asked, much less answered, the question of whether he travels there through Outer Space or Inner, via madness or flying saucer—or merely by means of Pop fiction, in which each of these is revealed as the metaphor of the other.

Perhaps Vonnegut does not know at all what he is really doing in his last book [*Slaughterhouse-Five*]. Perhaps he even believes what he so stoutly maintains in those sections of it which are more reminiscence and editorial than invention and fantasy; believes that he is at last writing the book he ascribed to John-Jonah in *Cat's Cradle*: the book which he precisely cannot, should not write, which is called archetypally *The Day the World Ended*, and which comes to him not out of his writer's imagination, but out of the duty he feels imposed on him by the fact that he himself lived through the fire-bombing of Dresden.

But though, like his author, Billy Pilgrim lives through that event—and returns to it eternally in contempt of time—he, like his author once more, can only return to it the way of Tralfamadore, which is to say, a world more comic and terrible and real than that of apocalyptic history. And if at last Vonnegut does not understand, all the better for him and for us. What he does not understand is precisely what saves him for readers like me who are disconcerted and dismayed as he grows more and more conscious of more and more in himself, turns more and more from fantasy to analysis.

Perhaps the process has begun to reverse itself, however, in *Slaughterhouse-Five*, or at least in those pages of it in which Billy takes his author back with him into the world of Science Fiction. I at least find occasion for hope in such passages, as I do in some remarks Vonnegut has included in a recent statement about his future plans and prospects. "I expect," he writes, "to become more and more stupid as time goes by." God bless him.

Hurting 'Til It Laughs

The Painful-Comic Science Fiction Stories
of Kurt Vonnegut
Peter J. Reed

> As for the story itself, it was entitled "The Dancing Fool." Like so many Trout stories, it was about a tragic failure to communicate.
>
> Here was the plot: A flying saucer creature named Zog arrived on Earth to explain how wars could be prevented and how cancer could be cured. He brought the information from Margo, a planet where the natives conversed by means of farts and tap dancing.
>
> Zog landed at night in Connecticut. He had no sooner touched down than he saw a house on fire. He rushed into the house, farting and tap dancing, warning the people about the terrible danger they were in. The head of the house brained Zog with a golfclub.
>
> *(Breakfast of Champions*, 58–59)

Kilgore Trout's "The Dancing Fool" typifies Kurt Vonnegut's use of science fiction, above all in being funny. But beyond its being comical, it shows some other characteristics frequently seen in Vonnegut's short stories and in the science fiction episodes in his novels. Note, for example, that while this curt account provides a minimum of context, of "how" or "why," it includes the mundane detail that Zog's landing was in Connecticut. While comical, the story has a touch of pathos in Zog's ill-deserved fate. The humor relies on hyperbole, on comic exaggeration, for much of its effect, and is highly visual. One source of the humor is in disparity, particularly that between Zog's lofty purpose in visiting Earth and the manner of its communication, and between his noble intent to save lives and his ignominious braining. These are all characteristics frequently seen in Vonnegut's science fiction short stories. They may be even more obvious in the science fiction interludes, such as the Trout inventions, in the novels. Typically, "The Dancing Fool" is not essential to its novel's main plot: used in *Black Garterbelt* magazine as filler, it could be about anything. It is comic interjection. It does have thematic connections, however, in being about communication and failures of communication. That becomes a major theme in *Breakfast of Champions*, from the failures of Rabo

Karabekian's art to communicate to its audience, to Dwayne Hoover's inverting the message of Trout's "Now It Can Be Told." The story serves, then, not only as comic interlude, but in its thematic implications, as comic fable (perhaps for the moral that "No good deed goes unpunished"). All of these features are characteristic of Vonnegut's use of science fiction, evident from his earliest short stories to the later novels.

While Vonnegut has been characterized all too often as a "black humorist" and has been exaggeratedly classified as a science fiction writer, what remains distinctive in his method is the combining of these approaches. Vonnegut's recourse to science fiction, be it in a short story entirely in that mode or simply as interjection within a larger "realistic" work, is invariably comedic and usually humorous. While it often displays the properties of farce, as in "The Dancing Fool," his science fiction frequently has a tragi-comic tone. Much of it may be described aptly as "painful comedy," where the comical vies with the hurtful. Sometimes it derives its humor from an existential sense of the absurd, in the incongruity between human (or even robot) efforts and the forces that they strive to master. Good comedy holds within it the potential for tragedy, and derives its cathartic value from alleviating broadly perceived threats or dangers. That is certainly true of many of Vonnegut's stories.

Reflecting their times, they deal with Cold War fears, the Damoclean threat of the Bomb, the lurking dangers of overpopulation and food shortage on the one hand and on the other government's Big Brotherly efforts to assuage them. The threats to the individual, of being dehumanized in an anonymous technological world, of loss of identity, purpose, or power of choice, are implied repeatedly in even lightly humorous stories. Science fiction plots provide the perfect mode in allowing Vonnegut to treat these topics without becoming bogged down in the quagmires of logic that often inhibit their more serious discussion. He can touch upon issues of free will, population control or race and gender relations, for example, with hyperbole and humor. He can thus express a philosophical point of view or make moral judgment in a manner that may avoid the resistance argumentation might invite. He gains the freedom to play both sides of an issue, and by his humor he can enlighten or provoke while entertaining. Hence, these stories often function as parables, comic and fantastic, but with moral purpose.

The novels are the most familiar of Vonnegut's writings to the majority of his audience, and painful-comic science fiction appears in them from the start. *Player Piano* (1952) has its share of both pain and humor written into its dystopian world. Its science fiction episodes usually adhere to the novel's theme of the human in combat with the machine: Paul Proteus' challenging "Checker Charley" at chess, and winning after Ed Finnerty hobbles the machine, or the Shah of Bratpuhr's challenging the mighty EPICAC XIV with a rhyming puzzle as incomprehensible to the machine as to anyone else. Sometimes "animal vs. machine" dramatizes the human conflict. The plant cat's surviving the robot sweeper only to die scaling the fence roughly parallels Paul Proteus' course in this novel, much as the luckier animal in the short story "Deer in the Works" amplifies the situation of that tale's protagonist.

The second novel, *The Sirens of Titan* (1959), moves further into the realm of science fiction, and the painful comic elements become even more conspicuous. One of the central science fiction creations of this novel is the Tralfamadorian robot Salo. This remarkable machine is described as "eleven million Earthling years old" and "four and a half feet tall." He has "a skin with the texture and color of the skin of an Earthling tangerine" and "three light deer-like legs." His inflatable feet enable him to walk on water or up walls. Salo has no arms, three eyes, and a head that is round and hung on gimbals (*Sirens*, 267–268). When anxious he lifts his feet up and down, making a squelching sound. He has been stranded on Titan for centuries for the lack of a part as simple as a beer can opener, and his Odyssey across the universe has been "a fool's errand"—his closely guarded secret message is simply "Greetings." The comic aspects of his plight are enhanced by the messages the Tralfamadorians send him by manipulating massive human constructions on Earth. Stonehenge reads "Replacement part being rushed with all possible speed." The Kremlin walls spell out, "You will be on your way before you know it" (*Sirens*, 271). While often the source of comedy, Salo also brings sentiment, even pathos, to the novel. He is loyal, compassionate, and feeling, emotions stronger in him than in the humans around him and that bring him to self-destruct. But in true comedic fashion he is repairable, and he creates the novel's happy ending by leaving Malachi Constant with a heart-warming illusion of reunion with his old friend Stony Stevenson and the message that "somebody up there likes you" (*Sirens*, 319).

While less familiar to most readers, the short stories are worth examining because many come early in Vonnegut's career where he evolves and develops his science fiction technique. Also, the short stories sometimes contain more sustained employment of science fiction than occurs in the short episodes, like the Kilgore Trout plots, that are found in the novels. There are marked similarities, however, and the characteristics briefly noted as occurring in "The Dancing Fool" emerge early in Vonnegut's work. In those early years he was working for the General Electric Company where, as he has said, he saw new technology and its implications for the future emerging all around him.[1] As a high school and college journalist Vonnegut had often used fantasized and hyperbolic renditions of events to make commentary. Combining that bent with projections of an evolving technological society quickly leads to his own style of comic but dystopian science fiction. In the early stories the technique sometimes seems aimed at engaging the interest of an audience still in the grip of a postwar "can-do" faith in scientific innovation. Later it more often expresses cynicism, anger, or even ridicule, its laughter more bitter. It can become sharper, compressed, and more fantastic as the pretense of plausibility yields to the rapidly sketched plots of Kilgore Trout. But that is to jump ahead, and it is best to start at the beginning, with Vonnegut's first published short story.

"Report on the Barnhouse Effect," which appeared in *Collier's* on February 11, 1950, records the experiments of Professor Arthur Barnhouse as presented by his assistant. Barnhouse achieves what he calls "'dynamopsychism,' or force of the mind," by following a "thought train that aligned the professor's brain cells" (18).

He then has the power to move physical objects. He begins by manipulating dice; eventually he becomes "about fifty-five times more powerful that a Nagasaki-type atomic bomb," able to destroy objects thousands of miles distant (18). The professor wants to use his power for peaceful purposes such as "moving cloud masses into drought areas," but the armed services become "interested in dynamopsychism as a potential weapon." Barnhouse resists sharing the secret of his powers, but agrees to a demonstration, destroying fleets of aircraft and warships. But in the midst of his triumph he slips away into hiding and sets about destroying the weapons of the world's powers in an effort to bring about global peace. Barnhouse's endeavors are threatened by the efforts of governments to hunt him down and by the fact that he is "of short-lived stock." While his death would mean the end of his single-handed imposition of peace, at the end of the report the writer reveals that he has decoded the last message Barnhouse left him and is now increasingly able to exercise "dynamopsychism" himself. With the clear implication he will take up Barnhouse's role, he ends the report with a simple "Good-bye."

Much of the humor in this story resides in its far-fetched plot, which nevertheless retains enough plausibility to sustain interest and suspense. Fascination with the potential of psycho-kinetic powers tends to persist, recurring in fiction and even fueling rumors of Russian experiments with it for military purposes. Its use in this story injects an element of the American "tall tale" tradition, coupling the comic use of science fiction with an established and familiar form of humor. Typically, Vonnegut quickly dispenses with seemingly logical explanations of "dynamopsychism," offering simply the throwaway note that Barnhouse achieves his power by "aligning the brain cells." The title of the process—"dynamopsychism"—is another example of Vonnegut's love of inventing comic words and language. Comic descriptions are scattered throughout the story, such as the notation that at one point Barnhouse "had the range and power of a 37-millimeter cannon, perhaps" (18). The scale of the ultimate experiment is itself comic in its sheer excess, with everything carried to a hyperbolic extreme, a carnage of ships, planes and rockets, as the delighted general chortles, "Well, sir, by George, by George, by George!" like a gleeful Sidney Greenstreet.

Barnhouse's escape and solo campaign to disarm the opposing forces before any of the competing sides can capture him and avail themselves of his powers creates the suspense in the story and is heightened with the revelation of Barnhouse's coming from "short-lived stock." That circumstance inserts a genetic joker into the plot, and introduces a human element into a science fiction setting. The solution to the problem is easy and predictable: the young narrator will carry on the professor's work. It is a surprise turn in the plot at the end that is not really a surprise, and that in itself is a comic device. Vonnegut's short stories often have a sudden turn in events that has the appearance of a surprise ending, but that we have been let in on earlier. We gain the double satisfaction of the relief that a last minute reversal typically gives, plus the rather smug satisfaction of having suspected what was to come.

The story functions as comedy in that it confronts the familiar "bogey-men" of that Cold War era and overcomes them. The pervasive fears of war, the Bomb, a military-industrial complex or an intrusive Big Brother government are dispelled—and by a human power. The professor remains invulnerable—except to his own humanity. Just as in *Player Piano*, it is human failings that at once thwart the revolution but affirm its humanity, so here Barnhouse's genes confirm his humanity against the dispassionate forces of science and militarism. Barnhouse's potential mortality threatens to turn the story toward tragedy. But the emergence of the underling, the student who will by cunning thwart the figures of authority, is a reversal in the best traditions of comedy.

"Report on the Barnhouse Effect" embodies science fiction with parapsychological overtones, and "Thanasphere," which appeared in *Collier's* on September 2, 1950, takes this direction further. Major Allen Rice, an astronaut in orbit two thousand miles above the earth, begins complaining of hearing voices that drown out those from mission control. When the ground personnel check out names that Rice hears mentioned, they find that the speakers he hears are dead. It emerges that Rice has entered a sphere populated by the spirits of the dead. These spirits bombard Rice with messages for people living on earth. Much of the humor derives from the mounting obsession of Rice with the phenomenon he has encountered played against the hysterical frustration of the ground team. The latter find the prospect of Rice possibly going crazy or that he is sane and his discovery will be revealed universally through the radio operators trying to listen in equally appalling. Once again there is the comic figure of a blustering general, yelling at the astronaut, "I don't know what your angle is, but I do know I'll bring you back down and slap you on a rock pile in Leavenworth so fast you'll leave your teeth up there" (60). The tension mounts when the spirits later manifest themselves as beautiful shimmering phantoms, with Rice's late wife Margaret appearing among them. While the ground crew try to keep the mission a secret, they can do nothing except jam the transmissions and bring Rice down.

Their fears that the orbiting Rice may prefer to crash and thus join his wife are duly realized. His death provides a macabre comic resolution of the story, ensuring the continued secrecy of the mission and of the existence of the "Thanasphere," and permitting Rice to rejoin his wife. Vonnegut inserts an ironic underlining to the comic nature of the story by having the supervising scientist of the project tell the suspicious newsmen, "You people read too many comic books" (62).

Being written more than a decade before the first manned space flight, some aspects of "Thanasphere" may appear accidentally humorous to us now. But humor is implicit in the science fiction elements of the story. The whole concept of a "dead zone," where spirits compete to be heard by an astronaut, is comic in itself. The particulars, like the late Hollywood actor trying to rectify his nephew's tampering with his will, and the amateur radio operators trying to make sense of this when they intercept a transmission, add delightful touches of the absurd. This will not be the last time Vonnegut will entertain with comic visions of an afterworld or communications with it. Other renditions occur in the play *Happy Birthday, Wanda June* (1970), where scenes are set in a shuffleboard-playing heaven, and in *Slapstick* (1976), where the scenes of Wilbur Swain communicating with his dead sister via the "Hooligan" take on the character suggested by the novel's title.

"EPICAC," which first appeared in the November 25, 1950, *Collier's*, owes its genesis to Vonnegut's inevitable involvement with technology while working for General Electric. In his *Playboy* interview he says, "There was no avoiding it, since the General Electric company was science fiction."[2] EPICAC, the subject of the story, is a huge computer that cost $776,434,927.54 and occupies "about an acre." It is intended to "plot the course of a rocket from anywhere on earth to the second button from the bottom of Joe Stalin's overcoat, if necessary" (36). Its great size in itself seems comic in an era of microcircuitry. So does the specific figure of its cost, down to the last cent. Moreover, EPICAC falters in its task because it is unhappy in its work. Until, that is, its operator tells it of his love for Pat Callaghan, a woman colleague. The machine then writes copious romantic poems that the narrator claims as his own and uses to woo Pat. EPICAC has fallen in love. When the narrator tells EPICAC that Pat believes that the poems are from him and that she cannot love a computer anyway, EPICAC commits suicide.

One might argue that Vonnegut shows characteristic foresight, and that a situation like this might yet arise in the interaction between humans and artificial intelligence. One advantage to Vonnegut's comic shaping of science fiction is that he can be predictive without the same requirements of plausibility or technical accuracy that might be expected of serious science fiction. Most of the specifics of this plot take on their character because of the dependence of this story's humor on comic exaggeration. "EPICAC" is another story that invites suspension of disbelief, again given touches of brass-tacks plausibility. One such—itself comic— is that the mathematically accomplished operator and the supercomputer can come up with no more sophisticated means of communication than "a childish numbers-for-letters code: 1 for A" and so on. There is comic hyperbole in the sheer volume of poetry that EPICAC produces, in the computer's astronomical price, even in the devastation produced by its suicide.

"EPICAC" depends heavily upon the effectiveness of its narrative persona. A factual, third-person omniscient reportage of the events would fall flat. So Vonnegut establishes a characterization behind the narrative voice from the first sentence: "Hell, it's about time somebody told about my friend EPICAC" (36). The careless informality creates a different level of acceptance from that applied to an objectively stated story. It makes the giving of EPICAC gender, personality, and relationship plausible, too. Further, the narrator saves the story from succumbing to its sentimentality. The emotions are his: we may share in them, but are not asked to be the primary receptor of them as would be the case without his presence. Vonnegut sometimes seems sentimental in his earlier work. Frequently, though, he undercuts the sentiment with humor and with something rather off-handed or rough-hewn in the narration, as in "EPICAC." The machine's falling in love, its being told it cannot be loved because it is a machine, and that it is inferior because it is not protoplasm is poignant—but still a joke.

"The Euphio Question" (*Collier's*, May 12, 1951) is presented as a report to the Federal Communications Commission about a physicist who has picked up radio signals from space. The hiss that emanates from his equipment induces a state of supine euphoria in the listening audience. The physicist and two friends, their sights set on making themselves fortunes with a scheme to market guaranteed happiness, come up with a "euphoriaphone" and run a home test. The scene that results becomes a mix of Laurel and Hardy and the Three Stooges, as more and more people arrive and fall under the sound's spell. In careless abandon they trash the house and would continue in their hypnotic state indefinitely, it seems, but for a tree's falling on the power lines to cut off the machine. The end of the story has a characteristic Vonnegutian twist. The unscrupulous radio announcer giving the FCC report plans to push ahead with the euphoriaphone and mounts a demonstration model in the hearing room. We are left to imagine the consequences.

"The Euphio Question" illustrates a theme frequent in Vonnegut's work: the downside of the pleasure principle, or the Utopian becoming nightmare. While that theme obviously has serious implications, Vonnegut relishes treating it with comic exaggeration in slapstick scenes. While once again the science fiction concept—beaming a universal soporific from space—is comic, much of the story's humor derives not from the science fiction itself but from the slapstick events that ensue from it. Additionally, the comic resolution of "The Euphio Question" evades answering the moral issues the situation has raised. In that sense, "The Euphio Question" represents a variation on the shaggy dog story, the form explicitly invoked in Vonnegut's next story.

"Tom Edison's Shaggy Dog," which first appeared in *Collier's* on March 14, 1953, while not strictly science fiction, makes use of science for its main comic episode. Two retired men share a bench in a Florida park. Harold K. Bullard chatters endlessly of his past business successes. His captive listener merely wants to sit and read, but Bullard's dog keeps nuzzling his suspenders, while Bullard relentlessly pursues his self-aggrandizing monologue. The victim's move to another bench fails to deter either the dog or Bullard. In self-defense the stranger launches into a story of his own. He tells how when he was a boy he lived next door to Thomas Edison's laboratory. He made friends with Edison's dog, Sparky, which one day led to his meeting the great man. Edison showed him a black box called an intelligence analyzer. As a test they attached it to Sparky's head, and it at once read off the scale. It seems that dogs had been smarter than humans all along, giving humans the worry and stress of providing for them while they lived in comfort. To repay Edison for keeping this secret, Sparky told Edison to use carbonized cotton thread as a filament for the light bulb, and gave the boy the stock tip that had made him wealthy for the rest of his life. The unfortunate Sparky, however, was killed by a pack of dogs who had overheard him reveal the secrets of man's best friend.

Vonnegut has flirted with the shaggy dog story form before, but this self-proclaimed example is a classic. It is, after all, a shaggy dog story about a dog—and within a frame story also involving a dog. Part of our enjoyment comes from seeing the tables turned on the boring Bullard and his intrusive dog, and in watching his mounting incredulity as the stranger's story escalates. The climax of the stranger's tall tale sneaks up delightfully. Edison is lamenting that he has been working for the last year, "'Slaving to work out a light bulb so dogs can play at night.' 'Look, Mr. Edison,' said Sparky, 'why not—' 'Hold on!' roared Bullard" (49). The purple-faced Bullard's finally being caught as the story takes its last step over the edge of credulity is a masterfully contrived moment. Beside being one of the most amusing short stories with a science fiction element, "Tom Edison's Shaggy Dog" is noteworthy in another respect. By using within the narrative a storyteller who mixes scientific history and the far-fetched, this short story points toward the eventual use of Kilgore Trout and his vignettes in later novels.

"Unready to Wear" was the first of two stories Vonnegut would publish in *Galaxy Science Fiction*. A fine example of Vonnegut's comedic uses of science fiction, it appeared in the April 1953 issue and was subsequently reprinted in both *Canary in a Cathouse* and *Welcome to the Monkey House*. It depicts a future in which people have learned, thanks to a Professor Konigswasser, how to escape their bodies. Such people are called amphibians, in that they are like the first creatures that learned how to leave the water and live on land. Ironically, Professor Konigswasser has discovered how to do this by walking into water. Ever absent-minded—in fact, his absentmindedness is seen as the first step to his leaving his body—he has walked into a lake. Later he walks back out, sees a rescue team resuscitating a decrepit body, and realizes it is his, so to spare people any inconvenience, he gets back into it and walks it home. From then on he mostly leaves his body in a closet, keeping it on low maintenance. He writes a book on how to do all of this and soon has millions of followers, among them the narrator of the story and his wife Madge. The amphibians store some bodies for people to check out when they want. Despite discarding their bodies, some of the amphibians remain ironically obsessional about them. For the annual Pioneers' Day parade even old Konigswasser checks out the body of a tall, blond cowboy who crushes beer cans between his fingers. Madge shows a penchant for the body of a platinum blonde burlesque queen.

The amphibians' enemies are those humans who have resisted becoming amphibian. One day Madge and the narrator discover that the humans have built an elaborate body storage center, like the ones the amphibians maintain. Madge decides the enemy has seen the light and plans to become amphibians. She spots an irresistible body, "six feet tall and built like a goddess. . . . The body had copper-colored skin, chartreuse hair and fingernails, and a gold lame evening gown" (107). But it proves to be a trap. The ankles are tied so that an amphibian cannot take the first few steps required to leave a body. Trying to help Madge, the narrator enters another body that is also a trap. The humans stage a trial and convict the two trapped amphibians of desertion, but the amphibians counter that this will mean war, that other amphibians surround the building, and that if the two of them are not released amphibians will enter the humans' bodies and march them off the edge of a cliff. This, the narrator confides, actually would be impossible, since only one person can inhabit a body at a time! The bluff works, and the amphibians escape the bodies and human capture, but not before Madge has left instructions for the copper-colored chartreuse-haired body to be sent to her.

Once again, the central science fiction ingredient in the plot of this story is a throwaway device. The few absentminded steps necessary to set the would-be amphibian walking out of a body have about the same plausibility as Barnhouse's aligning his brain cells. The "how" of this central phenomenon is not important—Vonnegut needs only to establish the situation of "what if" humans could escape their bodies? It is the kind of "what if" comic situation he delights in creating, as we see later in *Slapstick*'s variable gravity or *Cat's Cradle*'s Ice-Nine, and in which science fiction serves him so well. Konigswasser is also a set-piece comic figure for Vonnegut, the absentminded professor in the mold of Barnhouse or *Cat's Cradle*'s Felix Hoenikker. There is other stock humor in this story, such as the descriptions of the bodies amphibians choose and how they behave in them, the Pioneers' Day parade, and the trial, with its parody of a McCarthy hearing.

While its plot is almost farcical, "Unready to Wear" nevertheless touches on some serious social issues such as overpopulation and the effects of biochemistry on human behavior. Konigswasser vainly delights in assuming the "macho" image of the husky cowboy and crushing beer cans. Women, we are told, relate identity even more to the body, and delight in trying new bodies and costuming them and making them up like oversized dolls. But bodies are the source of most human problems. "The moment you get in, chemistry takes over—glands making you excitable or ready to fight or hungry or mad or affectionate, or—well, you never know what's going to happen next" (101). This is the first instance of Vonnegut's speaking of people's being controlled by chemicals, something that he returns to quite often in later fiction. That concept becomes a major component of the plot of *Breakfast of Champions* and *Slapstick*, where chemicals' control of human behavior is seen as sometimes reducing them almost to being robots. That also touches on the issue of free will, and how much of it humans actually enjoy, which is another perennial topic with Vonnegut. While its subjects are comically treated, this story proves another example of Eliot Rosewater's grounds for complimenting science fiction writers in *God Bless You, Mr. Rosewater*: "You're the only ones who'll talk about the really terrific changes going on" (*Rosewater*, 13).

"Unready to Wear" works well as a comic parable about overpopulation while reveling in its own implausibility, in effect celebrating its own fictionality. Vonnegut rather resembles Konigswasser (who may even be seen as another German-named author-surrogate within a story) in his adolescent irreverence for the determined conditions of existence and the imagination to explore, if only in fun, what might happen if they were changed. This shows the same imagination that can conceive water that freezes at room temperature in *Cat's Cradle*, variable gravity in *Slapstick*, or chrono-synclastic infundibula in *The Sirens of Titan*. We recognize the parallel between Konigswasser's amphibian and the disembodied fictional character that an author creates, and just as the person "trapped" in a body and controlled by biochemistry lacks free will, so the fictional character faces the comic dilemma of being at the mercy of the author-creator. Vonnegut gives that situation extended treatment in the ending pages of *Breakfast of Champions*, in the amusing scene where Kilgore Trout and his creator come face to face.

The other story in *Galaxy Science Fiction* (January 1954, included in *Canary in a Cathouse* and *Welcome to the Monkey House* with the new title, "Tomorrow and Tomorrow and Tomorrow") similarly gives comic treatment to serious social issues, returning in its primary focus to the one of overpopulation. Set in 2185 A.D., "The Big Trip Up Yonder" depicts a world where the invention of anti-gerasone has enabled people to stop the aging process, resulting in overpopulation and the rationing of food and space. Life becomes miserable for most people, yet they remain reluctant to leave it, abandon their anti-gerasone, and take "The Big Trip Up Yonder." Lou and Emerald Ford share their grandfather's apartment with twenty-three other relatives. The 172-year-old Gramps rules the household ruthlessly, using the tyranny of his last will and testament, which determines who will succeed to his bedroom and who meanwhile will sleep on the prized daybed. Others sleep crowded on mattresses on the floor. Rivalries for favor in Gramps' eyes or to end his rule lead to subterfuges like attempts to dilute his anti-gerasone. Eventually Gramps uses a ruse of his own wherein he vanishes and appears to leave a suicide note dividing his belongings equally among all his descendants. This precipitates a riot among them that leads to them all being arrested. At the end Lou and Em are luxuriating in private eight-by-four prison cells with their own wash basins. They are hiring a good attorney to get them the longest sentence possible. Gramps retains his apartment, which is private at last, and sends off for the new Super-anti-gerasone, which not only stops aging but enables the user to recover youth.

Incidental humor abounds in this story, in addition to its central comic treatment of overpopulation. It satirizes the advertising world's promotion of the desire among people to look young and alike: "Wouldn't you pay $5,000 to be indistinguishable from everybody else?" the Super-anti-gerasone commercial asks (110). Even soap operas are satirized; "The McGarvey Family" has been running for at least 102 years. The situation in Gramps' apartment and the childish shenanigans of the five generations trapped there are sheer slapstick. The jailer threatens the celebrating family inmates with eviction if they do not keep quiet, and with lifelong exclusion if they ever disclose how good conditions are in prison. The post office box number for Super-anti-gerasone is 500,000! Only Gramps gets to eat real food; the rest get "buckwheat-type processed sawdust cakes" or "egg-type processed seaweed." The Indianapolis 500 has become the 5,000-mile Speedway Race. Typically, then, the humor depends heavily on hyperbole and the inversion of normal expectations. Traditional comic elements such as the cunning and tyrannical old patriarch, the resourceful younger couple, the treacherous snitch, and the surprise reversal that turns potential tragedy into a happy ending, all contribute to this story's appeal.

The two *Galaxy Science Fiction* stories give the Cassandra in Vonnegut freedom to alert his readership to issues confronting society, but also allow the comedian to enjoy comic situations and childlike deconstructions of traditional assumptions about life. He can use science-fictional terms and futuristic settings with a comic hyperbole that banishes resistance to their implausibility. These are stories that prefigure some of the earlier novels like *The Sirens of Titan* and *Cat's*

Cradle, where the same combination of science fiction tropes and comic hyperbole produces energetic novels that both entertain and educate.

"Harrison Bergeron" appeared in the October 1961 issue of *Magazine of Fantasy and Science Fiction* and was reprinted in *National Review* on November 16, 1965 (page number citations in this chapter refer to the *National Review* appearance), and then in *Welcome to the Monkey House*. It is a dystopian portrayal of a society premised on an idealistic vision that has turned into nightmare. The events take place in the year 2081 when "everybody was finally equal," as ensured by "the 211th, 212th, and 213th Amendments to the Constitution" and "the unceasing vigilance of the agents of the United States Handicapper General" (1020). The story is set in the home of George and Hazel Bergeron. Average Hazel remains unhandicapped, but clever George wears bags weighted with bird shot and an ear radio that transmits brain-shattering noises to diminish his powers of thought. The Bergerons' fourteen-year-old superhuman son, Harrison, has been arrested by the Handicapper General, Diana Moon Glampers. As the Bergerons watch a ballet on television, an announcer interrupts to say that Harrison Bergeron, dangerous athlete and genius, has escaped. At once Harrison makes a dramatic appearance on screen and, declaring himself "the Emperor!" tears off his handicaps, selects a ballerina to be his Empress, and proceeds to dance with superhuman grace and strength. As they kiss while suspended in an unimaginable leap, Diana Moon Glampers herself bursts in armed with a shotgun and shoots them down. George and Hazel return to watching the resumed program. Tears stain George's cheek, but with the sound of a riveting gun blasting in his ear, he has no idea why.

Visual humor dominates "Harrison Bergeron." Most of the action—all of that involving Harrison, the dancers and Diana Moon Glampers—appears on the Bergerons' television. Harrison enters looking "like a walking junk yard," required to wear "a red rubber ball for a nose, keep his eyebrows shaved off, and cover his even white teeth with black caps at snaggle-tooth random" (1021). When he dances with the ballerina they defy "the law of gravity and the laws of motion as well," leaping to kiss the thirty-foot ceiling until finally "they remained suspended in air inches below the ceiling, and they kissed each other for a long, long time." It is then that Glampers enters with her shotgun. "She fired twice, and the Emperor and the Empress were dead before they hit the floor" (1041). The sheer implausibility and exaggeration of all of this—the handicaps, Harrison's size and prowess, the astronomical leaps—create the comic spectacle. The story celebrates its very fictiveness: we know these things cannot happen. In depicting the action in a representational manner the story actually subverts its claims to realism by its sheer exaggeration. Rather than pretending to realism it actually declares its fictionality. Having the dramatic events within the story presented on television, two removes from reality, emphasizes this fictionality.

The "serious" topic that the story declares itself to be concerned with is equality. It satirizes an obsession with equalizing; the predominant images are of the ludicrousness of the mental and physical handicaps, the grimness of reducing a population to its lowest common denominator, and the Big-Brotherly oversight that results. But the topic's main emphasis is comic. "Harrison Bergeron" may be a satirical fable, like George Orwell's *Animal Farm*, but the balance between comical rendering and moral message in the fable becomes almost the opposite in the two stories. Take Vonnegut's view of what passes as average in America: "Hazel had a perfectly average intelligence, which meant she couldn't think about anything except in short bursts" (1020). The observation on the ballerinas continues the undercutting humor: "They weren't really very good—no better than anybody else would have been, anyway" (1020). There is heavy irony in the plodding Hazel's missing the point, as when she sympathizes with the stuttering announcer for trying "real hard" to do his best, or when she suggests George might remove some of his weights in the evenings. Compounding the irony she says, "'I think I'd make a good Handicapper General.' 'Good as anybody else,' said George" (1041). The range of sounds and the comic brutality of their effect provides another source of humor. We may recall that Vonnegut as a youth enjoyed the often painful comedy of such teams as Laurel and Hardy, Abbot and Costello, and the Three Stooges, whose physically violent slapstick was often accompanied by appropriately barbarous sounds. One of George's winces prompts Hazel to ask the cause. "Sounded like somebody hitting a milk bottle with a hammer," he replies. Another sounds like a twenty-one gun salute that leaves George "white and trembling" and two of the ballerinas on the floor clutching their temples. The final one is a riveting gun.

"Gee—I could tell that one was a doozy," said Hazel.
    "You can say that again," said George.
    "Gee—" said Hazel— " I could tell that one was a doozy." (1041)

So "Harrison Bergeron" represents another of Vonnegut's painful comic renderings of a dystopian vision. Its technique on this occasion might be more accurately described as fantasy than as science fiction, particularly with its handsome, super-humanly endowed young hero who liberates his lovely young empress. The elements of dance, music, and staging all suggest that mode, as does the wicked witchlike presence of Diana Moon Glampers. But as with the science fiction, the fantasy tropes are transformed by slapstick undercutting and hyperbolic distortion.

"2BR02B" appeared in *Worlds of If* in January 1962 and returns to the portrayal of a dystopian future world governed by a good idea gone mad. (Vonnegut will use "2BR02B" again as the title of a Kilgore Trout story in *God Bless You, Mr. Rosewater*.) The good idea carried to excess is population control. As in "The Big Trip Up Yonder," a way has been found to stop the aging process, necessitating laws requiring that no child can be born until the parents can certify that someone else agrees to die. This story also features Ethical Suicide Studios staffed by efficient and welcoming young "gas chamber hostesses" who wear purple. A dispirited husband sits in a waiting room of the Chicago Lying-in Hospital, while above him a "sardonic" old painter works on a stepladder. The painter is completing a mural of a formal garden, with gardeners dressed in purple.

Among those depicted stands Dr. Benjamin Hitz, the Chief Obstetrician, who at this point in the story actually enters the room in person. He announces to the waiting husband that his wife as expected has delivered triplets, and asks if the family has found three candidates for the Ethical Suicide Studios. The husband has found only one, so faces having to choose two of the triplets to die. But instead he produces a gun, shoots Hitz, and then himself. The old painter, having watched silently from above, descends, picks up the gun, lacks the nerve to shoot himself, and instead calls "2-B-R-0-2-B," the telephone number of the ethical suicide service. The answering hostess arranges an appointment, then delivers the story's ironic final lines: "Your city thanks you; your country thanks you; your planet thanks you. But the deepest thanks of all is from future generations" (65).

As in "The Big Trip Up Yonder," Vonnegut uses painful comedy rather than didacticism to point out the dangers of overpopulation and, through the distortions of hyperbole, some of the difficult choices it imposes. In this story, the imposition of population control averts a disastrous situation where drinking water was already running out and people were eating seaweed. The negative aspects of population control are epitomized in the necessity to kill a baby if no volunteer for death can be found, and by the references to the euphemistically named Ethical Suicide Studios as gas chambers, calling up all the horrors of Nazi exterminations. The hyperbole heightens both sides of the issue to the point of absurdity. The story, like others on this topic, draws attention to one of the most serious issues facing human kind, but one that governments, religions, politicians, and people generally show a remarkable reluctance to consider. Vonnegut's dark humor permits an approach to a topic that generally invites instant resistance.

Some of the circumstances of "2BR02B" are repeated or extended in a Kilgore Trout story in *God Bless You, Mr. Rosewater* and in "Welcome to the Monkey House" some six years later, including what become Ethical Suicide Parlors. The hostesses wear purple there, too, and in each case the unnaturalness of this reversal of their human maternal functions is signaled by their unsexing. In "Welcome to the Monkey House," chemicals stop all feeling below their waists, while in this story they all develop facial hair—"an unmistakable mustache, in fact"—after a few years in the job. Vonnegut uses the name of his Shortridge High School chum, Ben Hitz, who was later best man at his first wedding, for one of the characters. Dr. Hitz stands seven feet tall, another instance of Vonnegut's use of hyperbole for comic effect. He creates other seven footers, such as Harrison Bergeron, or Wilbur Swain of *Slapstick*, and some midgets, too, like Newt Hoenikker of *Cat's Cradle*.

Despite the rather grim consequences in this story, "2BR02B" is told brightly, with a cheery tone and brisk, short sentences. The relative brevity of the story, combined with its pace, prevents its taking on the dour quality to which its content could lead. The opening sets the tone:

Everything was perfectly swell.
There were no prisons, no slums, no insane asylums, no cripples, no poverty, no wars. (59)

The comic note is established early. The waiting husband, we are told, is a "mere stripling" being fifty-six where the average age is one hundred and twenty-nine. Then there are the lyrics of a currently popular song in which a lover threatens to go to "a girl in purple" if he is rejected. The mural on the hospital wall is ironically titled "The Happy Garden of Life." The Suicide Studios are run by a "Federal Bureau of Terminations," and the popular sobriquets for them include "Easy-go," "Catbox," "Kiss-me-quick," and "Why Worry." As with the other stories dealing with overpopulation, much of the humor derives from hyperbole and inversion, and there is an exuberance in treating serious subjects with flippancy. The ending falls short of the comic resolution of "The Big Trip Up Yonder," but is less clouded than that of "Welcome to the Monkey House." While the latter story (which appeared in *Playboy* in January 1968) has a futuristic setting, ethical suicide parlors, anti-aging pills and overpopulation, it appears less science fictional than social, and less comic than satiric. Its resolution, with the main female character having been raped for her own good, in effect, remains troubling, and diminishes the sparkle of the incidental humor along the way.

A short satirical piece written in 1962 is called "HOLE BEAUTIFUL: Prospectus for a Magazine of Shelteredness," published in *Monocle* (Vol. 5, no. 1). This satire presents another comic banishing of the current Cold War fears. The proposed magazine's title obviously derives from *House Beautiful*, and its subject is fallout shelters and activities surrounding them. It will be "the magazine of gracious survival." As a general public relations consultant the magazine would employ "a leading undertaker" who, "with his valuable experience in the field of putting people underground, will be helpful in overcoming the negative image that death has in this country" (46). Singing commercials might include "Hole is where the heart is" or "There's no place like hole." The publisher would be a separate corporation called Subterranean Publications, Inc., with offices in Mammoth Cave, Kentucky. "Cost per issue will be 50¢ in subways and $1.00 above ground." Because of negative connotations, the word "bomb" will never be used and instead it will be referred to as "the Big Fella." The editorial policy will be to oppose the government's community shelter program with the aid of the American Medical Association's attack on it as "socialized sheltering." The magazine would promote "Shelter Hopping Kits" designed to gain access to other people's shelters in time of attack by using various devices such as Cyklon-B gas or imitations of the pleadings of a beloved family pet. A sample theater review focuses on the theater's emergency exits, lighting, and proximity to a fallout shelter. Editorials projected include "Unilateral Disarmament by the Russians—Does It Violate the American Sense of Fair Play?" (50). So it goes on, irreverent and inventive, in the best comedic tradition of meeting society's worst fears head on with laughter. Once the premise has been established, much of the humor of this piece depends on the evolving details, and it is not difficult to see how this text could have become one of the comic subplots that often run through the novels.

Those comic subplots are well illustrated by the science fiction portions of *Slaughterhouse-Five* and *Slapstick*. Significantly, the main plots of these two novels are among the most bleak in Vonnegut's canon, with settings of war, destruction, and death. In *Slaughterhouse-Five*, the Tralfamadorian segments provide the reader with relief from the war scenes much as they do for the protagonist Billy Pilgrim himself. While humorous, the science fiction subplot is shorn of the painful elements so often present in the short stories. Billy's life under the Tralfamadorians' geodesic dome, safe from the acidic atmosphere outside and with every need provided for, is pure wish fulfillment. Its humor—the watching plumber's-friend Tralfamadorians and their wishes to see the humans mate, the night cover, Billy's startled awakenings from time-traveling—seems mellow and reassuring in its contrast to the war scenes. Admittedly, the Tralfamadorian subplot includes a vision of the end of the world and the perpetuation of war, but these seem distant threats compared with the miseries of battlefield, prison camp, and firestorm. The Tralfamadorian philosophy of coping with life by thinking only of the good times seems less cynical than healing in this context. The incorporation of the science fiction subplot in such a way that it could all be read as Billy's imagining underscores the sense that the human mind can only tolerate so much pain. Thus, science fiction fulfills a similar role within Billy's personal drama that it often does in Vonnegut's fiction.

In *Slapstick*, the science fiction is not always as benign in its comic contributions. Variable gravity is one of the science fiction devices that sets up much of the plot of the novel, much as Ice-Nine does in *Cat's Cradle*. Both of these transformations of nature have their comic potential as well as their catastrophic consequences. Both display Vonnegut's characteristic tendency to ask the almost childlike question that challenges adult assumptions—what if ice could be frozen at room temperature? what if gravity varied, like the wind? The questions are comic in essence and may seem absurd, but they underline that we do, day in and day out, in effect gamble that such assumptions hold true until they do not—until the stable earth beneath us buckles in earthquake or sinks in flood, or the unnoticed breeze becomes a life-shattering tornado. Thus, variable gravity destroys bridges and crushes tunnels. But it also can be humorous in its effects, as when we learn that "All males have erections on days like this. They are automatic consequences of near-weightlessness" (*Slapstick*, 23–24). The fantastic events of *Slapstick* include Chinese who can miniaturize themselves, a new solution to the perennial overpopulation problem. There are rampant diseases like the Green Death and the Albanian Flu, the former caused by inhaling miniaturized Chinese. There is also the invention of "the Hooligan," a device that accidentally permits communication with the dead, whose world we learn sounds like a badly run turkey farm. The protagonist Wilbur Swain and his sister cut fantastic figures, being Neanderthaloids over seven feet tall with extra fingers, toes, and nipples. *Slapstick* then, abounds in the comic hyperbole that typically embraces pain and laughter—and that may lead to instruction—so often found in his science fiction and fantasy.

Beyond such subplots that carry science fiction motifs throughout their novels, however, there is a continuation of the short stories in the form of vignettes, plot outlines, or allusions within the novels. These sometimes function as parables and are frequently the invention of the ubiquitous Kilgore Trout. "The Dancing Fool," with which this chapter began, is a typical example. Kilgore Trout himself, of course, in his various shabby manifestations, might be seen as the embodiment of painful comedy. His plight as neglected science fiction writer, ever-accepting of the wonders of life, expecting the worst but always undaunted, surprised only by recognition, makes him the ideal persona through whom Vonnegut can insert his science fiction mini-stories when needed.

An example of how the Trout stories in the later fiction work much like parables is one in *Timequake* called "The Sisters B-36."[3] It tells of three sisters, two pleasant and one evil, on a matriarchal planet named Booboo. One of the good sisters is a painter, while the other is a writer. The third is a scientist who talks mostly about thermodynamics. People find her boring and shun her. In an obvious parallel to humans, Booboolings' minds are programmed by what they are told in words during their infancy. Booboolings are thus trained how to look at pictures or print, and they develop circuits that Earthlings would call "Imagination." To make her own impression on Booboolings, the bad sister, "Nim-nim B-36," invents television. Booboolings then no longer need imagination, and only the older ones, whose circuits were formed before television, can appreciate pictures and writing. The two good sisters are reduced to feeling abandoned and neglected, just as B-36 wished, but still no one appreciates the scientific sister. So B-36 invents the land mine, barbed wire, the machine gun, the flame-thrower, the computer, and automation. Then Booboolings kill one another other readily, feeling nothing because they had no imaginations. They had lost the ability of their forebears to see a story in the face of another person, to vicariously feel what others might feel. Hence, they had lost any capacity for mercy.

"The Sisters B-36" is clearly a parable about our own society, where young people kill one another on the streets in extraordinary numbers, and where political bombings and other acts of violence proliferate. It urges the crucial role that writing and other arts play in the development of the imagination. It proclaims the dreadful cost to the culture and to the individual of the loss of the imagination and the capacity to recognize and respect the feelings of others. It reiterates Vonnegut's frequent denunciations of the negative impact that television has had on society. It also returns to two even older themes in Vonnegut's work—pacifism, and the failure of the public to respond with understanding to scientific knowledge. It is a classic example of the insertion of a painful comic science fiction story into a novel to introduce at once laughter and message.

Naturally, the larger the role Trout assumes in the novel, the more frequently his stories appear, and hence they occur most often in *God Bless You, Mr. Rosewater, Slaughterhouse-Five, Breakfast of Champions*, and *Timequake*. Other science fiction tales, or at least episodes, occur in the novels, though few so specifically in this mode as in the Trout stories. In *Galápagos*, for instance, when the collapse of the international financial structure precipitates chaos and conflict, Vonnegut makes use of a typical science fiction perspective on things. From the violence people were doing to each other, and to all other living things, a visitor from another planet might have assumed that the environment had gone haywire, and that people were in such a frenzy because Nature was about to kill them all (*Galápagos*, 25).

In like mode, a war is started when radars misidentify a meteorite shower as incoming missiles, and the earth is depopulated by a corkscrew-like virus that destroys human ovaries. Cruel jokes, indeed, but characteristic macabre humor. Also in that vein is the placing of asterisks beside the names of characters who will die in the course of the novel. In lighter tone, the computer Mandarax supplies wryly appropriate quotations for various occasions, in a manner reminiscent of the Tralfamadorian messages in *The Sirens of Titan*. Thus, when Peruvian rockets wipe out Ecuador, Mandarax quotes: "Happy is the nation without a history. Cesare Bonesana (1738–94)" (*Galápagos*, 175).

In sum, the more frequent characteristics of the comic science fiction short stories carry through into the science fiction subplots and the mini-stories contained in the novels. They share the same mix of the humorous, be it ironical or slapstick, and the painful, be it pathetic or threatening. They make use of hyperbole and disparity, and in so doing often invite visualization. The other-worldly or fantastic in their fundamental elements are often counterbalanced by mundane details that connect the situation with the familiar and add plausibility. That connection is enhanced where there is a narrator or a voice that assumes a persona, these typically adopting some of the folksy tone of the yarn-spinner. Such affirmation as occurs in these stories may stem from the sense of undiminished human aspiration that often runs through them. Vonnegut has written of his admiration for Laurel and Hardy for their invariably "bargaining in good faith with destiny" (*Slapstick*, 1). He recounts his fondness for the cartoon that shows two prisoners chained at ankle and wrist to a dungeon wall, with only the smallest barred window far above, and one saying to the other, "Now here's my plan."[4] Similarly, there is that persistent voice that keeps asking "What if?" in the face of the comfortable assurances and platitudinous answers.

Our age questions whether tragedy can still be written, but the times are scarcely more kind to comedy. In many respects, though, Vonnegut's science fiction stories meet the classic requirements. Perhaps they can because they so often offer an alternative world. But the alternative worlds are almost always closely connected with our own, in theme and moral if not in feature, and their threats identifiable with those we know. While Vonnegut's fiction may serve to remind us of the nature and severity of those threats, it will also, in the best comic tradition, manage to surmount them with laughter or a momentary triumph. For Vonnegut, the reminder is frequently the important thing, calling attention to our neglect or overconfidence. As Northrop Frye wrote many years ago, "Comedy is designed not to condemn evil, but to ridicule a lack of self-knowledge."[5] Sometimes, as in "Report on the Barnhouse Effect" or "The Big Trip Up Yonder," we even see the classic pattern of the younger man triumphing by his wits over the patriarchal figure who embodies a corrupted social status quo. Often the story will reach a formal comedic resolution even if the portended circumstances left at the end are not promising. While Vonnegut is often satirical, many of the short stories, lacking specific targets of satire, fit that categorization less well than that of a comedy that, encompassing the threats and dissonance of a contemporary chaotic world, remains painful. The metaphorical distinction drawn by James Hall still stands: "comic novels find garlic and sapphires in the mud, satiric ones find mostly garlic and blame it for not being sapphire."[6]

What does the science fiction ingredient contribute to this brand of comedy? It certainly affords Vonnegut a greater freedom in addressing issues. While he shows little reluctance to address current social issues directly, science fiction becomes an effective device for achieving distance from which to address an issue that, close up, may be too controversial or confused. Issues projected into a science fiction setting can be simplified and exaggerated to expose or highlight their characteristics. They can be removed sufficiently from the controversies of their immediate contexts to be examined with detachment, and the consequences on one, the other, or both sides of the issue may be projected to extremes that reveal or emphasize their true nature. Science fiction becomes the perfect mode for allowing Vonnegut to move the examination of such issues into a realm where they can be treated, often hyperbolically, without the constraints normally attending their discussion. Science fiction, and the use of humor, allows him to speak of overpopulation, voluntary suicide, governmentally imposed contraception, or pacifism, for example, without necessarily invoking the entrenched resistance often surrounding such topics. In the short stories placed in the wide circulation glossy magazines, using science fiction enables him to extend the scope afforded him by the traditional domestic subjects, or to render them in a new light.

What I have called Vonnegut's painful comic science fiction writing has become, by whatever appellation, perhaps the most characteristic and identifying aspect of his work. To a great many readers Vonnegut is either a comic writer or a science fiction writer or both, and the works they are most likely to remember him by are *Cat's Cradle, Slaughterhouse-Five, Breakfast of Champions*, or maybe an anthologized "Harrison Bergeron." Perhaps it is ironic that the classification of Vonnegut as a science fiction writer tends to persist. Ironic, anyway, that it tends to persist as a narrowing definition, one that pigeonholes him when, in effect, his uses of science fiction have enabled him to broaden the scope of his work. In the short stories it is the science fiction plots, or elements in the plots, that are most likely to reach beyond the kinds of domestic dramas that constitute the stuff of most of his other stories. It is the science fiction that transcends the local to look at the future consequences of global patterns of human behavior, or of technological change, or of new knowledge. In the novels, the interjection of science fiction episodes extends their scope beyond their main plot and setting. It gives the freedom to amplify and broaden, to extend the context in which issues are presented and to create new perspectives. Even where the science fiction interludes seem largely for comic effect, which Vonnegut has spoken of as being like sending in the clowns, the comedy is often like that of the Fool in *King Lear*, seeming folly but with a moral message.[7]

Vonnegut's mode of science fiction has proved an excellent medium for him, a principal component of a postmodern technique for dealing with a postmodern world. For Vonnegut, chaos theory must seem not an abstraction but a reality manifest in the startling deaths within his family and in his own wartime experiences. He has seen the operations of chance in the hazards of war, with its random meting out of death and destruction. Well may his characters ask, "Why me?" Even the peace has been chaotic, from the Great Depression of his youth to an era of constantly accelerating change reflected in ever-more dramatic scientific insights into the nature and origin of our universe and the dizzying rapidity of technological evolution. At a time when, on the one hand, individual human destiny is being seen more and more as genetically determined and when, on the other, many people seek to escape the anguish of an incomprehensible world in chemical dependency, Vonnegut's focus on biochemistry and human behavior seems all the more appropriate. While science fiction helps Vonnegut to observe and comment on such a universe, his painful comic rendering of the form acknowledges not just the suffering existence may impose, but the essential absurdity of the situation in which its randomness and incomprehensibility frequently place us. Vonnegut persists, nevertheless, in seeing the funny side of that situation. The comedy in his fiction expresses a resistance to accepting the logic of the horrors it depicts. His ability to create comedy from the frightening implications of the human condition as he sees it may only be a form of gallows or trench humor. But it may imply some measure of confidence that the same aspiring human spirit that so often lands us in trouble can say once more, "Now here's the plan."

NOTES

1. Laury Clancy, "Running Experiments Off: An Interview," in William Rodney Allen, ed., *Conversations with Kurt Vonnegut* (Jackson: University Press of Mississippi, 1988), 51.

2. David Standish, *"Playboy* Interview," in William Rodney Allen, ed., *Conversations with Kurt Vonnegut* (Jackson: University Press of Mississippi, 1988), 93.

3. This story was recounted by Vonnegut to Marc Leeds and Peter Reed and is reported in *The Vonnegut Chronicles* (Westport, CT: Greenwood Press, 1996), edited by Reed and Leeds, 42. It was also seen by this writer in manuscripts of *Timequake* shown to him by Vonnegut in 1996.

4. Standish, 91.

5. Northrop Frye, "The Argument of Comedy," in Leonard F. Dean, ed., *Shakespeare: Modern Essays in Criticism* (New York: Oxford University Press/A Galaxy Book, 1967), 81.

6. James Hall, *The Tragic Comedians* (Bloomington: Indiana University Press, 1967), vi.

7. Standish, 94. In this interview, Vonnegut says: "And the science fiction passages in *Slaughterhouse-Five* are just like the clowns in Shakespeare. When Shakespeare figured the audience had had enough of the heavy stuff, he'd let up a little, bring on a clown or a foolish innkeeper or something like that, before he'd become serious again. And trips to other planets, science fiction of an obviously kidding sort, is equivalent to bringing on the clowns every so often to lighten things up."

WORKS CITED

Novels by Kurt Vonnegut

Player Piano. New York: Charles Scribner's Sons, 1952.
The Sirens of Titan. New York: Dell, 1959.
Canary in a Cat House. Greenwich, CT: Gold Medal/Fawcett, 1961.
Cat's Cradle. New York: Holt, Rinehart and Winston, 1963.
God Bless You, Mr. Rosewater. New York: Holt, Rinehart and Winston, 1965.
Welcome to the Monkey House. New York: Delacorte Press/Seymour Lawrence, 1968.
Slaughterhouse-Five. New York: Delacorte Press/Seymour Lawrence, 1969.
Happy Birthday, Wanda June. New York: Delacorte Press/Seymour Lawrence, 1970.
Breakfast of Champions. New York: Delacorte Press/Seymour Lawrence, 1973.
Slapstick. New York: Delacorte Press/Seymour Lawrence, 1976.
Galápagos. New York: Delacorte Press/Seymour Lawrence, 1985.

Short Stories by Kurt Vonnegut

* Also reprinted in *Canary in a Cat House.*
\# Also reprinted in *Welcome to the Monkey House.*
"Report on the Barnhouse Effect." *Collier's*, February 11, 1950, pp. 18–19, 63–65.*#
"Thanasphere." *Collier's*, September 2, 1950, pp. 18–19, 60, 62.
"EPICAC." *Collier's*, November 25, 1950, pp. 36–37.#
"The Euphio Question." *Collier's*, May 12, 1951, pp. 22–23, 52–54, 56.*#
"Tom Edison's Shaggy Dog." *Collier's*, March 14, 1953, pp. 46, 48–49.*#
"Unready to Wear." *Galaxy Science Fiction*, April 1953, pp. 98–111.*#
"The Big Trip Up Yonder." *Galaxy Science Fiction*, January 1954, pp. 100–110.*#
    ("Tomorrow and Tomorrow and Tomorrow" in *Welcome to the Monkey House*.)
"The Powder Blue Dragon." *Cosmopolitan*, November 1954, pp. 46–48, 50–53.
"Deer in the Works." *Esquire*, April 1955, pp. 78–79, 112, 114, 116, 118.
"The Manned Missiles." *Cosmopolitan*, July 1958, pp. 83–88.*#
"Harrison Bergeron." *Magazine of Fantasy and Science Fiction*, October 1961, pp. 5–10.
    Reprinted in *National Review*, November 16, 1965, pp. 1020–1021, 1041.#
"HOLE BEAUTIFUL: Prospectus for a Magazine of Shelteredness." *Monocle*, 1962, pp.
    45–51.
"2BR02B." *Worlds of If*, January 1962, pp. 59–65.
"Welcome to the Monkey House." *Playboy*, January 1968, pp. 95, 214.

Other Works Cited

Allen, William Rodney, ed. *Conversations with Kurt Vonnegut.* Jackson: University Press
    of Mississippi, 1988.
Frye, Northrop. "The Argument of Comedy." In Leonard F. Dean, ed., *Shakespeare:
    Modern Essays in Criticism.* New York: Oxford University Press/A Galaxy Book,
    1967.
Hall, James. *The Tragic Comedians.* Bloomington: Indiana University Press, 1967.
Reed, Peter, and Marc Leeds, eds. *The Vonnegut Chronicles.* Westport, CT: Greenwood
    Press, 1996.

It's All Play-Acting

Authorship and Identity in the Novels of Kurt Vonnegut

Michelle Persell

There are few more mundane observations to offer of Kurt Vonnegut than the fact that he writes about writing. Between flourishes of Nazi propaganda, Howard Campbell, Jr., of *Mother Night* (1961), generates turgid Medieval romance and ludicrously chaste pornography. Rudolph Waltz's solitary dramatic production, *Katmandu*, haunts *Deadeye Dick* (1982). *Slaughterhouse-Five* (1966) is a novel about Dresden whose unnamed narrator is writing a novel about Dresden. Eliot, the titular protagonist of *God Bless You, Mr. Rosewater* (1965), is a "poet" of "lavatory walls" who appropriately introduces *Slaughterhouse-Five*'s Billy Pilgrim to the scatological dementia of science-fiction writer Kilgore Trout (*Rosewater*, 68). So, of what import are these ersatz literary figures? Are these fictional authors updated David Copperfields, heroes of their own lives? If so, their function could be easily encapsulated into a tight psychoanalytic argument. That is to say, we might blithely label each artist as an example of mere "narcissistic doubling of the creative experience" (Dällenbach, 16). Under these circumstances, Vonnegut could be said to be vicariously acting out the anxieties and consequent triumph of his narrative method onto characters bearing suspicious similarities to his own biography. Leave that self-justifying strategy to Charles Dickens, however, because this is precisely what does not occur in the novels of Kurt Vonnegut.

Instead, Vonnegut is a master of encrypting failed artistry into his novels. Campbell's carefully crafted speeches qualify him as an anti-Semitic shill; Stepan Bodovskov achieves his greatest success plagiarizing Campbell's most maudlin pabulum; painter George Kraft-Potapov ascends to Modernist-chic during a stint in Leavenworth; Otto Waltz would be a dilettante except he could not squander talent he never had; the entire body of work of Kilgore Trout constitutes a stylistic monstrosity. Still, these men are not just patsies against whom we judge the triumph of the novels containing them. The effect of their presence enables Vonnegut to explore the inherent inadequacies of both deploying or resisting traditional narrative strategies. Consider that the raison d'être of Vonnegut's novelistic project is to question the cultural shibboleths that permeate such standard genres as science fiction, combat stories, and historically set pieces including the conceits of cohesive subjectivity and the concept of a just war, each of which is "exploded" by Billy Pilgrim in *Slaughterhouse-Five*. It is not so much that Vonnegut sets out to justify his own artistry against the ramblings of a Reverend Jones or even Kilgore Trout, but that the author himself must guard against a mindless adherence to inherited aesthetic form as a flimsy bulwark against insanity, schizophrenia, and moral incertitude, without succumbing to those threats in the process of revealing them.

In *Mother Night*, for example, Vonnegut needs to be able to pan the vapid neo-romanticism of an early Campbell play without accepting the concomitant self-destruction of the disillusioned middle-aged Campbell who, in the absence of formal constraints upon expression—a role to play—slips into paralysis and eventual death. Freed from the sting operation that swept up Jones and his entourage, Campbell stands immobilized at his drop-off point outside the Empire State Building. "What froze me was the fact that I had absolutely no reason to move in any direction" is his explanation (*Mother*, 167). Campbell pointedly dismisses guilt, loss, fear of death, heartbreak, and despair at injustice as factors in his behavioral breakdown. Forced to desist his loitering, he eventually finds himself at the Epsteins' apartment where he hopes to turn himself over to Israeli authorities. Significantly, this event occurs after one of the tritest exchanges in the novel where Campbell and a patrolman trade penetrating observations like war is "hell" and "You think there'll be another one?" (*Mother*, 170). Triggered by this banal dialogue, Campbell breaks out of his nihilistic torpor long enough to set off to find a slightly more sophisticated text to inhabit. "And you really want to be punished?" inquires Dr. Abraham Epstein when Campbell presents himself. "I want to be tried," Campbell responds to which the physician sneers, "It's all play-acting" and "It proves nothing!" (*Mother*, 186). Epstein wants some expression of will outside of this self-justifying, trite little dramatic scenario of closure for the "undiluted evil" christened "Kahm-boo" (*Mother*, 184). Campbell requires, however, just such a life script.

On the one hand, this need itself comes across as contemptible and dangerous. As Mrs. Epstein observes to her son:

This is not the first time you've seen eyes like that . . . not the first man you've seen who could not move unless someone told him where to move, who longed for someone to tell him what to do next, who would do anything anyone told him to do next. . . . You saw thousands of them at Auschwitz. (*Mother*, 185)

There, at the camps, walking corpses as well as their vile Nazi guards were reduced to mindless automatons. This absolute loss of autonomy is indistinguishable from death. On the other hand, the comparative freedom of chaos is not the most logical palliative to prevent this horrific extinguishment of life because it is not survivable either, as we see when Campbell arrives at his building in New York City. The younger Epstein wants to dismiss his directionless neighbor, the self-proclaimed "friendly robot," as psychologically disturbed. In contrast, Campbell recognizes,

Mrs. Epstein "understood my illness immediately, it was my world rather than myself that was diseased" (*Mother*, 185). Campbell is less a madman without a locus for allegiance than a man in search of a context in which to be a diabolical madman. That is to say, even though the former playwright is not the embodiment of unadulterated malice (he *did* serve as a double agent under the auspices of the U.S. government and for which Wirtanen-Sparrow will vouch), he would seek to assume that guise anyway.

Like Howard Campbell, Jr., Arthur Garvey Ulm of *God Bless You, Mr. Rosewater* is bereft without a proscribed role, no matter how repugnant or stifling that role may seem to be. Ulm is no Nazi (although, interestingly "Ulm" is a city in Germany), he is rudderless without some form of artistic fascism to direct his literary output. His very name, Ulm, is an *onomatopoeia* for the sort of gulp one makes when in a quandary, not knowing how to proceed. Ulm's patron, Eliot Rosewater, naively imagines that giving people what they say they want and need will actually fulfill their wants and needs. What Ulm wants, ostensibly, is to write great poetry, unfettered. Eliot's financial largesse should liberate Ulm to pursue this course. Instead, the uncomprehending Ulm begs to indenture himself to Eliot in homage for the act of buying his artistic freedom. Eliot demurs, but Ulm perseveres, exalting Rosewater's "divine assistance" for motivating his eight-hundred page tome (*Rosewater*, 70). Given the absence of an authority figure, Ulm conjures one up with the face of Eliot Rosewater. The latter is the arbiter of virtue, some god-like figure whose oppression is laudable because the bondage is voluntary.

The novel, *Get With Child a Mandrake Root*, writes Ulm, could not have been created by me without you [Eliot] and I do not mean your money. (Money is shit, which is one of the things I have tried to say in the book.) I mean your insistence that the truth be told about this sick, sick society of ours, and that the words for the telling could be found on the walls of restrooms. (*Rosewater*, 69)

Ulm cheerily perverts Eliot's credulous advice until the "truth" becomes synonymous with whatever Ulm imagines Eliot wants to hear, for his patron is the source of "creation." Given this derivative premise, one is not surprised to witness the novel's soporific effect upon Eliot who finds not penetrating insight, but stories of penetration in what turns out to be soft-core pornography. Ulm interprets Rosewater's absurdist penchant for the guileless restroom aphorism (e.g., the *chiasmus*, "We don't piss in your ashtrays, / So please don't throw cigarettes in our urinals" [*Rosewater*, 68]) as a general call for bathroom reading. That is to say, rambling, penny-ante vulgarity is what Ulm would fob off as an indictment of a "sick society." Ulm does not even discern the basic contradiction in his rhetoric wherein he wants to exploit traditional revulsion at dirty words with condemnatory phrases like "Money is shit," then to claim that very same gutter vocabulary contains the proper "words for the telling" of truth. Does he prefer readers to be shocked by the scatology or not? Without content, these exclamatory phrases will no longer be so, once used ad infinitum. Even if the "truth" were inherent in the act of provoking distaste, that effect would be lost through the din of repetition.

Vonnegut responded in *Palm Sunday* (1981) to charges of mindless provocation in his own use of salty language. Already in his fifties, he writes, "It has been many decades since I have wished to shock a teacher or anyone. I didn't want to make the Americans in my books talk as Americans really do talk. I wanted to make jokes about our bodies" (*Palm Sunday*, 221). Herein, Vonnegut confronts the conundrum of pretending to "shock" an audience, claiming all the while that epithets are the unexceptional language of realism. He turns that very contradiction into a source of humor. Familiar words to which the trace value of immorality clings have less the capacity to scandalize than to embarrass, and that is the ripest territory for comedy.

In contrast, Ulm's smug disclosure of lewdness, as if it were some perspicacious revelation, will not give rise (pun intended) to any creative literary production just as the phallic mandrake root will never bear offspring. Ulm's chosen title, borrowed from John Donne, mires him in a mixed metaphor representative of his whole novel—overlong and full of words that snare him in paradoxes rather than providing a call for social change. Unaware of his dilemma, Ulm treats his novel as something akin to Christ attacking the money-changers when it doesn't even constitute "fair-to-middling Pharisee-baiting" (*Rosewater*, 74). Granted, only a book with those qualifications could ever attain the status of featured text with a "major" book of the month club (*Rosewater*, 69), that is, a work of utter conformity convinced of its mutinous posture.

Ulm's demigod, Rosewater, himself favors Kilgore Trout's brand of pornography, which "wasn't sex but fantasies of an impossibly hospitable world. . . . Trout's favorite formula was to describe a perfectly hideous society, not unlike our own, and then, toward the end, to suggest ways in which it could be improved" (*Rosewater*, 20). Despite his beneficent projects, Trout is relegated to smut-shops where both Billy Pilgrim and Eliot's would-be nemesis, Norman Mushari, manage to purchase his "anti-social" texts. Vonnegut deploys in *Slaughterhouse-Five* and *Rosewater* a pair of standard satirical themes: (1) what is clearly recognizable to the reader as mundane goodwill becomes revolutionary when actually put into practice and (2) the sane are insane in an insane world. If the "truth" that Rosewater and Billy seek were that simple we could, with some sense of closure, file them away in the Lemuel Gulliver school of naiveté, and we would do so with kudos from Vonnegut since Jonathan Swift (1667–1745) remains one of the reigning members admitted to his pantheon of favorite authors (*Palm Sunday*, 255–259). But the fact remains that the augur of Billy's and Eliot's visions, ostracized artist Kilgore Trout, is, at base, an absolutely terrible writer. Just when we are ready to sneer at Vonnegut for trumping up this poet-prophet, he sabotages the impulse by calling our attention to it and casting doubt upon it.

Trout arrives in the final chapters of *Rosewater* like a *deus ex machina* sent for by Eliot because "Trout could explain the meaning of everything" (182). Indeed, Trout wastes no time conjuring up a philosophy for Eliot's random acts of kindness, that is, a philanthropic scheme to help the perpetual failures of society.

Overwhelmed at this flourish of deception, and deaf to the grain of truth in Trout's pronouncement, Senator Lister Rosewater pays the ultimate compliment to the novelist: "You should have been a public relations man! You could make lockjaw sound good for the community!" (*Rosewater*, 185). Dazed, the congressman's son Eliot, who has just emerged from a year-long blackout, can only ask why the novelist shaved off his beard. To this Trout responds: "Think of the sacrilege of a Jesus figure redeeming stamps" (*Rosewater*, 185). Kilgore, his very name belying the notion of a Christlike savior, is a parody of a sage who nonetheless remains far short of charlatanism. Of course, the boozy Eliot has no conception of why he is driven to be a martyr to the cause of good Samaritans. Yet, Trout's speculation that Rosewater has conducted an experiment in the heretofore unsounded depths of human kindness accurately describes Eliot's practice if not his conscious motivation. Trout is both lying and imparting the truth—a fair characterization of novel-writing itself.

Had not Eliot experienced his serendipitous amnesia and forgot his acquaintance with Kilgore, he risked becoming a kind of Ulm character who waits upon the prophet for revelations. The fact is that even if Trout were able to reveal all, that would not be what humanity requires. In one of Trout's science fiction adventures, *Pan-Galactic Three-Day Pass*, telepathic space aliens from across the universe seek instruction in the uniquely human creation, language.

The reason creatures wanted to use language instead of mental telepathy was that they found out they could get so much more *done* with language. Language made them so much more *active*. Mental telepathy, with everybody constantly telling everybody everything, produced a sort of generalized indifference to all information. But language, with its slow, narrow meanings, made possible to think about one thing at a time—to start thinking in terms of *projects* [Vonnegut's italics]. (*Rosewater*, 173)

Paradoxically, if one were actually to provide the unmitigated "truth" that Ulm sought, one would merely generate a meaningless mass of sensory impulses. It is the imposition of form that "narrow[s]" random thoughts ("telling everybody everything") into comprehensible units. These structures, plots, or "*projects*," convey a sense of significance because they emphasize certain ideas at the expense of others. Ironically, it is the resulting lacunae that produce an "*active*" effect upon the mind of the reader. At the very least, this passage advocates that lies, in the sense of omission, are the mainstay of literature, the most highly stylized mode of communication. Rendering every possible or even probable sensation, nuance, and circumstance is the equivalent of scatter-shot thinking that neutrally evokes a "generalized indifference to all information."

In this context, Eliot's defense of Kilgore's atrocious literary style is rendered explicable. Eliot proclaimed that although

science-fiction writers couldn't write for sour apples . . . it didn't matter. He [Eliot] said they were poets just the same since they were more sensitive to important changes than anybody who was writing well. "The hell with the talented sparrowfarts who write delicately of one small piece of one mere lifetime, when the issues are galaxies, eons, and trillions of souls yet to be born." (*Rosewater*, 18)

This passage is typical of Rosewater's penchant for histrionic gestures. But it reiterates the centrality of the act of discernment. One comes closer to generating meaning by leaving information out of a "big picture" than by pursuing the conventional practice of fully encompassing one's minuscule subject. The idea of providing the whole truth is itself an illusion, resulting in, at best, a chronology of data. This niggling definition of "writing well" through obsessive detail makes form an end unto itself. "Did you ever," inquires Vonnegut in a 1980 essay, "admire an empty-headed writer for his or her master of the language? No" (*Palm Sunday*, 77). Trout may be an aesthetic failure, but he fails big, which is always preferable to "sparrowfarts" who are under the mistaken impression that they can entirely master a subject if its scope is sufficiently diminished. Their triumph is that given a universe, they can reduce it to a grain of sand.

If Pan-Galactic telepathy was amenable to scatter-shot firearm metaphors, then Rudy Waltz, the "Deadeye Dick" of Vonnegut's 1982 novel, gives us the literal thing. He suffers his whole life long for another act of arbitrariness by discharging a gun out a window striking down the pregnant Eloise Metzger in her home miles away. Years after the event, the still guilt-ridden Rudy is attracted to the formulaic genre of drama. Novels attempt to naturalize the voices of characters and lyric poetry claims the unmediated language of the heart. A theatrical script, though, is written with such obvious evidence of its contrived nature as to include the names of speakers and stage directions. The purpose here is not to argue drama's lack of verisimilitude (it is no less or more "real" than any other art form), but to note that its transparently structured nature is the very thing that Rudy clings to in response to the meaninglessness of his deed. At moments of stress, such as Celia Hoover's funeral at which Felix experiences a mental collapse, Rudy breaks out of his confessional prose autobiography. He remarks, for example, during the aforementioned episode, "If this confrontation scene were done as a playlet, the set could be very simple" (*Deadeye*, 201). What follows is an actual scene from the proposed piece.

Why present these contrived dialogues in the middle of Rudy's comparatively seamless narration? These texts within texts, *mise-en-abymes*, draw attention to the constructedness of the novel itself as a means of organizing experience. Fabrication becomes, of necessity, a theme in itself. The writer, after all, must shuttle between (1) the necessity to edit and overstate in discourse and (2) the danger of mindless enslavement to conventions (even conventions of rebellion) of plot and rhetoric to which Arthur Ulm and the youthful Howard Campbell, Jr., succumbed. Not surprisingly, specifically at moments of identity crisis, when proscribed roles are most fragile, Rudy introduces the script conceit. In response to the prelude to the divorce of Genevieve and Felix or Celia Hoover's transformation into a cadaverous junkie, a more obvious gesture of organization is required to make the center hold.

As Vonnegut explains in a written interview for *Paris Match* (1977),

I guarantee you that no modern story scheme, even plotlessness, will give a reader genuine satisfaction, unless one of those old fashioned plots is smuggled in somewhere. I don't praise plots as accurate representations of life, but as ways to keep readers reading. (*Palm Sunday*, 110)

For Rudy to keep on "reading" his life, living it out as a narrative worthy of examination, he needs to render it sensible and imbue it with the energy to continue. That is something that plot, which implies purpose, provides. "Accuracy" calls for "plotlessness," but signification demands a "story scheme."

Ironically, when finally given the chance to stage his play *Katmandu* in New York City, Rudy finds himself benumbed by his anonymity in the vast city. "I no longer cared about the play," he confides. "It was Deadeye Dick tormented by guilt in Midland City, who had found old John Fortune's quite pointless death in Katmandu, as far away from his hometown as possible, somehow magnificent. He himself yearned for distance and death" (*Deadeye*, 130). Rudy uses one alter ego, Fortune, to confront another, Deadeye Dick, resulting in the neutralization of both. Fortune's quest-journey puts a laser-light on that aspect of capricious Deadeye Dick's experience centering around the need to overcome the "pointless" vagaries of existence. The result of staging the play is a sort of triangulation in which Rudy's epiphany is in *not* recognizing himself in Fortune because he has become so "distanced" from Deadeye Dick. The price, however, for breaking free of his character is the inability to mount a successful production.

Rudy is, in fact, barred from rehearsals by the company. "It wasn't," he explains, "that I had made impossible demands. My offense was that I seemed to know less about the play than anybody" (*Deadeye*, 130). The cast wants Rudy to be the high priest of their interpretive community, but he has absolved himself of any authority and has no more insight, indeed less, than the other participants. Not unreasonably, the actors demand a more dictatorial writer to furnish some motivation for what seems to them a rather repetitive and superficial plot. "What would you like to say?" responds Waltz credulously (*Deadeye*, 132). Refusing to structure the dialogue, Rudy cements his incompetence as a playwright.

Away from his parasitic parents and vindictive heart(less)land neighbors, he "regresses to being the boy he used to be" before the homicidal incident at twelve, which is to say that he assumes a more amorphous identity (*Deadeye*, 134). This sort of infantilization hardly seems a liberating moment, but the fact is that for a brief time Rudy Waltz has lost the need to impose this degree of, in Trout's terms, "slow, narrow meanings" through dramatic language (*Rosewater*, 173). The very organizational scheme of the play that explained his life to him, made it bearable, was the thing that could limit him as well. As Vonnegut humorously remarks in a speech collected in *Palm Sunday*, "Healthy people exposed to too many actors and too much scenery may wake up some morning to find their own imaginations dead" (164). Oxymoronically, art (dependent upon the relationship of form and content) sparks the imagination by focusing it while always potentially imprisoning the very creativity it nurtured through the strictures it imposes.

For instance, composing a role that parallels himself in *Katmandu* releases Rudy from the oppressive fiction of being Deadeye Dick. But the ease of role-playing itself proves irresistible, and his moments as an undefined entity, Rudy Waltz, are short-lived. On opening night, Rudy happens upon a marital spat at his brother's duplex in which Felix's wife, Genevieve, verbally assaults the Waltz family. Stunned, Rudy falls back to the path of least resistance, a playlet in which he enacts his familiar character of Deadeye Dick. At the dénouement, Rudy confides the truth of the Mrs. Metzger episode to Genevieve. "I had to let my sister-in-law know," he declares, "that I was somebody to be reckoned with—that I was a murderer. That was my claim to fame" (*Deadeye*, 147). The language of the passage, "claim to fame" and "somebody to be reckoned with," is embarrassingly trite, something out of a play even worse than *Katmandu*. There is an irony to its conventionality of phrasing, as if the dialogue were so much pastiche without any specific authorial impetus behind it. In essence, the formulaic writing takes on a life of its own. "I wrecked the marriage," Rudy observes. "It was an accident-prone time in my life, just as it was an accident-prone time when I shot Mrs. Metzger. That's all I can say" (*Deadeye*, 147). Claiming to be at a loss for words in an absurd yet deterministic universe, Rudy would absolve himself of self-authorship. In its stead, he would live out a pre-proscribed position in a plot that is "prone" to occur.   Of course, the very fact that he has just conveyed this scene of confrontation in the form of a play puts the lie to this approach.

Rudy is caught between regulating life into stories to create a space that imbues his life with some coherence and purpose and being held hostage by these spaces. Notably, there is no possibility of living without at least the conceit of a cohesive identity, so Rudy's moment of retreat into the (imagined) unselfconsciousness of childhood is a chimera. Rudy must arrest himself into some form of role-playing to have an identity while allowing for mutability. The desire for this balance may explain Rudy's diffidence at the offer of Haitian witch-doctor and Oloffson employee, Hippolyte Paul De Mille, to resuscitate Celia to comfort the weeping Felix. The Waltz brothers demur, but Hippolyte assures them that the "ghost would be nothing more than illusion, based harmlessly on whatever Celia used to be" (*Deadeye*, 238). "To Felix," explains Rudy, "it seemed that our Haitian headwaiter was offering to make him insane" (*Deadeye*, 238). Perpetually recapitulating a role, even an "illusory" one, is the most destructive act imaginable—the very definition of madness. To pacify Hippolyte, Rudy allows that he might revive someone, but only if the Waltzes are unacquainted with the individual. Using this strategy, Rudy can construct an entirely new "legend" to account for the roaming of barnstormer Will Fairchild (*Deadeye*, 239). It is a story he can change on a whim since he does not know the man in contradistinction to being saddled with the endless repetition of Celia's past. Jesting, Rudy calls himself the "William Shakespeare of Midland City" for composing this narrative (*Deadeye*, 239). Yet even through the self-deprecation, it is clear that Rudy is, for once, able to pose himself as the generator of discourse instead of the passive victim of it.

This is the sort of compromise that many of Vonnegut's characters fail to achieve—using illusions for the betterment of circumstances rather than to mire them further in repressive conditions. The concept is important enough that Vonnegut seeks out a nonfictional example of identity-ossification culled from the New York literati scene. He chooses William F. Buckley, the Yale-man-in-perpetuity, whose "intellectual voyage [through life] has been one of confirmations rather than discoveries" (*Palm Sunday*, 120). Having the good sense to have been born into better circumstances than Rudy Waltz and Billy Pilgrim, Buckley does not suffer from his unfaltering adherence to the priggish high-brow persona who hosts *Firing Line*. This "pinball machine" of conservatism, as Vonnegut terms him, programmed to credit more points the closer one's rhetoric adheres to social Darwinism, only tyrannizes others with his unforgiving constancy of identity (*Palm Sunday*, 121). That is not to suggest that much more ideologically protean figures like, for instance, Howard Campbell, Jr., are models to emulate. Campbell's lack of consistent "character" (is he a Nazi or a democratic patriot?) makes him an excellent double-agent but also a contemptible accessory to mass murder. Genevieve, another character marked by shallowness (although, obviously, of a vastly different degree and kind from that depicted in *Mother Night*), is given the contemptible title "Anyface" because she can play "Mrs. Waltz" as well as any of the nondescript women who precede or follow her (*Deadeye*, 134). In fact, that very indistinctness is almost a prerequisite for Felix who must perceive some horrible deficiency in his love object to elicit a marriage proposal. Hence, we have Felix's marriage to Donna whom he maimed in a car accident and his obsession with the constitutionally embittered, and later thoroughly tranquilized, Celia. Other of Vonnegut's disturbed creatures, Eliot Rosewater and Billy Pilgrim, lose touch with a coherent identity as they suffer, alternately, from alcohol-related blackouts and delusions of parallel universes. Granted, each of these characters offers inspired moments of insight. Yet these men and women are more compelling in their pathos than in their ability to generate a model of both ethically and pragmatically sustainable subjectivity. Again, one might wish to argue that Vonnegut's sole point is to rail against an irrational, unjust world that persecutes authentic goodness of people like Eliot Rosewater. However, by Vonnegut's own admission, based on his eldest son's psychopathology, he is loathe "to romanticize mental illness" and "to imagine a brilliant and beguiling schizophrenic who makes more sense about life than his or her doctor or even the president of Harvard University" (*Palm Sunday*, 241–242). The cliché is certainly attractive, but ultimately too façile a rationalization for Vonnegut to embrace uncritically.

Particularly in *Slaughterhouse-Five*, there is little in the way of coherent characterization and plot in the conventional sense because Vonnegut has destroyed the concept of linear time turning the protagonist Pilgrim into a schizophrenic. Billy maintains alternate lives as a young soldier, an optometrist in New England, and an inhabitant of a zoo exhibit on the planet Tralfamadore (a scenario he has lifted from a Kilgore Trout novel). Might these multifarious existences not be creative liberation for the self? That is not what one gleans from Pilgrim's creator, the author-surrogate narrating *Slaughterhouse-Five*.

He provides his reason in the form of a biblical analogy for telling the tale of Pilgrim's perpetual place in the destruction of Dresden, an event decades past even at the time of the first publication of the text.

And Lot's wife was told not to look back where all those people and their homes had been. But she *did* look back, and I love her for that, because it was so human.

So she was turned to a pillar of salt. So it goes.

People aren't supposed to look back. I'm certainly not going to do it anymore.

I've finished my war book now. The next one I write is going to be fun. This one [novel] is a failure, and had to be, since it was written by a pillar of salt. (22–23)

In essence, the categories of success or failure have no meaning because the task of authorship is already doomed to deficiency. Few beyond the eighteenth-century epistolary novelists or the pure stream-of-consciousness authors of modernism ever claimed to write to the moment. Indeed, to write one has to "look back," assess circumstances in retrospect, and then impose some form upon them adding, almost by definition, some element that perhaps was not even there to begin with, for example, a saving grace for Sodom and Gomorrah or Nazi Dresden. Vonnegut only facetiously promises never to recover the past; the specter of World War II remains a mainstay of his fiction. That is part of the humanism of his work, to relive the experience, this time with feeling. If every text is a flawed human production by virtue of this intentional misunderstanding and misremembrance, then the binarism of artistic triumph versus defeat becomes useless. The Platonic ideal of a "true" selfhood revealed and sustained in art is sheer sophistry. Nevertheless, art can at least reveal that what we have *is* a misrepresentation, a shadow on the wall of the cave. Do not, however, become beguiled by the shadows themselves. Billy Pilgrim's problem is that he has become like one of the shadow-ghosts that Rudy and Felix Waltz did not want to see walk the earth; he pointlessly recapitulates the same experience. But the person who wrote that story, who created the theme of infinite sadness/repetition, gained from it (as do readers), just as Rudy's moment of sanity was in making up the legend of Will Fairchild.

In his discussion of a later novel, *Galápagos* (1985), Peter Freese generalizes that from *Player Piano* (1952) onward, Vonnegut has posited that "the tension between the human mind and the given world cannot be alleviated by any attempt at imposing the mind's order upon the contingency of matter" (Freese, 168). Hence, one finds Vonnegut's penchant for apocalyptic scenarios as if "only by abdicating the irritating abilities of man's troublesome brain" could the need to impose false regulatory schemes (fiction) onto reality be contained (Freese, 168). Of course, the point is that it is Vonnegut who cannot help but give us renewal after the apocalypse, be it Rudy Waltz's deliverance to a tropical paradise after the destruction of Midland City or the survival of human language after the annihilation of the Milky Way galaxy in Trout's *Pan-Galactic Three-Day Pass*. Even in *Galápagos*, observes Freese, Kilgore's ghostly progeny, Leon, "in story form, tell us about future story-less times—thus contradicting its message [Darwinian-laced Schopenhauerian pessimism] by the choice of its medium"

(Freese 170). Notably, Kilgore's space aliens reject telepathy in favor of this flawed mechanism of communication, language, patched together by mere "pillars of salt." It is not, I would add, despite but because the narrative mechanism distorts reality, by giving it a form that allows us to imbue it with values that are not inherently there, that Vonnegut can consistently "articulate faith in the redemptive power of language and the sense-making ability of story-telling" (Freese, 170). Or, in the more homely phrase of Rudy Waltz, "We all see our lives as stories . . . and I am convinced that psychologists and sociologist and historians and so on would find it useful to acknowledge that" (*Deadeye*, 208).

This inexorable impulse to make the world intelligible through necessarily reductive narrative is revealed in *Palm Sunday* when Vonnegut states, "I do not really consider this [collected works-cum-autobiography] to be a masterpiece. I find it clumsy. I find it raw. It has some value, I think, as a confrontation between an American novelist and his own stubborn simplicity" (xvii). Subordinating experience into readable volumes, making one's own life formulaic to a degree, necessarily reduces the nuances and complexities of possibility. But it also imposes a degree of legibility, "simplicity" or sense in Vonnegut's nomenclature, onto disparate events, even if the paradigm does not encompass all truth(s). Pointing out the inadequacies of one's own method avoids the exaltation of oppressively overly deterministic life-plots like the tragi-comedy of *Deadeye Dick*. It also sabotages the perverse appeal of the hegemonic fascism of *Mother Night* wherein the "classic totalitarian mind" proceeds like a well-oiled machine (*Mother*, 162). The predictability is reassuring, but those machines are "missing teeth" otherwise known as "truths available and comprehensible even to ten-year-olds" (*Mother*, 162). The purpose of writing is not ruthlessly to sustain a seamless piece of reasoning or an aesthetically perfect object like the blue vase that obsesses Werner Noth while the human being who is carrying it is soundly abused. A neat structure is a means, but not an end unto itself. Its very tidiness almost brings it under suspicion. Arguably, that is why Vonnegut, who is well aware of the dangers of schizophrenia, keeps breaking in on himself in such works as *Slaughterhouse-Five* (e.g., "That was I. That was me. That was the author of this book" [125]). Vonnegut needs to have this second (indeed, multiplicatus) voice(s) in his own story of Dresden because the parable of Billy's insanity—that old juggernaut from *Mother Night* that war is hell—is true, but not true enough, because nothing ever is.

The alternatives, however, are either (1) to say nothing, and suffer the Kafkaesque inability of the narrator to write of Dresden at the opening of *Slaughterhouse-Five*, or (2) to delude oneself with the technical proficiency of Kraft-Potapov, which is just a self-referential modern aestheticism. "None of this [fascism, the Holocaust, oppression] really concerns me," the Russian asseverates, "Because I'm a painter. . . . That's the main thing" (*Mother*, 165). This is precisely the dichotomization between artistry and morality, particularly with respect to honesty, that Vonnegut is intent upon avoiding. Typically whimsical and self-deprecating, he does not claim to have succeeded in this endeavor. But his success *is* grounded in posing the problem of veracity in fictions of the self both at the level of subject matter, via the portrayal of would-be creative producers, and at the level of discourse, the fragmented structure and narrational stance of the plots themselves.

WORKS CITED

Dällenbach, Lucien. *The Mirror in the Text.* 1971. Trans. Jeremy Whitley and Emma Hughes. Chicago: University of Chicago Press, 1989.

Freese, Peter. "Surviving the End: Apocalypse, Evolution, and Entropy in Bernard Malamud, Kurt Vonnegut, and Thomas Pynchon." *Critique: Studies in Contemporary Fiction* 36.3 (1995): 14. Online. Melvyl System of University of California Libraries. Internet. 29 Apr. 1997.

Vonnegut, Kurt. *Deadeye Dick.* 1982. New York: Laurel-Dell, 1985.

———. *God Bless You, Mr. Rosewater, or Pearls Before Swine.* 1965. New York: Laurel-Dell, 1991.

———. *Mother Night.* 1961. New York: Laurel-Dell, 1991.

———. *Palm Sunday: An Autobiographical Collage.* 1981. New York: Laurel-Dell, 1984.

———. *Slaughterhouse-Five, Or The Children's Crusade.* 1966. New York: Laurel-Dell, 1991.

The Paradox of "Awareness" and Language in Vonnegut's Fiction

Loree Rackstraw

> Do I contradict myself?
> Very well then
> I contradict myself,
> I am large, I contain multitudes.
> —Walt Whitman

The writer may invent a story as a way of looking at the world—only to find, like Jorge Luis Borges, that the world he portrayed "traces the image of his face." Nonetheless, imaginative literature distills the experience of a culture into images that can shape its identity and transform its future. It can subvert the power of an enemy who would destroy and move a reader to rebellion or introspection, to laughter or to tears. Even if we may doubt the Aboriginal belief that the world must be sung into existence, most of us are still awed by the mysterious generative power of the word.

Persons outside academic institutions may not know (or care) that a renewed concern about the nature of language, reality, and literature has been blustering about the academy in the past decade or so. The speech of English professors at traditionally tedious meetings has been known to grow strident over the issue of whether words can refer to anything other than themselves. Recently, a stormy concern about the need for cultural literacy and a common national language has even made its way onto political ballots. A confused observer of this tempest, which seems to recur periodically in literate cultures, may study difficult critical theories about the nature and function of language and literature, theories like that of Jacques Derrida's "deconstructionism" that drifted across the Atlantic from France in the 1970s. Or one can avoid the philosophical bluster and instead consult novelistic versions of what Kurt Vonnegut might call "colorful weather maps" to see whether they offer any insight into the prevailing conditions.

That has been my pleasant task since first being introduced to "nontraditional fiction" as a student of Vonnegut in the mid-1960s at the Iowa Writers' Workshop in Iowa City. It was then that I first became intrigued with Vonnegut's form of mind, his endlessly playful way of viewing the world.

That period was also a time of tempestuous concern about language on university campuses. Part of the distress came then, as now, from the recognition of the impending information explosion and acceleration of technological change—as described in *Future Shock* by Alvin Toffler in 1970. But part also came from a related recognition of the importance of diversity: the cultural richness of racial plurality and gender distinctions made visible by civil rights movements; the differences in kinds and relationships of species needed to maintain ecological systems; and new political complexities that arose from the growing United States involvement in Vietnam. Language was inevitably a dynamic participant in these recognitions—articulating, altering, and being transformed by them. It was in that context that I came to appreciate what was for me a dramatically different and valuable way of seeing and being in the world that Kurt Vonnegut and his fictions represented.

Then, it was no more unusual on a late fall afternoon than it is now at the University of Iowa to see students protesting on the central campus or listlessly dozing in the lounge of the Memorial Union. As a student in the Writers' Workshop, I was walking through the Union after class with Vonnegut, my Workshop mentor, when he pointed out Nelson Algren, then also on the Workshop faculty, motionless and prone on a couch back in a corner of the lounge. His slight frame was spotlighted by a floor lamp. Vonnegut suggested a detour to be sure he was all right. In a less benign setting, Algren might have been a park bench bum on one of those Chicago streets he knew so well. His pale, wizened face was softened by sleep into an uncharacteristic innocence. One arm dangled to the floor with his hand curled on the cover of the book he was reading—*In Cold Blood* by Truman Capote.

"That's sweet—he's reading Capote," whispered Vonnegut. We walked on. "There ought to be some kind of pension fund for poets so they wouldn't have to grow old like this," he said quietly.

Somehow that little cameo of a scene stays in my mind as a harbinger of the change that was occurring in literature as well as in the culture as a whole. In literature, here was Nelson Algren, one of America's best writers of modern realism, nodding over the "new journalism" that Capote's *In Cold Blood* heralded, a book Vonnegut regarded as very significant to 20th-century literature. Both writers would become friends of Vonnegut, then a little recognized author and, at the time, working on his *Slaughterhouse-Five*, a novel that would shake the American literary traditions Algren and Capote helped establish.

In fact, within the next five years, Vonnegut would become a nationally known campus guru for youngsters struggling with the absurdities and paradoxes of global cultural change that were more insistent and destructive than those of the usual sophomoric crisis. But in 1965, with *Slaughterhouse* still resisting its liberation onto the page, he caused only a minor stir on the Iowa campus. It is true that he took a different approach to writing than other Workshop lecturers from whom one enjoyed the assurance that writing was a nearly sacred profession and way of life.

Instead, he seemed to regard fiction-making more practically—as a respectable enterprise like any other business. He said any writer had an obligation to fulfill certain expectations for the reading customer, and there surely was no reason to write if one did not have "something"—and publication—on one's mind. He even was skeptical about the self-effacing voice of Henry James, a Workshop idol whose soul hovered almost visibly in the warm moist air of the World War II Quonset huts that housed writing classes.

On the other hand, he had an extraordinary creative intelligence that resonated, if whimsically, with universal profundities of world literature. His conversations and writings celebrated the fundamental creative process in all its forms—whether it was operating in the body or cultural change or scientific inventiveness or in the literary and fine arts. He loved music, and played clarinet in occasional jam sessions at fellow Workshop lecturer Vance Bourjaily's country schoolhouse studio with other pick up musicians who found their way out to the farm. Indeed, jazz was one of the happier ways he found to celebrate life rather than take it seriously.

These were serious times, however, and he listened with grim and sympathetic outrage to a young student, Steve Smith, the first of the university protesters to burn his draft card in renunciation of U.S. involvement in the Vietnam War. He contributed canned goods to a campus program sending aid to voter registration activists who were at that time being gravely threatened in Selma, Alabama.

Nonetheless, his playful way of looking at the world—his form of mind as expressed in the ideas and structures of his novels—seems prophetically intertwined with changing visions about the nature of consciousness occurring in the humanities as well as in the sciences. Despite a dark concern for the future of the planet, his vision celebrates the diversity and adaptability so important for sustaining life, and it invents models of reality that are life enhancing rather than life controlling. They recapitulate current scientific models of a dynamic cosmos in its eternal processes of self-organization, rather than the static, mechanistic models of 17th-century Newtonian science.

While an emphasis upon the artifice of language and life is now an important focus in contemporary literary criticism, it was not in academic vogue in American universities when Vonnegut was making his way into literary history. Thus, it is worth noting that Vonnegut was one of the first American writers to make explicit through his self-reflective fiction the irony that he was using language to explore the curious and powerful and sometimes even dangerous nature of language itself—how it functions as "signs" or symbols that can influence our perceptions and what we take to be real, and thus can actually shape our system of values and ethics.

One can see the beginnings of this concern in his earliest novels—for example in *Mother Night* (1961), with the dilemma of American counterspy, Howard W. Campbell, Jr., a popular American playwright living in Germany, who agrees to provide coded information to officials in his own country via anti-Semitic propaganda messages he writes and broadcasts by radio for the Nazis. In responding to the call to exploit his gift as a writer and actor for the patriotic cause,

Campbell suffers the paradox that his use of language makes him adored by the Nazis and reviled by his own countrymen. He comes to the unbearable realization that his naïve use of language has caused him to actually be what he thought he was only pretending to be, a Nazi Jew-hater. The novel leaves readers with the chilling awareness of how history, to say nothing of personal identity, can be transformed by the way humans use and interpret language.

It seems likely that Vonnegut experienced something similar to the irony of Campbell's dilemma during his formative years. Stung by anti-German sentiment during the world wars, most German-American parents, including his, discouraged their children from speaking the German language. As a young enlisted soldier he must have been amazed by the paradox of his own capture, imprisonment, and abuse in Germany by what could have been his countrymen, an irony compounded when, as a prisoner of war, he was one of the few survivors of the Dresden fire-bombing by what actually were his own countrymen.

As Vonnegut has often said, his formal study of cultural anthropology at the University of Chicago influenced his interest in cultural relativism and his skepticism about absolutes. But his concerns with those who feel righteous about moral "Truth"—as he has said many times—obviously have earlier roots as well. In addition to being descended from a long line of Free Thinkers, he was deeply impressed by what he learned about the Bill of Rights as a high school student. His adamant public defense of the First Amendment underlines a motif threading through all his fiction: freedom of thought and expression are fundamental to human awareness and survival, no matter the risks these freedoms might create. For him, language is an intimate and curious aspect of the creative nature of humanity closely associated with consciousness or awareness. In this sense it has powers that resonate with the daemon or creative muse in classical Greek myth and thought.

So while the biblical—or any other—"Word" did not impress him as divine truth, the ironic intellectual and ethical problems that words create became important to his work as an artist, as did the profound philosophical and political questions language could both reveal and hide. As his talent in writing satirical fiction developed and his vision matured, his work dealt increasingly with the technical problems of how language—that human invention that creates rational order and meaning out of chaos—can also distort the clarity of our awareness. Through irony and satire he came to excel in making language reveal its inherent paradox: to function simultaneously with *daemonic* creativity or *demonic* destructiveness.

One of his most successful early efforts to show how stories can affect the way people perceive reality was *Cat's Cradle*, the 1963 "black humor" novel in which he created a new language and a new religion to convey how language and religion help to invent beliefs that provide meaning and purpose in the face of life's paradox. When the narrator begins the story with the quietly loaded statement, "Call me Jonah," Vonnegut launches a literary irony of several dimensions. One aspect is of course that of the Old Testament prophet who was punished for his failure to carry God's message of mercy to the Assyrians by being cast off a ship into a storm, swallowed by a whale, and then coughed up on dry land—a remarkable gesture of compassion. Second, the narrator's statement echoes Melville's *Moby-Dick*, a well-known story about human honor, revenge, and death in a battle against a whale and the mysterious powers of nature, which another outcast survivor begins to tell with nearly identical language: "Call me Ishmael." A third level is drawn from both these literary contexts, by putting Jonah or John, the fictional protagonist/narrator of a story about the day the world ended, into the same role as protagonists in these two powerful stories from the past. At the novel's end, John even wants to leave some "magnificent symbol" atop a whale-shaped mountain.

To add to the complexity, the narrator John's surname is never given, except to imply that it is a German name, most likely that of Vonnegut himself. (Thus, he foreshadows the style he introduces later in *Slaughterhouse*, of entering the novel himself as a character.) It also should be noted that the German form of Jonah is Johann, the first name of the great German author, Goethe. It is also the name of Johann Faustus, the actual historical model for Faust in Goethe's masterpiece of that name. (Not only does Vonnegut refer to Goethe on several occasions in his writing and interviews, but the title and central theme of his previous novel, *Mother Night*, is actually taken from Faust.)

As narrator of *Cat's Cradle*, John tells us his name is also the same as that of Bokonon, another Jonah (real name: Lionel Boyd Johnson), who was washed up on the shore of San Lorenzo Island where he established himself as a holy prophet and invented a new religion called Bokononism. John comes to believe in Bokononism because it seems to explain coincidences and help soften contradictions in his life. Thus the three named Jonah/Johns—the Old Testament figure, the narrator, and Bokonon—can all be seen as daemonic muses or masks of Vonnegut in their creative, authorial roles as writers or myth-makers. Likewise, he reminds us of the great biblical and secular literatures and themes of Western tradition that have all had a role in creating meanings that give comfort or direction to an otherwise paradoxical and absurd human life. Tangential to them must surely be the New Testament genesis story in the Gospel of John, which assigns generative divinity to the biblical word for the Christian world.

The narrator tells us he intended his book as a factual account of the bombing of Hiroshima with a title of *The Day the World Ended*. Instead, the novel unfolds another kind of apocalypse in which the world is destroyed by Ice-Nine, likely a metaphor of Vonnegut's experience of the Dresden fire-bombing (with the epigraph disclaimer that "nothing in this book is true"). In the story, this fictional world ends when the children of a great scientist find themselves on the tropical island of San Lorenzo where they accidentally release their father's invention of Ice-Nine which turns the earth into ice (rather than into fire as it had in Dresden and Hiroshima)—but not before the narrator-protagonist discovers the new religion of Bokononism that has given a sense of purpose to the miserable life of San Lorenzons.

The central theme of Bokonon's scriptures is drawn from Charles Atlas' comic book ads for muscle building through the exercise of "dynamic tension." Thus, Vonnegut satirizes the logic of the principle of opposites and makes his point: the purpose of a text, holy or profane, is to help strengthen the reader's sense of power and purpose in a world of accidents and contradictions, whether through building muscles or spiritual atonement. The narrator comes to the bittersweet realization that it is through Bokononist "foma" (harmless untruths) that humans can find the energy to play out the joke, the absurdity, the purposeless polarity that makes up the cat's cradle game called Life. (Perhaps the greatest irony of *Cat's Cradle* is that it eventually qualified as a master's thesis, giving Vonnegut a delayed but earned graduate degree in cultural anthropology from the University of Chicago!)

The inherent paradox of language and of life is an ironic theme and aesthetic central to the Vonnegut oeuvre. Insight into and resolution of this paradox was probably most clearly articulated in the 1973 novel, *Breakfast of Champions*, when the intractable abstract expressionist painter Rabo Karabekian defends his painting, "The Temptation of Saint Anthony," to a skeptical audience at an arts festival. Present in that audience is another guest of the festival, the fictional author Kilgore Trout, and none other than Vonnegut himself who "literally" appears as a character disguised by mirrored sunglasses.

The huge Karabekian painting is comprised of a green background bisected by a single vertical stripe of "day-glo orange reflecting tape," likely a Vonnegutian parody of the aesthetic concept of the "golden section," the geometrical proportion believed to be universally pleasing. In reading Karabekian's speech, one may also be hearing Vonnegut's own defense against critics who were by then beginning to be quite volatile about his nontraditionalism. He has Karabekian say that his painting:

shows everything about life which truly matters, with nothing left out. It is a picture of the awareness of every animal—the "I am" to which all messages are sent. It is all that is alive in any of us—in a mouse, in a deer, in a cocktail waitress. It is unwavering and pure, no matter what preposterous adventure may befall us. A sacred picture of Saint Anthony alone is one vertical, unwavering band of light. . . . Our awareness is all that is alive and maybe sacred in any of us. Everything else about us is dead machinery. (*Breakfast*, 221)

Now read the description of the "fire-storm of Indianapolis" that another Vonnegut character from an earlier novel, Eliot Rosewater, envisions in a hallucination that derives from his "inexplicable guilt and anxiety." In *God Bless You, Mr. Rosewater* we are told that Eliot:

was awed by the majesty of the column of fire, which was at least eight miles in diameter and fifty miles high. The boundaries of the column seemed absolutely sharp and unwavering, as though made of glass. Within the boundaries, helixes of dull red embers turned in stately harmony about an inner core of white. The white seemed holy. (201)

I think it is safe to say that this description, published eight years before *Breakfast*, gives a close approximation of the Rabo Karabekian painting. When we link it with a factual, eyewitness description of the Dresden fire-bombing quoted in *Rosewater*, Vonnegut's intent seems evident:

As the many fires broke through the roofs of the burning buildings, a column of heated air rose more than two and a half miles high and one and a half miles in diameter. . . . In a short time the temperature reached ignition point for all combustibles, and the entire area was ablaze. In such fires complete burnout occurred; that is, no trace of combustible material remained. (201)

This horrific baptism by fire seems to be the ironic vehicle for an unexpectedly Platonic aesthetic—a vision of the form of life spirit or soul abstracted from "combustible material," that is, freed of the literary conventions, sensory illusions and truth-altering institutions that limit and distort. It seems to be Vonnegut's vision of what the daemonic life essence actually is, unlimited by biological or any other encumbrances. The irony is that it is apparently a vision Vonnegut has abstracted from his own painful experience of surviving what he called the "moral zero" of the Dresden holocaust in which thousands of humans perished.

That column of light, then, represented by "day-glo orange reflecting tape," may be his way of expressing the paradox that new life stems from primordial chaos—and that just as planetary life and awareness arose out of the cosmic chaos, so his own renewal comes from inventing new forms out of the turbulence of his experience. And, not incidentally, it is to express the irony that it was the disaster of Dresden that helped him gain this insight. This story, then, like the Karabekian painting, is to transform into an artistic aesthetic the tragic experience of the chaos represented by the Allied bombing of Dresden, which did indeed cause the purposeless, rapid combination of all substance with oxygen, the holocaust of death. As usual with Vonnegut, however, there is a further irony: While death is what human life in its awareness attempts to avoid, inherent in what we call life is also the bodily process of dying, that is, a slower but similar process of oxidation. In short, we are born to die and doomed by our human evolution to a painful awareness of that paradox.

But there is yet a further paradox that takes this vision a step beyond what the Greeks celebrated in their great tragic dramas: that column of light representing life's consciousness was visible to Dresden survivors only because of fire and as a characteristic of it. That is, light is radiant energy that accompanies the oxidation process in combustion. Light—and the life that is aware of it—cannot occur separate from that process of oxidation. Or, as Jorge Luis Borges said in his *Labyrinths*, "Time . . . is a fire which consumes me, but I am the fire. The world, unfortunately, is real; I, unfortunately, am Borges" (234). That is to say, Vonnegut celebrates that daemonic life essence of awareness represented in Rabo Karabekian's painting, but the origin of the image in the Dresden holocaust confirms his recognition of the ultimate paradox: the very essence that makes life awareness sacred is inevitably of those same transforming processes. Light cannot be separate from fire. We are the profane and consuming fire, and at the same time, the sacred light.

This paradox is similar to that described by psychoanalyst C. G. Jung when he spoke of the "primordial experience" of the poet as:

the source of his creativeness, but . . . so dark and amorphous that it requires the related mythological imagery to give it a form. . . . It is nothing but a tremendous intuition striving for expression. It is like a whirlwind that seizes everything within reach and assumes visible form as it swirls upward. Since the expression can never exhaust its possibilities, the poet must have at his disposal a huge store of material if he is to communicate even a fraction of what he has glimpsed, and must make use of difficult and contradictory images in order to express the strange paradoxes of his vision. (Jung, 198)

Thus, we have Karabekian, the invented creator of the profound painting, who is, after all, drawn by Vonnegut as a cruelly insensitive and humorless man—in marked contrast to the beatific image of his vision. People in the bar where this artist gives Vonnegut-the-narrator his "rebirth" experience are themselves glowing—not from sacred light, but rather from the pollution of chemicals in their clothing created by the earnest (and paradoxical) productivity of their community. To abstract an immutable image of the sacred life essence as separate from the paradox of mortal life is likewise a humanly created artifice like Karabekian's painting and of the novel itself. It is created in such a way as to alert readers to its sacred symbolism but also its difficult and contradictory artificiality, and thus to the profaneness of its inventor. The epiphany Vonnegut celebrates is the awareness of primal life energy. His renewal comes from the creative ability to articulate that awareness, even if what he invents is limited and may be short-lived. To be a conscious participant in this creative process is a renewing experience to be cherished and protected at all cost—for the sake of life itself.

With this view, I differ only in emphasis with Kathryn Hume in her insightful discussion of Vonnegut's congruities with the Greek perception of cosmic flux. She emphasizes the distinction between the positive Heraclitean view of fire as divine and generative, and Vonnegut's view of fire as "the ultimate nightmare," but notes that "fire's visible element, purified and intensified, with its wavering and fluctuations gone, is light. Light is not so destructive. Light has associations with spiritual enlightenment, with rising above the self. . . . In *Breakfast of Champions* he affirms the identity of individual consciousness with this band of light" (Hume, 223).

In this affirmation, I think Vonnegut is as closely aligned with Borges as with Heraclitus, and perhaps even more so with the physicist and Nobel laureate, Ilya Prigogine, whose paradoxical "chaos theory" research focuses on the complex order that arises out of chaotic systems, an apparent contradiction between the biological sciences and 19th-century thermodynamics. Prigogine is among those exploring how complexity and life itself can spontaneously emerge in the face of the universal tendency of heat energy to dissipate (leading to the "heat death" of the universe). Prigogine reconceptualizes the Second Law of Thermodynamics (in a closed system, entropy or disorder always tends to increase) to argue that in turbulent systems, this entropic tendency is so great that it actually can power a non-linear transformation toward self-organization. Prigogine says, "This description of nature, in which order is generated out of chaos . . . leads to the conception of matter as active, as in a continuous state of becoming" (13).

In discussing the cultural ramifications of Prigogine's work, cultural critic N. Katherine Hayles says,

The reconceptualization of the void as a space of creation has deep affinities with the postmodern idea of a constructed reality. . . . This reconstitution makes clear that the world as humans experience it is a collaboration between reality and social construction. . . . Prigogine's vision illuminates and validates the dialectic between order and disorder by finding analogous processes in physical systems. Moreover, it imparts an optimistic turn to such processes by positing them as sources of renewal for the universe. (14)

Vonnegut points toward the collaboration between reality and social construction when he titles Rabo Karabekian's painting the "Temptation of Saint Anthony," perhaps to remind us of Gustave Flaubert's play of the same name, in which the asceticism of the protagonist actually generates the illusions that tempt him. Finally, exhausted by these enticements, Saint Anthony is able to perceive in the ubiquitous chaotic flux the beauty of "being matter" (i.e., Prigogine's "continuous state of becoming")—the beauty of seeing and being part of the "birth of life . . . the beginning of movement" and to celebrate the absolute generative sensorium of his own body-mind. Likewise, Vonnegut seems to say that by embracing the paradoxical nature of our generative awareness (instead of trying to transcend it) we might live more humbly and gracefully with the ambiguities of life and death, and of the profane and sacred. Again, this may be why Rabo's brash personality is drawn as the opposite of what his painting celebrates. The paradox of Rabo is, I think, confirmed by Vonnegut's later treatment of this character and his paintings in his 1987 novel, *Bluebeard*, in which Rabo strives to achieve paintings that express soul, which he identifies as both life and death.

The rich ambiguity of the symbol in Rabo's painting of the unwavering band of light might also be more fully appreciated when viewed in (dare one say it?) the light of Goethe's *Faust*, which I believe figures as a parodic context to *Breakfast of Champions*. Early in the play Faust used the "triply burning light" or the sign of the Trinity in order to conjure Mephistopheles into materializing out of his canine form. Saluting Faust, Mephisto confesses his paradoxical identity—that he is "part of that Force which would do evil yet forever works the good." Which is to say, his efforts to destroy life result in the opposite of what he intended. Echoing the Dresden band of light and Prigogine's chaos theory, he says he has arisen out of the absolute primal chaos and, like man, he is:

Part of the Darkness which gave birth to light,
The haughty Light, which now seeks to dispute
The ancient rank and range of Mother Night,
But unsuccessfully, because try as it will,
It is stuck fast to bodies still.
It streams from bodies, bodies it makes fair,
A body hinders its progression; thus I hope
It won't be long before its scope
Will in the bodies' ruination share.
(II. 1350–1354)

That is, once consciousness evolved out of the cosmic chaos and became self-aware, it inevitably invented distinctions with language—differentiations between self and other, night and day, life and death, good and evil—which, with its enlightened ego, it took to be absolute. Goethe's "haughty" man (Faust) with his Light/consciousness has not recognized that he is inherently part of the undifferentiated primal source, the absolute Darkness; he suffers the illusion that he is distinct from that Darkness or that he can transcend it because of his consciousness, his intelligent ability to invent words to create reason. But his Light is "stuck fast" to the body and is subject to the cosmic paradox: consciousness by its very nature, cannot exist apart from body. Mephisto—perversely annoyed by the naïve arrogance of man and committed to annihilating his volatile paradoxes and tiresome cycles—complains that life keeps unfolding (the Heraclitean flux and Prigogine's chaos generating order) despite his efforts:

> I don't get far, when all is said and done.
> This stupid earth, this Somethingness,
> For all that I have undertaken
> Against it, still remains unshaken . . .
> And so it goes. Sometimes I could despair!
> In earth, in water, and in air
> A thousand growing things unfold,
> In dryness, wetness, warmth and cold!
> Had I not specially reserved the flame
> I wouldn't have a thing in my own name.
> (II. 1373–1378)

If Vonnegut's portrayal of the Dresden paradox is read in the context of *Faust*, then Mephistopheles whose flame represents death, and the Trinity whose "triply burning light" represents the creative life force, can both be synonymous with the paradoxical Dresden flame: all three derive from the primal cosmic void and have transforming abilities. But Mephistopheles is no more able to stop the creative flux than Rabo Karabekian (or Saint Anthony!) was able to live by pure awareness. The generative life/death paradox is central to both Goethe's and Vonnegut's work. Read in this light, Vonnegut's repetitive "So it goes" that occurs after every death in *Slaughterhouse-Five* may express cynical resignation, as many critics saw it, but could also be read as a celebration of the immutable life process, even if, in his view, that process is essentially purposeless. Regardless, like Goethe, Vonnegut seems always to have celebrated those who would strive on in the face of life's absurdity.

Critic Peter Reed perceived this early on. In his discussion of Vonnegut's 1962 novel, *Mother Night*, he argued that Vonnegut "does not submit to the darkness of nothingness as Mephistopheles does. . . . He recognizes that we are each a part of that original darkness, but affirms 'that supercilious light' in its struggles against 'Mother night'" (118).

Vonnegut's whimsical recapitulations of honored literatures like *Faust* affirm the continuity as well as the transforming cultural powers such archetypal figures have had and will continue to have. Humanity is unified and renewed—at least temporarily—by participating in this literary continuity with its generative transformations of language and "truths" that shape and are reshaped by human awareness and action. This seems particularly evident in *Breakfast of Champions* when he enters the novel's text to explain what he is actually doing. That is, Vonnegut as the "holy" ghost writing the novel also echoes the creative role of Goethe. He may even impishly have perceived himself as a spin-off of the actual historical figure who inspired Goethe and the many other legendizers of Faust: the 16th-century German magician and presumed companion of Satan, Doctor Johann Georgius Sabellicus Faustus, Junior. This "real" Doctor Faustus, a contemporary of Martin Luther, was a star-gazer and fortune-teller, as well as a teacher and professor, who dabbled in alchemy on the side. He was said to have spiced up his classroom performances by producing Homeric heroes alive, and supposedly once summoned up the form of Helen of Troy. Like many protagonists in Vonnegut's early novels, he was often accompanied by a dog, believed by Faustus' superstitious peers to be his satanic supernatural guardian.[1]

Of course Goethe's version of that dog in his *Faust I* is the poodle transformed into Mephisto. In *Breakfast*, it appears in the epilogue when Vonnegut as narrator tells us he is waiting to intercept Kilgore Trout as he walks in the eerie center of a Midland City whose description resembles the setting for a Raymond Chandler novel. As Creator of the novel (and of Kilgore Trout, identified here with Vonnegut's father), his purpose will be to tell Kilgore his future and then to free him from any further use in his stories. That is, Vonnegut's patriarchal authority conflict as a driving force in his fiction has apparently been resolved. The scene is one of Vonnegut's funniest, as he turns his own suave private-eye imitation into slapstick. When he steps out of his rented car in a dark section of Midland City to address Kilgore Trout, he unknowingly alerts a fierce Doberman pinscher guard dog who is poised to attack him from behind a fence. The dog, surely a spin-off of the satanic figure in the old Faustus stories, is named Kazak, echoing the loyal space hound from *The Sirens of Titan*. The devilish dog springs, alerting the flight chemistry of Vonnegut the Creator, who leaps completely over the automobile and lands on all fours in the street. Fierce Kazak is flung back by the fence and, defeated by gravity, knocked senseless.

To see this scene as a parody of Faustian themes, one can recall that Mephistopheles lost his power over Faust to God because his magical enchantments failed to keep Faust from actively striving in life; in *Breakfast*, the satanic canine loses his power over Vonnegut—not to God, but to a (de)fence the author invents with language, and to the natural force of gravity. Furthermore, Vonnegut as narrator tells us he has invented a way to keep striving and to avoid suicide by bringing chaos to traditional literary orders, so as to create new fictions that can make life more humane and harmonious (*Breakfast*, 210). In *Faust II* the heavenly ascension of the soul of Faust is by the power of divine love, whereas in Vonnegut's text, the Faustian narrator is bodily resurrected, if temporarily, by the automatic response of his own biochemistry triggered by terror, that is, by his awareness of danger.

But it seems that Vonnegut also performs another kind of resurrection by freeing Kilgore Trout, here the mask of patriarchal authority, from his psyche and from his literary form. First, like the historical Faustus, Vonnegut as mock magician does all manner of tricks to Kilgore, to convince him he is Kilgore's Creator. He says he could reproduce Helen of Troy before Trout's very eyes, even as the real Faustus was said to have done, and even as Mephistopheles did for Faust in Goethe's play.[2]

Then Vonnegut tells Kilgore to "look up" at the apple he holds, possibly as a parody of the last scene of Gothe's *Faust II* in which "Doctor Marianus," the teacher of the mysteries of the creative force, admonishes heaven-bound penitents to "Gaze upward to that saving glance" from the Eternal-Feminine (I. 12097). But in Vonnegut's narrative, the divine saving glance is replaced by an apple, the obvious symbol of discrimination and knowledge—that seducer of Adam and of Faust—which he uses to satirize Goethe's and our insistence on images of divine truth and salvation. He tells Kilgore that the apple is the "symbol of wholeness and harmony and nourishment. . . . We Americans require symbols which are richly colored and three-dimensional and juicy. Most of all, we hunger for symbols which have not been poisoned by great sins" (*Breakfast*, 293). Vonnegut's apple is, I think, to remind us to be conscious of our persistent and paradoxical need to invent new works of art and bodies of knowledge to transcend our awareness of mortality and impotence, and to recognize that the epiphany we create with language is inevitably doomed to be temporary, given the ironic flux of life that awareness reveals.

Having freed the patriarchal aspect of his psyche, Vonnegut himself floats pleasantly through the void with the angst-ridden Kilgore Trout, surely suggesting a parody of "Pater Ecstaticus," Goethe's epithet for Saint Anthony, who likewise appears at the end of *Faust II*. Stage directions say Pater is "floating up and down," suspended in the ecstatic torment of martyrdom. Pater says, "Lightning bolts, shatter me! So the All may utterly/ Abolish the Nullity,/ Gleam the fixed star above,/ Essence of endless love" (*Faust II*, II. 11861–11865). Vonnegut's understanding of that "gleam" is the light of life's essence: the awareness that makes creative and adaptive life possible. It has freed him from such martyrdom so he is now comfortably attuned to the nullity in which he dreamily levitates. In the distance he hears Trout call out, in his father's voice, "*Make me young, make me young, make me young!*" (*Breakfast*, 295). It is the voice of "logical" patriarchal civilization with its ecstatic torment and mortal need—if not for transcendence, at least for the power to find renewal and direction in the void.

Kilgore Trout, the incorrigible science fiction writer, has been Vonnegut's daemon and doppelgänger who has "kept striving" through a number of his novels. In *God Bless You, Mr. Rosewater* (1965), he makes his living working at a trading stamp redemption center, giving away harmless gifts. It is he who assumes a Christ-like benevolence to pronounce the sanity of "flamboyantly ill" Rosewater, the alcoholic philanthropist who went insane partly because of the social strain of loving other strivers against paradox: science fiction writers, volunteer firemen, and useless paupers.

In *Slaughterhouse-Five* (1969), he is Billy Pilgrim's favorite author of science fiction about people like himself who were "trying to re-invent themselves and their universe" to help deal with life's absurdity and war's irrational cruelties. Kilgore's stories spring up throughout the novel as mini-illustrations of how the ideas of science, religion, and politics become the lenses that alter human perception and shape values and "truth."

In *Galápagos* (1985), Kilgore Trout is the deceased father of the "ghost writer" of the story who was accidentally beheaded while working as a shipbuilder on the *Bahia de Darwin*, a Swedish ship wrecked on a Galápagos island. Despite outraged summons from his father who beckons from the "blue tunnel to the Afterlife," Leon Trotsky Trout inhabits the head of Captain Kleist (a Vonnegut look-alike), whose inept navigation caused the wreck—and the survival of a bizarre group of people who will evolve into a harmless race of small-brained, handless "fisherfolk." Leon Trout's irrepressible need for creative expression parallels the biological need to reproduce, both leading to the novel's thesis that how we perform the generative dance of life is largely a matter of luck, accidents, and genes.

In *Jailbird* (1982), Trout appears only briefly as the pseudonym of convict Bob Fender, a gentle and generous friend to all inmates, who is serving a life term for treason. Never mind that his "treason" was his brief cohabitation as a soldier in Korea with a beautiful Korean spy disguised as a nightclub singer. At that time, he was a shy, virgin veterinarian who had been drafted to be a meat inspector for the army, and who was set up to be the brunt of a joke by fellow officers who told the singer he was an elite commander of an atomic bomb guard unit. Now in prison for life, he has taken up writing science fiction. Walter Starbuck, the protagonist of *Jailbird*, tells us that Trout/Bob Fender wrote Walter into one of his stories about a judge from the planet Vicuna whose soul was flying about the universe looking for a habitable planet and body after his own planet was destroyed. People on Vicuna, who could easily leave their bodies, became "weightless, transparent, silent awarenesses and sensibilities . . . when they floated around without their bodies" (56). The judge's soul floats into a jail on the planet earth, which he mistakes for a meditation center for philosophers, and ends up stuck in the head of aging Walter Starbuck, imprisoned on false charges of being a participant in the Watergate cover-up.

Stuck in the head of Kurt Vonnegut for all these years, it appears, is the same daemonic soul of awareness and sensibility that finds its apparently final inscription as Kilgore Trout in *Timequake*, Vonnegut's 1997 novel, which he insists is his last. In the Preface he claims this book is a story of how he failed to write a novel he now calls *Timequake One*. The protagonist, eighty-four-year-old Kilgore Trout, described the nature of the timequake as "a cosmic charley horse in the sinews of Destiny" in his unfinished memoir entitled *My Ten Years on Automatic Pilot*. This cosmic event occurred in the year 2001 when "a sudden glitch in the space-time continuum, made everybody and everything do exactly what they'd done during a past decade . . . a second time" (xii). A total of sixteen hilarious Trout stories and a play are drawn upon by Vonnegut to reveal the ineptitudes of human awareness, but also to set up a happy fate for Kilgore, who emerges as a tenacious model of hope after Vonnegut's literary career of misanthropic worry about determinism and random accidents. Kilgore becomes a hero through his humanitarian use of free will.

The timequake is Vonnegut's metaphorical device to defamiliarize the disintegrating cultural condition of America, in the hope that it might shock readers into an awareness of their careless disregard of human potential and indifference to the ideals of human dignity and unanimity in our society. Now an old man, Kilgore Trout is so cynical that when he is hauled with other homeless bums to a shelter in upper Manhattan (the former Museum of the American Indian, which has been moved to a safer location downtown), he makes a habit of dumping every story he writes into a wire waste receptacle in front of the fortified headquarters of the American Academy of Arts and Letters next door to the shelter. The academy's executive secretary is Monica Pepper. Those stories are read with delighted awe by her husband, Zoltan, a man she had paralyzed from the waist down in an accident, and who once plagiarized a Kilgore Trout story when he was a boy.

After "free will kicks in again," and unsuspecting folks on "automatic pilot" crash their cars and airplanes, or fall down at the foot of escalators, the only person who seems able to take control of himself again is none other than Kilgore! To mobilize people to put their free will to use and restore order, he shouts out a mantra that soon is broadcast over the media to the whole world: "You were sick, but now you're well again, and there's work to do" (*Timequake*, 178). This mantra, which becomes "Kilgore's Creed," is too late to help Zoltan, the disabled plagiarizer, however. He is killed the instant the timequake is over by a berserk fire truck that smashes his wheelchair into the steel door of the academy headquarters. But with that fortress now blasted open, Kilgore uses the building as a morgue and sets up a triage hospital in the homeless shelter next door, after organizing the bums into rescue teams.

Lest we get too optimistic about the beneficial use of free will at this point in Vonnegut's storytelling, we are favored with a flashback that reveals how Kilgore's father accidentally became a specialist in ornithology by discovering birds that were making themselves extinct or causing chaos by choosing easier methods of survival than those deterministic instincts of natural selection that had sustained their species for eons (*Timequake*, 159).

Never mind, it all ends happily. Happily? Perhaps for the first time in his writing career, Kurt Vonnegut has found a "gaily mournful" way to actually end a novel! Order is restored, and Kilgore is driven in widow Monica Pepper's armored limousine to the kind of retirement setting Vonnegut had wished for Nelson Algren decades earlier: the Ernest Hemingway suite of the writers' retreat Xanadu, in the summer resort village of Point Zion, Rhode Island. The retreat appears to be a reward for his heroic efforts during the disaster that ensued once the timequake finished its ten-year rerun and free will kicked in again. There he is welcomed by a loving extended family including members of the Pembroke Mask and Wig Club, the Xanadu household staff, members of Alcoholics Anonymous and Gamblers Anonymous, which meet in the Xanadu ballroom, and battered children, women, and grandparents who also have found shelter there and are grateful for Kilgore's Creed.

Kilgore's biggest achievement, however, is more subtle—Vonnegut tells us that he never lost his self-respect: "His indestructible self-respect is what I loved most about Kilgore Trout" (*Timequake*, 183). This quality surely resonates well with Goethe's celebration of the stalwart Faust, ever striving in the face of demonic adversities.

The final reward for Kilgore is his role as the provider of sound effects in the last act of the Pembroke Mask and Wig Club's production of *Abe Lincoln in Illinois* by Robert E. Sherwood. It is an epiphanic scene that represents Vonnegut's celebration of the nobility made possible by humanity's capacity for awareness and language. Kilgore is to blow the antique steam whistle that signals Lincoln's departure by train from Illinois to assume the presidency in Washington on the eve of the Civil War. The scene allows Vonnegut to quote Lincoln's eloquent farewell message in which he recounts the ideals of the American Union. Then, in a rousing farewell, the crowd breaks into the singing of "John Brown's Body" as Lincoln gets into the car. The song signals our memory of the Stephen Vincent Benét poem in tribute to John Brown's anti-slavery heroism and in compassion for both sides of the disastrous Civil War. It is a moment not lost on the sound effects man:

That was when Trout was supposed to blow the whistle, and he did.

As the curtain descended, there was a sob backstage. It wasn't in the playbook. It was ad lib. It was about beauty. It came from Kilgore Trout. (*Timequake*, 203)

And after the play, a triumphant Kilgore gets to go to the cast party clambake on the beach, a party at which many of Vonnegut's own family and friends are present. There, proudly adorned in the tuxedo of Monica Pepper's deceased husband, he offers his and Vonnegut's star-gazing benediction to the uniqueness of human awareness in the universe: "Let us call it soul" (*Timequake*, 214).

Thus, Vonnegut echoes the revelation first offered by Rabo Karabekian in his "Temptation of Saint Anthony" painting nearly twenty-five years earlier. Like Rabo and Kilgore, he has never ceased striving, nor has he ever betrayed his gaily mournful respect for the daemonic awareness that has driven his half century of literary effort to create aesthetic form and a humane culture out of the chaos of life's paradox.

Kilgore's Creed may have kept him going, too.

NOTES

1. For an apparent biographical account of the life and exploits of this remarkable figure, see William Rose, ed., *The Historie of the Damnable Life and Deserved Death of Doctor John Faustus*.

2. A print-maker of some accomplishment and productivity, Vonnegut includes among his portfolio of works a picture entitled "Helen," reprinted in *The Vonnegut Chronicles*, edited by Peter Reed and Marc Leeds.

WORKS CITED

Borges, Jorge Luis. *Labyrinths: Selected Stories and Other Writings.* Donald D. Yates and James E. Erby, eds. New York: New Directions, 1962, 1964.

Flaubert, Gustave. *The Temptation of Saint Anthony.* Kitty Mrosobsky, trans. Ithaca, NY: Cornell University Press, 1981.

Goethe, Johann Wolfgang von. *Faust: Part One and Part Two.* Charles E. Passage, trans. Indianapolis: The Library of Liberal Arts/The Bobbs-Merrill Company, Inc., 1965.

Hayles, N. Katherine. *Chaos and Order: Complex Dynamics in Literature and Science.* Chicago: University of Chicago Press, 1991.

Hume, Kathryn. "The Heraclitean Cosmos of Kurt Vonnegut," *Papers on Language and Literature* 18.2 (Spring 1982): 208–224.

Jung, C. G. *Psychological Reflections.* Jolande Jacobi and R.F.C. Hull, eds. New York: Bollingen Foundation, 1953; Princeton: Princeton University Press, 1970.

Melville, Herman. *Moby-Dick; or The Whale.* New York: Heritage Press, 1943.

Prigogine, Ilya. "Man's New Dialogue with Nature." *Perkins Journal* (Summer 1983): 4–14.

Reed, Peter J. *Kurt Vonnegut, Jr.* New York: Thomas Y. Crowell/Warner Books, 1972.

Reed, Peter J., and Marc Leeds, eds. *The Vonnegut Chronicles.* Westport, CT: Greenwood Press, 1996.

Rose, William, ed. *The Historie of the Damnable Life and Deserved Death of Doctor John Faustus.* 1592. Notre Dame, IN: University of Notre Dame Press, 1963.

Vonnegut, Kurt. *Bluebeard.* New York: Delacorte Press, 1987.

———. *Breakfast of Champions.* New York: Delacorte Press/Seymour Lawrence, 1973.

———. *Cat's Cradle.* New York: Dell Publishing, 1963.

———. *Galápagos.* New York: Delacorte Press/Seymour Lawrence, 1985.

———. *God Bless You, Mr. Rosewater.* New York: Holt Rinehart, 1965.

———. *Jailbird.* New York: Delacorte Press/Seymour Lawrence, 1979.

———. *Mother Night.* New York: Harper and Row, 1961, 1966.

———. *The Sirens of Titan.* New York: Dell Publishing, 1959.

———. *Timequake.* New York: G. P. Putnam's Sons, 1997.

Kurt Vonnegut's Bitter Fool: Kilgore Trout

Peter J. Reed

By now Kilgore Trout must be almost as well known as his creator. This bedraggled fictional alter-ego has persisted in Kurt Vonnegut's books since his first appearance in *God Bless You, Mr. Rosewater* (*GBR*), most reports of his demise proving premature. Trout made his first appearance at about the time that Vonnegut starts to speak directly, first-person, in his own fiction, that is, soon after revisiting *Mother Night* (*MN*) with an introduction added in 1966. That coincides, he recounts, with his colleagues at the Iowa Writers' Workshop telling him it was all right to abandon his journalist's anonymity and speak in his own voice.[1] Vonnegut felt increasing freedom to write autobiographically in introductory pages, or to include intermittent interjections, as in *Slaughterhouse-Five* (*SL-5*) or *Breakfast of Champions* (*BC*). Yet he obviously found advantage in the use of the alternative voice, the persona, afforded by Kilgore Trout. So where does Trout come from, and why is he there?

Vonnegut may have come close to the name—certainly found the same initials—when writing for the *Cornell Sun* as far back as 1941. In one of his humorous columns he invented a parody of Superman with a bumbling anti-hero named "PEACHY-FELLOW."[2] This pitiful figure's plain-clothes name is Kent Trent—clearly a play on Clark Kent. While the source of the name is obvious, it is an intriguing coincidence that Vonnegut arrives at the initials "KT" for a pathetic figure of parody, and sets him in a short episode as hyperbolic and satirical as the plots that later are to come from the pen of Kilgore Trout himself. Much later, in a 1987 interview with Hank Nuwer, Vonnegut indicated that Trout had his origins in an actual writer, the science fiction writer Theodore Sturgeon. That association was even noted in Sturgeon's obituary in the *New York Times*.[3] It is generally accepted that Trout represents a kind of alter ego for Vonnegut, a combination of a self-mocking parody of himself, an embodiment of his worst fears of becoming a denigrated science fiction writer, and a voice for some of his own most impish and inventive ideas.

The impulse that finally takes form in the persona of Kilgore Trout is surely the comic spirit evident in Vonnegut from childhood, the baby of the family who clowns for some attention at the dinner table. The particular nature of that sense of humor, shared with his sister Alice, favors slapstick. He describes their delight in witnessing a woman, her heel caught, coming out of the door of a streetcar horizontally. A fan of Laurel and Hardy, he appears an adherent to the "Here's another fine mess you've gotten us into" school of humor in some of his high school and college writing. In the *Cornell Sun* columns there are comic scrapes—in a seedy bar, getting back to college from vacation, in the infirmary—in which he creates himself the persona of a hapless innocent overtaken by circumstances. "The child is father to the man," and this figure may be the ancestor to the equally hapless Kilgore Trout, the wise naïf never quite in step with the world around him.

The are other figures in the ancestral line of Trout in Vonnegut's short stories. Vonnegut frequently uses first-person narrators to create the comfortable, informal voice of the storyteller, usually for plausibility or for humor. Some of his best-known stories, like "Report on the Barnhouse Effect," "EPICAC," "Unready to Wear," and "More Stately Mansions," benefit from that narrative device. Two of Vonnegut's favorite narrative personae are the man who sells and installs storm windows, screens, and bathtub enclosures—a profession Trout pretends to in *Breakfast of Champions*—and the investments counselor. Both jobs offer the advantage of a plausible way for the narrator to gain an intimate view of other people's domestic affairs. The salesman, perhaps understandably given his involvement with bathtubs and bedroom windows, tends to find himself caught up in tricky situations in stories like "Lovers Anonymous" and "Go Back to your Precious Wife and Son." The investments man more often remains observer, though the strained situation in which he sometimes finds himself, as well as his ironic tone, adds to the humor of the story. "Custom-Made Bride," "Unpaid Consultant," and "The Foster Portfolio" are classics in this mode. These narrators can heighten the comedy of the stories by their abilities as yarn spinners and by interjecting the kind of colorful vernacular not typical of an omniscient third-person narrator. Their own dilemmas—Will they make the sale? Will the secret get out? Will their words of down-to-earth common sense go unheeded? Will the situation unravel?—add to the tension of the near-calamity implicit in this kind of humor. As storytellers whose own fraught circumstances and particular ways of looking at things shape the humor of the story, they function rather as Trout does in his stories. There are other interlocutors in the stories who also have their place in the family tree. These are characters like Mr. Hinkley, the drugstore owner in "Miss Temptation," or the other druggist in "The Powder Blue Dragon," who, while not narrators, have roles as comic commentators making pithy, undercutting observations on the actions of the protagonists. They point toward the outside observers to come later in the novels, a role that Trout sometimes plays.[4]

One of the manifestations of Vonnegut the short story writer that occurs in the novels is the interjection of stories or other short texts by writers who appear as characters. Various reasons for these inclusions suggest themselves. On one level, when their authors appear as surrogates for Vonnegut himself, or represent aspects of him, they may make comment on the writer's craft. Sometimes they do indeed appear to be for light relief.[5] Frequently, they are useful for lending another perspective. Particularly in the earlier novels, Vonnegut uses an outside observer to provide just such another point of view. The Shah of Bratpuhr in *Player Piano* and the Tralfamadorian Salo in *The Sirens of Titan* serve that purpose. Those two make their observations in the dialogue, but in other instances the commentary comes in written inclusions. They enable Vonnegut to have another voice, in effect. He can say things in a different manner or from a different perspective from that established in the novel's narrative voice, and, importantly for a writer who reaches far in his social commentary, they enable him to get at other topics that may lie beyond the compass of his setting.

Ed, the writer who does *not* appear in *Player Piano*, refuses to compromise his standards by writing what the book clubs want—dog stories or adventure tales. His novels are rejected as too long, too intellectual, and too anti-machine, so he fails to qualify for the grade of "fiction journeyman," let alone the higher rank of "public relations." Vonnegut parodies his own situation here, since he has been both fiction journeyman and public relations writer at this stage of his career.

Howard Campbell of *Mother Night* personifies other moral ambiguities surrounding the writer. A playwright, he embodies Vonnegut's assertion that people tend to make dramas or fictions of their own lives. He does this first by making a diary of the variety of roles he and his wife Helga invent to keep their sex life vital, called *Memoirs of a Monogamous Casanova*. In time the *Memoirs* become not a diary but a fiction self-consciously created, a real-life drama performed for the writing. Eventually the manuscript is plagiarized and published throughout eastern Europe as pornography, with lurid illustrations. Campbell's fate not only resurrects the writer's fears of being relegated to hack status, but of being transformed out of necessity or by misperception. Hence, the moral that Vonnegut says the novel asserts: "We are what we pretend to be, so we must be careful about what we pretend to be" (*MN*, v).

There are also writers within *Cat's Cradle*. John, or Jonah, the narrator, embarks upon writing *The Day the World Ended*, which seemingly turns out to be *Cat's Cradle* itself. The other writer is Bokonon, priest-philosopher-charlatan, who writes his *Books of Bokonon*, whose tenets and calypsos are quoted frequently in the novel. He declares that all of his truths are foma, or shameless if harmless lies, once again raising the issue of the ethics of the writer. Like Vonnegut's subsequent favorite writer-character, Kilgore Trout, Bokonon is a debunker, a demystifier, a mocker, an alternative voice through which Vonnegut can find the freedom to be as iconoclastic as he pleases. Both Bokonon and Trout invent versions of history and explanations of various of life's mysteries with alacrity. In so doing they share a similar—and apparently conscious—disregard for distinctions between fact and fiction. Bokonon is perhaps both more cheerful and more cynical than Trout in this role.

Kilgore Trout makes his appearance in *God Bless You, Mr. Rosewater*, which also features another writer-within who should be noted first. This is the disreputable Arthur Garvey Ulm. A struggling writer, Ulm tells the millionaire

Eliot Rosewater that he wants to be free to tell the truth, relieved of financial dependence. The ever-naïve and hopeful Eliot writes him a huge check on the spot, whereupon Ulm spends eight years only to eventually produce for a book club an eight-hundred-page pornographic novel called *Get with Child a Mandrake Root*. Ulm becomes the inverse of *Player Piano*'s Ed, not a writer who refuses to write marketable trash out of economic need, but who does so as an expression of his financial independence. The image of writer reduced to pornographer persists. Trout, of course, represents the writer reduced to what Vonnegut says the critics regard as lower than the pornographer; the science fiction writer. In fact, one of the measures of Trout's low esteem is that his stories are often used as fillers in pornographic publications.

Trout varies in his successive incarnations throughout Vonnegut's fiction. His most consistent characteristics are that he writes science fiction stories at an astonishing rate, that he appears a disheveled older man, and that he remains impecunious and generally unknown. Other constants are that he was born in Bermuda, the son of Leo Trout, an ornithologist who studied the Bermuda ern, and that he in turn has a son, also named Leo or Leon. The son has run away and generally despises him, and three marriages have failed, so he lives alone. In *God Bless You, Mr. Rosewater* he ekes out a living as a clerk in a trading stamp redemption store, in *Slaughterhouse-Five* he supervises newspaper delivery boys, and in *Breakfast of Champions* he sells combinations storm and screen windows. Trout has a major role in *Timequake* (*TQ*), a book that is in many ways his novel, and which contains numerous plots of the stories he writes ceaselessly and then discards.

In *God Bless You, Mr. Rosewater*, Trout is the favorite author of Eliot Rosewater, who lavishes praise on science fiction writers, despite admitting that they "couldn't write for sour apples," by saying, "I love you sons of bitches. . . . You're the only ones who'll really talk about the really terrific changes going on" (12–13). Trout's stock in trade is to stand back and take a deconstructive look at something long accepted. His story *2BR02B*, a title Vonnegut had used himself three years previously, sounds like a mix of Vonnegut's plots: it features an America where all the work is done by machines, the only people with work have three Ph.D.s, there is overpopulation, and there are ethical suicide parlors next to Howard Johnsons. One customer plans to ask God, "What in hell are people for?" (16). That question underscores the search reiterated in *God Bless You, Mr. Rosewater* for meaning and substance in the lives of so many. In another Trout story, *Oh Say Can You Smell?* the ruler of a country sets out to eliminate all odors and orders research to that end. Finally the dictator ends the search himself, not by discovering a chemical to eliminate all odors but by eliminating noses (164–165).

The briefly summarized *The First District Court of Thankyou* deals with ingratitude. In this setting there is a court where people can take those they feel have not been properly grateful for a good deed. Those convicted have the choice of thanking the plaintiff publicly or being sentenced to a month in solitary confinement on bread and water. Eighty percent choose the latter (*GBR*, 173). Recounted in more detail, *Pan-Galactic Three-Day Pass* tells of an interstellar expedition to the outer rim of the universe. The Tralfamadorian commander of the expedition calls its only human member to tell him he has some bad news from back home. The earthling asks if someone has died. The commander responds, "What's died, my boy, is the Milky Way" (*GBR*, 185).

As these examples illustrate, Trout's stories typically contain elements of violence or apocalypse, and their science fiction dimensions often permit a distancing that reduces the everyday to the absurd. They may well give expression to Vonnegut's experiences in having witnessed the wrecking of the American economy and his own family's normal functioning by the Great Depression, the suicide of his mother, the chaos of war, and the nightmarish incineration of Dresden. Trout's bizarre tales show the wisdom to recognize the absurd in the operation of such a universe. They find the humor in the utter randomness of existence, the joke in both its unpredictability and its coincidences that suggest the working of some irresistible pattern. Often Trout views things with the detachment of an undeniable logic combined with a naiveté that makes them seem hilariously absurd. Hence the joke of the spaceman's discovering not just his family but his galaxy died, while cruel, puts things in a certain perspective. It offers a characteristic macabre humor, like that of the gallows or the trenches, against the whimsies of an unpredictable existence.

Some of the humor does focus on more immediate or domestic phases of life, even if it uses the hyperbole of science fiction to comment on them. *The First District Court of Thankyou* is one such. If it seems a touch bitter or cynical in its assumption that a majority of people would rather be sentenced to solitary confinement on bread and water than be properly grateful for a kindness received, we recognize the grain of truth it contains and may well have come close to proclaiming the same judgment ourselves a time or two. It is in moments like this that Trout sounds most like the fool in Shakespeare's *King Lear*. There is propriety in that, of course, since both the play and the novel have to do with parents and children and above all inheritances. In Shakespeare's play it is the fool who under the guise of jest tells Lear of his folly and some home truths about the propensities of human behavior. "A bitter fool," Lear calls him. In Vonnegut's novel, Trout can show some of the same cynicism about human behavior, but he eventually is listened to and his wisdom accepted. At the end of the novel, Trout is brought in to provide a rationale for Eliot Rosewater's benevolence. He, too, offers some astute if bitter observations on his society: "'Americans have long been taught to hate all people who will not or cannot work, to hate even themselves for that.'" Or: "'Poverty is a relatively mild disease for even a very flimsy American soul, but uselessness will kill strong and weak souls alike, and kill every time'" (*GBR*, 196). The practical wisdom he offers is to proclaim that Eliot's behavior has been in the nature of a social experiment seeking to find an answer to the question, "How to love people who have no use?" (*GBR*, 195). This so delights Eliot's father that the senator proclaims, "'By God, you're great! You should have been a public relations man!'" (*GBR*, 197).

In some ways most interesting of the inclusions in *God Bless You, Mr. Rosewater* is Trout's novel *Venus on the Half-Shell*. Fred Rosewater furtively picks this off a newsstand when he thinks his daughter is not watching, and reads on the back cover "an abridgment of a red-hot scene inside. It went like this:

Queen Margaret of the planet Shaltoon let her
gown fall to the floor. She was wearing nothing
underneath. Her high, firm, uncowled bosom was
proud and rosy. Her hips and thighs were like an
inviting lyre of pure alabaster. They shone so whitely
they might have had a light inside. "Your travels are
over, Space Wanderer," she whispered. (119)

The quotation actually goes on for twenty-three lines. After that the back cover photograph of Trout is described as "like a frightened, aging Jesus, whose sentence to crucifixion had been commuted to imprisonment for life" (120). The unique aspect of this passage is that it offers an extended glimpse of a Trout story in his own words.

There is a further point of interest about this story, in that another writer, Phillip Jose Farmer, took up this extract and published a novel of the same title using the name Kilgore Trout. Thus did the fictional writer almost come to life, as it were, and in something like the kind of confrontation that occurs at the end of *Breakfast of Champions* where a bewildered Kilgore Trout comes face to face with his creator, Kurt Vonnegut. Trout has another fictional meeting with his maker in an interview in *Crawdaddy* for April 1, 1974. This was actually conducted by Greg Mitchell but is set up so as to look as if done by Trout. Vonnegut has commented on this piece saying that everything attributed to his characters in it is either a quotation or a paraphrase.[6]

In *Slaughterhouse-Five*, Kilgore Trout makes his appearance as the tyrannical supervisor of newspaper delivery boys, a necessary job since he makes no money from his writing. His stories are read, however, and once again by Eliot Rosewater. One of the stories Rosewater reads is *Maniacs in the Fourth Dimension*, about people whose mental illnesses could not be treated because the causes were all in the fourth dimension. Its appeal to the disturbed Rosewater is predictable. He also delights in its claim that vampires, werewolves, goblins and angels all exist, but are in the fourth dimension. "So was William Blake, Rosewater's favorite poet, according to Trout. So were heaven and hell" (*SL-5*, 90).

The moral of Trout's second story seems more clear, especially in context. Called *The Gutless Wonder*, it tells of a humanoid robot who is despised for his halitosis. The narrator finds the story remarkable for being written in 1932 and predicting napalm. The robot pilots an airplane and drops napalm on people without conscience. Despite this, the curing of his halitosis assures his acceptance into the human race. Bombing people may be socially acceptable, but bad breath never. In the context of this novel, whose central event is the fire-bombing of Dresden, this story's moral is obvious. Once again Trout enables Vonnegut to offer a parable that underlines one of the messages of the novel.

The remaining Trout story in *Slaughterhouse-Five*, *The Gospel from Outer Space*, tells of a visitor from outer space who makes a study of Christianity. In particular he seeks to learn what made it so easy for Christians to be cruel. He concludes that the problem lies with careless narration in the Gospels. They are meant to teach mercy, even toward the humblest people. They have failed by inviting the interpretation that killing Jesus was wrong only because he was "the Son of the Most Powerful Being in the Universe." That leaves the impression that there are some people it is all right to kill, namely those not well connected. The space visitor leaves Earth a new gospel in which Jesus "really was a nobody," though he preached the same philosophy. At his crucifixion God thunders from the sky that he is "adopting the bum as his son," and decrees: *"From this moment on, He will punish horribly anybody who torments a bum who has no connections!"* (*SL-5*, 92–95). Here, too, Trout's voice supplements Vonnegut's. This novel depicts the mass slaughter of Dresden, dwells on the horrors of the thirteenth-century Children's Crusade, recounts one death after another, and chronicles the persecution of the frequently Christ-like Billy Pilgrim. Just as with *God Bless You, Mr. Rosewater*, it is a novel in which a serious, direct statement of the ethics implicit in it would seem didactic and false. Trout's simple, humorous, hyperbolic stories deliver the message effectively without changing the author's narrative stance in the novel.

Breakfast of Champions sees Kilgore Trout being given an even larger role in the novel as a character. As a consequence, a greater number of his stories occurs; more, in fact, than need to be recounted here. Trout makes no copies of the stories he sends off, mostly to "World Classics Library," which uses them to bulk pornographic books and magazines while paying him "doodley-squat." The stories, which usually have no female characters, appear with "salacious pictures" and are often retitled. Hence "Pan Galactic Straw-boss" becomes "Mouth Crazy." It is another overpopulation story, in which a bachelor produces endless offspring by mixing shavings from his palm with chicken soup and exposing them to cosmic rays. Instead of the society's taking a stand on overly large families, it bans the possession of chicken soup by single people (*BC*, 21).

"The Dancing Fool" gives vent to some of the frustration Trout-Vonnegut must feel when, Cassandra-like, their warnings go unheeded. Zog, from the planet Margo, comes to Earth to tell humans how to cure cancer and end war. He belongs to a species that communicates by means of tap dancing and farts. As he lands he sees a house on fire and rushes in, tap dancing and farting furiously to warn the occupants. The owner brains him with a golf club. Some plots are simply opportunities for brief comic jibes. In "Hail to the Chief" an "optimistic chimpanzee" becomes president. He wears a blazer with a presidential seal on the pocket. Wherever he goes bands strike up "Hail to the Chief." The chimpanzee is delighted and responds by bouncing up and down.

One summarized plot interests because it appears to prefigure the later novel, *Galápagos*. Trout's novel, *The Smart Bunny*, features a rabbit with the intelligence of Einstein or Shakespeare. (She is female, and the only female leading character in Trout's fiction!) She lives like other rabbits so she finds her brain useless,

Kurt Vonnegut

regarding it simply as a tumor. She heads for the town to have the tumor removed, only to be shot on the way. The hunter and his wife also conclude that the rabbit has a tumor, is diseased, and therefore they do not eat it. In *Galápagos* huge human brains are judged as excessive as the massive antlers of the Irish elk, a creature brought to extinction by over-specialization.

The Trout fiction that has greatest impact in *Breakfast of Champions* remains his novel, *Now It Can Be Told*. The premise of the book is that the reader is the only human; all others are robots, put there by the Creator of the Universe so that he can watch the human's responses. Dwayne Hoover reads this and, taking it as gospel that the robots can neither reason nor feel, dementedly sets off on a rampage. Trout's story splendidly complements major ideas within *Breakfast of Champions*. There are twin themes linked to the notion of people as robots. One envisions people as being robotlike in that they are chemically controlled. This grows out of Vonnegut's own experience in taking antidepressant pills and discovering that those chemicals can manipulate his mood. The other sees people as being robotlike in the way they are treated. They are made functions of their jobs, doing "women's work," for instance. Often people act as though they shared Dwayne's Trout-induced obsession, viewing the world solipsistically and making other people merely projections of their own visions of reality. Trout's piece of "solipsistic whimsy" makes graphic in its hyperbole the consequences of such not-uncommon attitudes.

Trout's seemingly naïve responses to things that he sees often trigger his imagination toward observations on society and the science fiction parables that illustrate his conclusions. The appearance of a truck with "PYRAMID" painted on its side in eight feet high letters puzzles him: "'I mean—this thing can go a hundred miles an hour, if it has to. It's fast and useful and unornamental. It's as up-to-date as a rocket ship. I never saw anything that was less like a pyramid than this truck'" (*BC*, 109). The bemused truck driver tells Trout at one point, "'I can't tell if you're serious or not'" (86). Trout allows that he won't know himself until he finds out whether life is serious or not, and we are told that after he was famous one of the greatest mysteries about him was whether he was kidding or not. As we do with King Lear's fool, we often have to pause for a moment with Trout's stories and pronouncements before we are sure whether it is a comic parable with a message or simply farce. While in *God Bless You, Mr. Rosewater* Trout brings wisdom that makes possible the resolution of the novel, in *Breakfast of Champions* his "solipsistic whimsy" brings chaos. While his *Now It Can Be Told* does indeed contain a wise and moral message, what happens as a result of Dwayne Hoover's literal reading of it warns of the dangers of making gurus of fiction writers. At this period when his anti-war *Slaughterhouse-Five* was at the peak of its Vietnam War–era popularity, and would-be disciples camped on his lawn, Vonnegut may be embodying another fear in this characterization of Trout.

In *Breakfast of Champions*, Vonnegut says he is getting rid of all of his characters, and tells Trout he is being set free, leaving him imploring, *"Make me young! Make me young! Make me young!"* (295). But it is far from the end of Kilgore Trout. *Jailbird* (*JB*) announces, "Yes—Kilgore Trout is back again. He could not make it on the outside" (ix). Once again his name is employed by another writer. In *Jailbird*, Kilgore Trout is one of two pen names used by Dr. Robert Fender. His story "Asleep at the Switch" is recounted at some length. It depicts a large reception center at the Pearly Gates "filled with computers and staffed by people who had been certified public accountants or investment counselors or business managers back on Earth" (*JB*,184). In a parody of the biblical parable of the talents, these officials give all new arrivals a thorough review of how well they have handled the business opportunities offered them on Earth. Repeatedly they point out each newcomers missed chances, to the refrain of, "And there you were, asleep at the switch again." The ghost of Albert Einstein emerges as the hero of the story. He is told that if he had taken a second mortgage and bought uranium commodities before announcing $E = mc^2$ he could have been a billionaire. And so on. Finally, Einstein gains admittance into heaven carrying his beloved violin, but Einstein recognizes the fallacy in the procedure.

He calculated that if every person on Earth took full advantage of every opportunity, became a millionaire and then a billionaire and so on, the paper wealth on that one little planet would exceed the worth of all the minerals in the universe in a matter of three months or so. (*JB*, 187)

So Einstein writes God a note, arguing that the auditors must be sadists, misleading new arrivals about their opportunities. But God sends an archangel to tell Einstein to be quiet or he will have his violin taken away, and he hushes.

This story obviously parodies the notion of a final accounting, and perhaps also mocks that particular set of preachers who make a large part of their appeal the notion that God *wants* people to get rich. It certainly recognizes the ironic fact that whatever kind of accounting people might expect to make in a next life, a good percentage act as if they were to be audited on their financial opportunism. Another point to be made about this story is the way it appears to be triggered simply by the phrase "asleep at the switch again," an expression that seemed to be enjoying a revival at the time. Many of Trout's stories apparently spring from this same kind of spontaneous response to an object, a saying, or a particular event, as also revealed in *Breakfast of Champions*. Trout becomes one of the ways that Vonnegut keeps alive the mischievous, adolescent irreverence, seen in his earliest writing and manifest again and again in his later work, that questions all assumptions and authorities.

One of Fender's other stories, supposedly to appear in *Playboy* under his alternative *nom de plume*, Frank X. Barlow, concerns a planet that runs out of time (*JB*, 54–58). Aptly named Vicuna (the animal of that name also may be running out of time), the planet disintegrates as its inhabitants mine time from its very substance. Eventually the Vicunans have to leave their bodies and, like the amphibians of the short story "Unready to Wear," go off as spirits in search of bodies. The central character, a judge, gets to Earth. What Vicunans did not realize was that, having entered through the ear of a human, they were unable to leave again. The judge sees what appears to be a happy old man in a quiet place, only to discover he is a criminal in a minimum security prison. The judge finds himself forever locked in the head of a man who is aimlessly and interminably repeating a silly scatological childhood rhyme. His situation seems apt retribution for a judge who has condemned the convicted to be stood up to their necks in a pond of excrement as deputies aim powerful speedboats at their heads. An interesting detail of this story is that Vicunans say "ting-a-ling" in place of "hello," "good-bye," "please" or "thank you." In the later novel, *Timequake*, Kilgore Trout does the same thing.

The Barlow story fits *Jailbird*'s subject matter of trials, convictions, and prisoners, but it also relates to this novel's return to that favorite Vonnegut theme of social inequality. Like the Trout story, it underlines the question of the distribution of resources among people. The Vicunans' exhaustion of time itself makes this a parable about human time running out with the exhaustion of resources. That the Vicunans once had bonfires of time when they still regarded it as limitless sends an obvious message about human consumption of things like fossil fuels. The holes that open up in Vicuna as they consume time might be analogous to the holes in Earth's ozone layer.

Perhaps the clearest example of how Vonnegut uses Trout stories as parables, that is allegories or near allegories that illustrated a religious or philosophical moral, occurs in his employment of one called "The Planet Gobblers." Originally cited in a commencement address at Hobart and William Smith Colleges on May 26, 1974, and collected in *Palm Sunday (PS)*, the story appears only as summary. In it humans are cast as "interplanetary termites," who arrive at a planet, use everything up, but always send space ships on to the next planet. They were like a disease, "since it was not necessary to inhabit planets with such horrifying destructiveness. It is easy to take good care of a planet" (209). In his address, Vonnegut quickly goes on to draw out the lesson from Trout's story. "Our grandchildren will surely think of us as the Planet Gobblers. Poorer nations than America think of America as a Planet Gobbler right now" (*PS*, 209). And he goes on to make willingness to change the concluding call of his address.

Kilgore Trout has a major role in the novel *Timequake* (1997). His son, whose ghost narrates the novel *Galápagos*, is still depicted as having been killed in a Swedish shipyard in 1975. Since that time, Kilgore Trout has thrown away his handwritten stories within hours of finishing them. He has been writing an average of a story every ten days since he was fourteen, so by 2000 he has written about twenty-five hundred. He is now an eighty-four year old homeless person, one of the "sacred cattle," as he calls them. Like Barlow's Vicunans in the story from *Jailbird*, Trout uses "ting-a-ling" as a general purpose greeting, just one of many echoes in this novel from previous ones.

Vonnegut refers to the published *Timequake* as *Timequake Two*, *Timequake One* being an earlier version that he could never complete to his satisfaction. It told the story of a timequake, an event caused by a sudden contraction in the universe so that time jumped back ten years. For a decade people repeated automatically and inescapably what they had done in those past ten years. Then suddenly they are catapulted into the resumption of time, and chaos ensues. Trout's account of the timequake, *My Ten Years on Automatic Pilot* (sometimes referred to as *MYTOAP*) runs throughout *Timequake* as Vonnegut's device for recounting many of the events of the earlier plot. Once again Trout serves as surrogate commentator and joke purveyor. A dozen or so Trout stories are recounted in *Timequake*.[7]

Perhaps the most memorable Trout story in *Timequake* is called "The Sisters B-36."[8] It tells of three sisters, two pleasant and one evil, on a matriarchal planet named Booboo. One good sister paints, the other writes. The third, whom in an earlier draft Vonnegut has Trout describe as beautiful as "an Abyssinian brick shithouse with square wheels and Venetian blinds," is a scientist who can only talk about provable facts, so she bores people to death.

In an obvious parody of the way people learn and form biases, Trout explains that Booboolings are programmed—circuits removed, new ones installed—by what they are told in words when young. Booboolings are thus trained how to look at pictures or respond to ink marks on paper, and develop what Earthlings call "imagination." So the bad sister, "Nim-nim B-36," invents television. Booboolings no longer need imagination, and only the older ones can appreciate pictures and writing. This makes the two nice sisters feel awful, as she wished, but still no one likes Nim-nim B-36. So she invents the landmine, barbed wire, the machine gun, and the flame-thrower. Then Booboolings kill one another readily, feeling nothing because they had no imaginations and so could not "read interesting, heartwarming stories in the faces of one another" (*TQ*, 18).

Quite clearly this story speaks, like a parable, to the extraordinary rate at which young people kill one another on American streets. It addresses the vital role that writing and other arts play in the development of the imagination and the crucial importance of that facility to the culture and the individual. It decries the negative impact that television has had on society, and it returns to two even older themes in Vonnegut's work—pacifism, and the failure of the public to respond with understanding to scientific knowledge. It is vintage Trout, a comic little science fiction story loaded with implication.

"Dog's Breakfast" tells of a scientist who questions whether the human brain, which he describes as a dog's breakfast or a blood-soaked sponge, is really capable of the greatest human accomplishments. Then he discovers a miniature pink radio receiver in brains taken from extra-intelligent people. He sets about writing up his discovery, convinced he is a cinch for a Nobel Prize. He writes with a fluency he has never known before, until he stops to ask himself where his newfound loquacity, or even his discovery, comes from. It has to be from a receiver in his own brain. He is, in Trout's (or Shakespeare's) words, "hoist by his own petard!" The realization causes him to jump to his death.

Two others Trout stories where a plot is summarized are "Empire State," about a meteorite the size of the Empire State Building heading toward earth, and "Dr. Schadenfreude," about a psychiatrist who forbids his patients to talk about themselves and who, if they do, will scream, "When will you ever learn that nobody cares anything about you, you, you boring, insignificant piece of poop?" (*TQ*, 61). Incidents or phrases from these stories are referred to throughout the novel. Vonnegut uses them to make a joke, to underline a point, or as a kind of refrain.

As in his earlier appearances, Trout supplies *Timequake* with much of its humor and a great deal of its energy, and as in *God Bless You, Mr. Rosewater*, he turns out to be a savior. Amid the mayhem caused when free will resumes after the timequake, Trout is the one who goes into the street to get people back on their feet and functioning with the message, "You were sick, but now you're well again, and there's work to do" (*TQ*, 167). It seems appropriate that this man, whose imagination finds anything possible, should be the one to accept the situation with some alacrity and carry on. His message, "You were sick, but now you're well again, and there's work to do," captures something fundamental in the nature of Trout himself. He has acted out that same message for Eliot Rosewater in the earlier novel, and he embodies it in his own resilience throughout his appearances. Perhaps he also embodies that part of his creator's constitution, too, expressing the spirit in Vonnegut that, despite his acknowledged deep depressions, rebounds to write and paint, to laugh and make others laugh, again and again throughout a long career. Trout's message also may come close to defining his function in the novels, to recognize the malaise of the world we inhabit, provide some wisdom and some healing laughter, and set us on our way again.

Vonnegut has consistently used Trout's quirky, rapid plots to inject vitality and pace. They contribute to tone with their often slapstick humor, their outrageousness, and their naïve but penetrating observations. Their frequently bizarre science fiction settings help establish mood in novels where Vonnegut unleashes the chaotic to destabilize habitual, unquestioned assumptions about society, the universe, life. Like the riddles Lear's fool uses to cajole and arouse his king, Trout's amusing and sometimes bitter little stories become parables that offer wisdom and insights into our condition. As his fan Eliot Rosewater proclaims, Trout's stories do concern the future. They take to their logical conclusions the consequences of our social and technological programs, and urge us to see the ultimate price of our behavior. Like Lear's fool, and as in his appearance in *God Bless You, Mr. Rosewater*, Trout repeatedly talks about inheritance. Sometimes that inheritance is the passing on of a habitable planet, and sometimes his emphasis falls on the more equitable distribution of the nation's wealth among Earth's inhabitants. In doing so he speaks for his creator, much as the fool does for Shakespeare, in situations where for both authors to speak more directly and seriously would be to risk becoming overly didactic. But the fool and Trout delight with their humor, leaving us the pleasure of finding the wisdom in their bitter laughter. They express an essential vitality that persists in the human spirit and that enlivens their authors. From seeming to be a kind of alter ego who first epitomized what the writer feared he might have become, Kilgore Trout has come to embody the questioning mind, the irreverent iconoclasm, and the moral conscience that are the quintessence of Kurt Vonnegut himself.

NOTES

1. *Kurt Vonnegut: A Self-Portrait*, produced and directed by Harold Mantell (Princeton, NJ: Films for the Humanities, 1976).

2. Kurt Vonnegut, "A Challenge to Superman! ! ! !" in the "Well All Right" column, *The Cornell Daily Sun* (November 11, 1941), 4.

3. Interview with Hank Nuwer, in William Rodney Allen, ed., *Conversations with Kurt Vonnegut* (Jackson, MS: University Press of Mississippi, 1988), 263.

4. For a more complete discussion of these narrator-characters and the short stories in which they appear, see Peter Reed, *The Short Fiction of Kurt Vonnegut* (Westport, CT: Greenwood Press, 1997).

5. David Standish, *Playboy* interview, in Allen, *Conversations*, 94. Vonnegut says that "trips to other planets, science fiction of an obviously kidding sort, is equivalent to bringing on the clowns every so often to lighten things up."

6. Charles Reilly, "Two Conversations with Kurt Vonnegut," in Allen, *Conversations*, 213.

7. *Timequake*, 15–18. For comparison, a version of this story as recounted by Kurt Vonnegut to Peter Reed and Marc Leeds in 1993 appears in Peter Reed and Marc Leeds, eds., *The Vonnegut Chronicles* (Westport, CT: Greenwood Press, 1996), 41–42. It also appears in the *Timequake* (*One*) manuscript.

8. The manuscript *Timequake* (*Timequake One*, seen by the author in manuscript in 1996 by kind permission of Kurt Vonnegut) had additional Trout stories, some little more than two-line jokes on their titles. For example, one story tells of a bank failure on another planet. The hero has kept his money in his mattress until his wife persuades him to put it in the bank. Now he is *Up Shit Crick Without a Paddle*. After telling about an incident in which an entrepreneur moves a factory and steals the pension funds, too, Vonnegut invokes the Trout title: *Why Mess Around?* Vonnegut caps another story by quoting from *Kiss Me Again*: "It might help at least a little bit if men and youths would be more reflective about where their jizzzzzzzzzum goes." One such story in the published *Timequake* is the play *The Wrinkled Old Family Retainer*, who turns out to be named Scrotum.

Timequake One brings back another previously seen writer, incidentally; Arthur Garvey Ulm of *God Bless You, Mr. Rosewater*. He is reincarnated as a poet and author of *Welcome to Earth*. Ulm is reputed to be the first American to contract and die of AIDS.

WORKS CITED

Novels by Kurt Vonnegut

Breakfast of Champions. New York: Delacorte Press/Seymour Lawrence, 1973.
Cat's Cradle. New York: Holt, Rinehart and Winston, 1963.
God Bless You, Mr. Rosewater. New York: Holt, Rinehart and Winston, 1965.
Happy Birthday, Wanda June. New York: Delacorte Press/Seymour Lawrence, 1970.
Jailbird. New York: Delacorte Press/Seymour Lawrence, 1979.
Player Piano. New York: Charles Scribner's Sons, 1952.
The Sirens of Titan. New York: Dell, 1959.
Slapstick. New York: Delacorte Press/Seymour Lawrence, 1976.
Slaughterhouse-Five. New York: Delacorte Press/Seymour Lawrence, 1969.
Timequake. New York: G. P. Putnam's Sons, 1997.

Short Stories by Kurt Vonnegut

"Custom-Made Bride." *Saturday Evening Post*, March 24, 1951, pp. 30, 86–87.
"EPICAC." *Collier's*, November 25, 1950, pp. 36–37.
"Go Back to Your Precious Wife and Son." *Ladies' Home Journal*, July 1962, pp. 54–55, 110.
"Lovers Anonymous." *Redbook Magazine*, October 1963, pp. 70, 146–148.
"Miss Temptation." *Saturday Evening Post*, April 21, 1956, pp. 30, 64.
"More Stately Mansions." *Collier's*, December 22, 1951, pp. 62–63.
"Report on the Barnhouse Effect." *Collier's*, February 11, 1950, pp. 18–19, 63–65.
"The Foster Portfolio." *Collier's*, September 8, 1951, pp. 18–19, 72–73.
"The Powder Blue Dragon." *Cosmopolitan*, November 1954, pp. 46–48, 50–53.
"Unpaid Consultant." *Cosmopolitan*, March 1955, pp. 52–57.
"Unready to Wear." *Galaxy Science Fiction*, April 1953, pp. 98–111.

Other Works Cited

Allen, William Rodney, ed. *Conversations with Kurt Vonnegut*. Jackson: University Press of Mississippi, 1988.
Farmer, Phillip Jose, using the nom de plume Kilgore Trout. *Venus on the Half-Shell*. New York: Dell/A Laurel Edition, 1974.
Reed, Peter. *The Short Fiction of Kurt Vonnegut*. Westport, CT: Greenwood Press, 1997.
Reed, Peter, and Marc Leeds, eds. *The Vonnegut Chronicles*. Westport, CT: Greenwood Press, 1996.

Mother Night: Who's Pretending?

Marc Leeds

> This is the only story of mine whose moral I know. I don't think it's a
> marvelous moral; I simply happen to know what it is: We are what we
> pretend to be, so we must be careful about what we pretend to be. . . .
>
> If I'd been born in Germany, I suppose I would have *been* a Nazi,
> bopping Jews and gypsies and Poles around, leaving boots sticking out
> of snowbanks, warming myself with my secretly virtuous insides. So it
> goes. (*Mother Night*, v, vii)

Vonnegut's introduction to *Mother Night* (*MN*) alludes to the timeless dynamic
tension pitting appearance versus reality. Musing about life as a German born and
bred parallel to his own time frame as a German-American reduces the issue of
identity into a single dimension. His fantasizing is in recognition of the fact that
one's place and function within a given moment of existence is simultaneously
defined by outsiders considering the facades we present and by ourselves
contemplating the various mitigating factors that prompt our actions. An obvious
dilemma arises when the spectators of our lives disagree with our own perceptions
about the motives and actions that define us. As difficult as life may be with those
critical of our actions, it is all the more contentious when we can't coalesce our
own motives and deeds with our preconceived notions of identity. Vonnegut's real
concern is with his hyphenated sense of self and, as a result, *Mother Night* is a
study of the stateless schizophrenic, Howard Campbell, Jr., trapped by the
peculiarities of heredity and environment that mitigate any attempt to produce a
satisfying self-image.

Though all of Vonnegut novels study individuals enmeshed within the
competing and compelling forces that are characterized as the structured moments
of destiny/history, *Mother Night* is the first of two works set in the Germany that
originally gave rise to Vonnegut's sense of the structural dynamics of his life. The
second of his two war novels, *Slaughterhouse-Five*, follows the German-American
Billy Pilgrim along his time-looped existence as an American scout captured during

the Battle of the Bulge, imprisoned in an ancient cultural capital of his ancestor and shuttled underground by his Teutonic guardians while the forces of his American homeland incinerate the descendants of their common past (including Billy's sixteen-year-old cousin, Werner Gluck). Billy's chrono-synclastic infundibulated existence is, in part, a metaphor for the schism of his many parts. By the time Vonnegut is ready to face his Dresden experience, the time-looped fatalism already explored in *The Sirens of Titan* provides him with a tool to split the many parts of his character and at the same time reform them into an integrated, explicable whole. Just as Winston Niles Rumfoord was scattered far and wide across the universe and simultaneously always present on Titan, Billy's schizophrenic time travel was part of what made his identity complete.

Vonnegut's initial exploration of his hyphenated genealogy through the creation of Howard W. Campbell, Jr., is more concerned with circumstances contributing to the establishment of identity than it is with coalescing one's multiplicity into a satisfying whole. In *Slaughterhouse*, the trapped German inside the American foot soldier Billy Pilgrim is in some ways a straight translation of Vonnegut's dilemma as he experienced it. In *Mother Night*, however, Vonnegut transposes his hyphenated self into the American-German Howard W. Campbell, Jr., in keeping with the convoluted thinking of the schizophrenic. Not only is Campbell incapable of distinguishing his core self in the face of his many parts, schizophrenia is presented as the predominant operational activity enabling all the characters to live in harmony with their many selves.

The framework of the story compounds the problem of appearance versus reality (perhaps nature versus nurture) since *Mother Night* is presented as the autobiographical confessions of a "dead" playwright and admitted schizophrenic. As Vonnegut the editor warns,

To say that he was a writer is to say that the demands of art alone were enough to make him lie, and to lie without seeing any harm in it. To say that he was a playwright is to offer an even harsher warning to the reader, for no one is a better liar than a man who has warped lives and passions onto something as grotesquely artificial as a stage.

And, now that I've said that about lying, I will risk the opinion that lies told for the sake of artistic effect—in the theater, for instance, and in Campbell's confessions, perhaps—can be, in a higher sense, the most beguiling forms of truth. (*MN*, ix)

To be sure, Campbell is by no means comprehensive when considering motives and character development, nor should the reader be deceived into thinking this is the ostensible purpose for the confession. Prompted by Israeli archivists for any writings Campbell may care to add to their collection documenting the activities of war criminals, the confession is less a chronological report complete with the twisted rationalizations of a totalitarian as it is a disarmingly transparent catalogue of persons with whom he shared significant moments. *Mother Night* chronicles the inertial forces which induce schizophrenia on a great number of people. Some appear to be more out of touch with a common reality than others, but their individual sensibilities create, for the most part, satisfying constructions of their own identities within a larger world view.

The introduction of each succeeding character reveals his or her dual identity not simply because it is written in the past tense, but because Campbell employs the same unity of vision across time afforded the Tralfamadorians in *Slaughterhouse-Five*. Swiftly moving from a thumbnail sketch of his youth as a second generation German-American in Schenectady, to the family's relocation in Berlin because of his father's reassignment by (the ever present) General Electric, Campbell supplies the following:

> In 1923, when I was eleven, my father was assigned to the General Electric office in Berlin, Germany. From then on, my friends, and my principal language were German.
>
> I eventually became a playwright in the German language, and I took a German wife, the actress Helga Noth. Helga Noth was the older of the two daughters of Werner Noth, the Chief of Police of Berlin.
>
> My father and mother left Germany in 1939, when war came.
>
> My wife and I stayed on. (*MN*, 32)

The importance of this minimalist offering is in the simple establishment of his having been of hyphenated stock, and that through the circumstance of his father's biculturalism he was transported through the ensuing political ruckus. By the time Major Frank Wirtanen appears in the Tiergarten and asks Campbell to stay on in Germany as an American intelligence agent, his answer reveals his known destiny, "'Oh Christ,' I said. I said it with anger and fatalism" (*MN*, 40). The confluence of heredity, opportunity, and political upheaval conspired to place him in *his* particular moment. As an element in the larger confession, this instance exposes an understanding of the structures we fall into which, when reviewed from his jail cell in Jerusalem, enables Campbell to sculpt at once all the elements conspiring to tear into him. Perhaps it is these conspiracies seen in retrospect that become the signposts of future conspiracies, convincing Campbell to commit suicide.

But before Campbell bids his readers *"auf wiedersehen?"* and we are left to ponder the reliability of his claim that another prospect of freedom nauseates him to the extent that he considers suicide, it is significant that his tale mirrors the naive-schizophrenic-resurrected structure of Vonnegut's other novels. Schizophrenia is quite obviously the focus, but it is only by traveling along Vonnegut's gauntlet that Campbell appreciates his moments variously and simultaneously as "beautiful and surprising and deep" as a Tralfamadorian novel (*Slaughterhouse-Five*, 76).

Campbell's civilian occupation in Germany was as a playwright of medieval romances—fantasies of good and evil, pure hearts and heroes, and love conquering all. Despite the intense race baiting and war preparations going on all around, Campbell intended to write a play "about the love my wife and I had for each other. It was going to show how a pair of lovers in a world gone mad could survive by being loyal only to a nation composed of themselves—a nation of two" (*MN*, 37). As he naively tells Wirtanen in the Tiergarten,

When I go home, it will be to have a fine meal with my beautiful wife, to listen to music, to make love to my wife, and to sleep like a log. I'm not a soldier, not a political man. I'm an artist. If war comes, it'll find me still working at my peaceful trade. (*MN*, 40)

When war came, Helga and Howard in their common naivete hoped to shut out the war frenzy by ignoring the import of their military functions: she, comforting and encouraging the troops at the front, while he exhorted the populace with radio broadcasts.

Oh, how we clung, my Helga and I—how *mindlessly* we clung!
    We didn't listen to each other's words. We heard only the melodies in our voices. The things we listened for carried no more intelligence than the purrs and growls of big cats.
    If we had listened for more, had thought about what we heard, what a nauseated couple we would have been! Away from the sovereign territory of our nation of two, we talked like the patriotic lunatics all around us. (*MN*, 44)

The schizophrenia enabling the Campbells to function for each other necessitated the denial of language as a communication tool; as playwright and actress they obliterate the core of their vocations and seek refuge behind the parts they (and the controlling forces around them) have created. For Helga, detaching herself from the public persona is no more difficult than assuming another theatrical role. Howard's ambivalence about such duality is softened yet anxiously anticipated by the prospect of crossing over from author to actor. Though Wirtanen expects Campbell to become a spy because of his naive vision of the world (as elicited from his plays), Howard sees the opportunity to let out the actor within the dramatist, "The best reason was that I was a ham. As a spy of the sort he described, I would have an opportunity for some pretty grand acting. I would fool everyone with my brilliant interpretation of a Nazi, inside and out" (*MN*, 41). As Wirtanen later points out, "Generally speaking, espionage offers each spy an opportunity to go crazy in a way he finds irresistible" (*MN*, 140).
    The second reason Campbell is capable of detaching himself from his public persona as a Nazi propagandist is that Wirtanen's offer had already killed off any presentable identity to which Howard may have clung.

You'll be volunteering right at the start of a war to be a dead man. Even if you live through the war without being caught, you'll find your reputation gone—and probably very little to live for. (*MN*, 41)

Espionage relieved him of the necessity of operating with a conscience. When Helga disappears in the Crimea while entertaining the troops, Howard's detachment becomes total, "I became what I am today and will always be, a stateless person" (*MN*, 44).
    Actually, the entire text of the stateless schizophrenic is laced with constant reminders by Howard that he is not operating in the world of the living. After the war, while living in Greenwich Village surrounded by army surplus furnishings, he thinks about taking the morphine he found in some of the surplus first-aid kits:

But then I understood that I was already drugged.

I was feeling no pain.

My narcotic was what had got me through the war; it was my ability to let my emotions be stirred by only one thing—my love for Helga. This concentration of my emotions on so small an area had begun as a young lover's happy illusion, had developed into a device to keep me from going insane during the war, and had finally become the permanent axis about which my thoughts revolve.

And so, with my Helga presumed dead, I became a death-worshiper, as content as any narrow-minded religious nut anywhere. (*MN*, 47)

When Howard creates a chess set from a war-surplus wood-carving kit, he "felt compelled to show somebody, somebody still among the living, the marvelous thing" he made (*MN*, 48). Later, when considering the chest of manuscripts brought by Resi-Helga, he "remembered when I'd closed it up at the start of the war, remembered when I'd thought of the trunk as a coffin for the young man I would never be again." The chest contained a self-inscribed epitaph, as well:

Here lies Howard Campbell's essence,
Freed from his body's noisome nuisance.
His body, empty, prowls the earth,
Earning what a body's worth.
If his body and his essence remain apart,
Burn his body, but spare this, his heart. (*MN*, 96)

The manuscripts are his plays, poetry, and the one secret text written for only Helga and himself, *Memoirs of a Monogamous Casanova*. As he had twisted the use of his language arts, his art had also become twisted and, as it turns out, the secret text was pirated and turned into an underground pornographic best-seller in Russia by Stepan Bodovskov, the Soviet corporal who found the trunk in a Berlin theater attic. (Bodovskov made a career of plagiarizing Campbell, though he was eventually executed for writing an original satire of the Red Army.)

Campbell's espionage destroyed language as the medium of his art, thus removing his core. Beyond his art lay the death of his personal commune and confidence with his wife. Having betrayed the tools of his craft, his artisan's desire for exhibition (even as a woodcarver) transposes his use of art and becomes the source of his own betrayal (this desire for exhibition leads him to an acquaintance with Kraft-Potapov and his subsequent extradition to Israel for trial as a war criminal). He mistakenly believed that the love exchanged with his false Helga, Resi, had the "power to raise the dead." Later, when in a cataleptic trance, Mrs. Epstein senses his deadened spirit and beckons for the three Jews who take him into custody by crooning "*Leichentrager zu wache*. . . . Corpse-carriers to the guardhouse" (*MN*, 187).

Senseless and detached from associating his wavering stance in the swirl of forces that dictated his activities, Campbell asserts that Mrs. Epstein "understood my illness immediately, that it was my world rather than myself that was diseased" (*MN*, 185). Howard is incapable of understanding that as a part of the world he can not help but be as diseased as those around him. His motivations may differ, but the effects of his public actions are a part of the record that cares little for understanding the underlying causes. As his best friend and Nazi/Israeli double agent, Heinz Schildknecht told Howard that during the war, "All people are insane. . . . They will do anything at any time, and God help anybody who looks for reasons" (*MN*, 90–91). To accept Campbell's diagnosis as he projects it through Mrs. Epstein is to accept the supposition that his egotistical desire to "ham it up" as a Nazi is a sane response to cure the ills of a mad world. Howard had never been interested in the supposed ills of the world, devoting himself instead to caricaturing romance through the uncomplicated clashing of stereotyped extremes of good and evil. Spying was his chance to keep Helga, become a great actor in a grand morality play of apocalyptic proportions, and at all times remain a contributor to the dynamic tensions that authored his role. Accepting his role meant destroying his identity as lover and artist. Is this the reasoning of one who can judge his own sanity in a diseased world? Howard's narrative attempt to project in Mrs. Epstein a shared recognition of the world's maladies (and thereby gain a measure of reconciliation with an Auschwitzer as a compatriot in their common victimization) is another manifestation of his schizophrenia.

Howard's first recognition of his own schizophrenia occurs in Dr. Jones's basement while recuperating from a beating at the hands of an outraged veteran. As an introduction to Campbell's reluctantly delivered eulogy of August Krapptauer, Dr. Jones plays one of Howard's wartime radio broadcasts complete with an anti-Semitic diatribe. Campbell offers this and all other recordings to his prosecutors as evidence against himself, and he makes the following surmise:

I can hardly deny that I said them. All I can say is that I didn't believe them, that I knew full well what ignorant, destructive, obscenely jocular things I was saying.

The experience of sitting there in the dark, hearing the things I'd said, didn't shock me. It might be helpful in my defense to say that I broke into a cold sweat, or some such nonsense. But I've always known what I did. I've always been able to live with what I did. How? Through that simple and widespread boon to mankind—schizophrenia. (*MN*, 133)

It is during his basement episode that Campbell learns just how difficult it was to fail at his assignment as a Nazi propagandist.

I had hoped, as a broadcaster, to be merely ludicrous, but this is a hard world to be ludicrous in, with so many human beings so reluctant to laugh, so incapable of thought, so eager to believe and snarl and hate. So many people *wanted* to believe me! (*MN*, 120)

While in the basement headquarters of the neo-Nazi Iron Guards of the White Sons of the American Constitution, Campbell returns to another reminder of his past and how his artistic talent had served the grotesque.

Pinned to the sandbags was a target in the shape of a man.

The target was a caricature of a cigar-smoking Jew. The Jew was standing on broken crosses and little naked women. In one hand the Jew held a bag of money labeled

"International Banking." In the other hand he held a Russian flag. From the pockets of his suit, little father, mothers, and children in scale with the naked women under his feet, cried out for mercy. . . . I offer it in evidence against myself. I presume my authorship of it is news even to the Haifa Institute for the Documentation of War Criminals. I submit, however, that I drew that monster in order to establish myself even more solidly as a Nazi. I overdrew it, with an effect that would have been ludicrous anywhere but in Germany or Jones' basement, and I drew it far more amateurishly than I can really draw. (*MN*, 116–117)

Though Campbell claims he strived for the ludicrous linguistically and artistically, and despite his avowed loss of imagination once he became a spy, his ready acceptance by the Nazis is due in large measure to his reputation as a playwright; Campbell was an old hand at creating stereotyped examples of good and evil, unfettered by any ambiguity of character. His images were comforting illusions of a fabled nemesis.

Campbell's basement refuge is shared with a large group of schizophrenics including:

- George Kraft, otherwise known as Colonel Iona Potapov, alcoholic, amateur painter, chess master and sleeper Russian agent. "It was typical of his schizophrenia as a spy that he would use an institution he so admired (Alcoholics Anonymous) for purposes of espionage" (*MN*, 51).
- Resi Noth, alias Helga, whose childhood infatuation with Howard enables her to assume her sister's identity in a plot (unknown to her) to capture Campbell for the Soviets.
- The Black Fuehrer of Harlem Robert Sterling Wilson (at various times a jailbird, Japanese agent, and personal valet to Dr. Jones) who viewed the Japanese as brothers of color and was awaiting the day "colored people" had their own atom bomb to drop on their noncolored enemy, the Chinese.
- The defrocked Paulist Father Keeley who advocated the murder of Jews.
- The Reverend Doctor Lionel Jason David Jones, D.D.S., D.D., who though trained as a dentist and not as a theologian (kicked out of school because of his radicalism), insisted "that the teeth of Jews and Negroes proved beyond question that both groups were degenerate" (*MN*, 58).

Before Campbell is freed from his underground asylum, he delivers August Krapptauer's eulogy with the same ambiguity that got him through the war, "saying, incidentally, what I pretty much believe, that Krapptauer's sort of truth would probably be with mankind forever, as long as there were men and women around who listened to their hearts instead of their minds" (*MN*, 133). This carefully constructed double entendre is countered by Wirtanen's informing Howard that one of his radio broadcasts contained coded information concerning Helga's disappearance in the Crimea.

This news, that I had broadcast the coded announcement of my Helga's disappearance, broadcast it without even knowing what I was doing, somehow upset me more than anything in the whole adventure. It upsets me even now. Why, I don't know.

It represented, I suppose, a wider separation of my several selves than even I can bear to think about. (*MN*, 136)

Whether crafty and sublime by the skillful use of his art or ignorantly quiescent to the demands of the moment, Campbell's unending facility to gratify the extremes of human nature aligns him with the philosophy of Adolf Eichmann (which he learns while incarcerated with Eichmann in Israel):

"Life is divided into phases," he said. "Each one is very different from the others, and you have to be able to recognize what is expected of you in each phase. That's the secret of successful living.

"I'm a writer now," he said. "I never thought I'd be a writer."

"May I ask you a personal question?" I said.

"Certainly," he said benignly. "That's the phase I'm in now. This is the time for thinking and answering. Ask whatever you like."

"Do you feel that you're guilty of murdering six million Jews?" I said.

"Absolutely not," said the architect of Auschwitz. (*MN*, 122–123)

As if to draw some distinction between Eichmann's brand of schizophrenia and his own unique blend of personality, Campbell offers charity and self-condemnation:

The more I think about Eichmann and me, the more I think that he should be sent to the hospital, and that I am the sort of person for whom punishments by fair, just men were devised.

As a friend of the court that will try Eichmann, I offer my opinion that Eichmann cannot distinguish between right and wrong—that not only right and wrong, but truth and falsehood, hope and despair, beauty and ugliness, kindness and cruelty, comedy and tragedy, are all processed by Eichmann's mind indiscriminately, like birdshot through a bugle.

My case is different. I always know when I tell a lie, am capable of imagining the cruel consequences of anybody's believing my lies, know cruelty is wrong. I could no more lie without noticing it than I could unknowingly pass a kidney stone. (*MN*, 123–124)

After Campbell's brief excursion out of Jones's basement to meet with Wirtanen, during which time he learns of the encoded message concerning Helga's disappearance in the Crimea, he returns because "the only place I wanted to be was back in Jones' cellar with my mistress and my best friend" (*MN*, 153). That part of him which knowingly loved his sister-in-law turned spy, Resi, and genuinely appreciated the painter and recluse George Kraft, mattered more than the part that had been deceived and conspired against. By returning underground, Howard began to understand the mechanization of his own schizophrenia. The raid by the FBI finally incites the proper image for Howard to appreciate the subtler underpinnings of existence. When the paranoid schizophrenic Dr. Jones protests the arresting agent's efforts, he banters about the grand conspiracies that have driven his life.

"Why bother us? Everything we do is to make the country stronger! Join with us, and let's go after the people who are trying to make it weaker!"

"Who's that?" said the G-man.

"I have to tell you?" said Jones. "Haven't you even found that out in the course of your work? The Jews! The Catholics! The Negroes! The Orientals! The Unitarians! The foreign-born, who don't have any understanding of democracy, who play right into the hands of the socialists, the communists, the anarchists, the anti-Christ and the Jews! . . ."

"You talk about the Catholics and the Negroes," said the G-man, "and yet, here your two best friends are a Catholic and a Negro."

"What's so mysterious about that?" said Jones. (*MN*, 161–162)

This conversation draws a stark contrast for Campbell concerning the malicious ignorance of those around him in relation to his own self-evident duplicity.

I have never seen a more sublime demonstration of the totalitarian mind, a mind which might be likened unto a system of gears whose teeth have been file off at random. Such a snaggle-toothed thought machine driven by a standard or even a substandard libido, whirls with the jerky, noisy gaudy pointlessness of a cuckoo clock in Hell. . . .

Jones wasn't completely crazy. The dismaying thing about the classic totalitarian mind is that any given gear, though mutilated, will have at its circumference unbroken sequences of teeth that are immaculately maintained, and that are exquisitely machined.

Hence the cuckoo clock in Hell—keeping perfect time for eight minutes and thirty-three seconds, jumping ahead fourteen minutes, keeping perfect time for six seconds, jumping ahead two seconds, keeping perfect time for two hours and one second, then jumping ahead a year.

The missing teeth, of course, are simple obvious truths, truths available and comprehensible even to ten-year-olds, in most cases.

The willful filing off of gear teeth, the willful doing without certain obvious pieces of information—

That was how a household as contradictory as one composed of Jones, Father Keeley, Vice-Bundesfuehrer Krapptauer, and the Black Fuehrer could exist in relative harmony.

That was how my father-in-law could contain in one mind an indifference toward slave women and love for a blue vase—

That was how Rudolf Hess, Commandant of Auschwitz, could alternate over the loudspeakers of Auschwitz great music and calls for corpse-carriers—

That was how Nazi Germany could sense no important differences between civilization and hydrophobia—. (*MN*, 162–163)

Countering those who willfully played with their gears, Campbell falls into self-mockery because he never did so, though his schizophrenia is admittedly less subtle.

Since there is no one else to praise me, I will praise myself—will say that I never tampered with a single tooth in my thought machine, such as it is. There are teeth missing, God knows—some I was born without, teeth that will never grow. And other teeth have been stripped by the clutchless shifts of history—

But never have I willfully destroyed a tooth on a gear of my thinking machine. Never have I said to myself, "This fact I can do without." (*MN*, 163)

Campbell's great revelation about himself is that biological and environmental promptings largely determined his fate. Shaped by the eternal dynamic tensions of human existence, "the clutchless shifts of history" become the structured moments of his personal existence. But beyond the external and visible designs used as a grid against which we measure our humanity, there is the more complicating dilemma of our personal chemistries interacting with all the other flesh covered chemistry sets walking around. Howard's conversation with the policeman provides a sidewalk dissertation on the philosophy of psychiatry and its chemical underpinnings, considering such extreme conditions as premenstrual syndrome, postpartum depression, and maternal infanticide, as well as the paradoxical friendliness of post-war Japan and its wartime ruthlessness, and concludes, "Maybe it's all chemicals. Maybe it's different chemicals that different countries eat that makes people act in different ways at different times" (*MN*, 171). Perhaps Howard is silently considering the hormonal splurges of youth when he says, "I doubt if there has ever been a society that has been without strong and violent young people eager to experiment with homicide" (*MN*, 120).

Though Campbell's confession illustrates schizophrenia in varying degrees and forms and considers a number of possible reasons for its prevalence, his theme is that we all suffer some form of schizophrenia (dissociation) due to the swirl of historic/genetic forces and that we are doomed to perpetuate such cycles. The resurrected, though incarcerated, Howard Campbell is free to consider the nature of his activities and his impact on others. For the most part, the confession discusses his life's journey from naïve beginnings, through an awareness of his schizophrenia, on to the great realizations of his entombment. It is those realizations that enable him to superimpose upon his story's chronology a universal understandings of the biological and environmental trap of humanity.

The resurrected Campbell, more rightly the doppelgänger of his dead soul, actually begins his story with a return to the naïve (and the naively schizophrenic). By introducing the four Israeli prison guards in the beginning of the tale, Campbell focuses attention on those who seem undisturbed by the same malady. Bernard Mengel had saved his life by playing dead as a German soldier pulled three gold teeth from his mouth. A more subtle demonstration of the separation of his several selves appears in his recollection of the death of Rudolf Hess. He had placed a leather strap around Hess's legs at his hanging, and within the same hour had similarly strapped his suitcase shut without sensing any difference between the activities. As he tells Campbell, "I was like almost everybody who came through the war. . . . I go so I couldn't feel anything" (*MN*, 25).

Andor Gutman lived through the hell of Auschwitz and, to his shame, had been a member of the Sonderkommando, the corpse-carrier unit. What could make him facilitate the death machine?

There were loudspeakers all over the camp, and they were never silent for long. There was much music played through them. Those who were musical told me it was often good music—sometimes the best. . . . There was one announcement that was always crooned, like a nursery rhyme. Many times a day it came. It was the call for the Sonderkommando. After two years of hearing that call over the loudspeakers, between the music, the position of corpse-carrier suddenly sounded like a very good job. (*MN*, 21)

Arpad Kovacs resented those Jews who passively became "briquets." He became an officer in the Nazi SS while simultaneously feeding information to the Hungarian Jewish underground. Hidden behind his execution of fourteen SS soldiers are the numerous duties he most probably accomplished on behalf of the Nazis. Is it possible to compare the relative guilt or innocence of these two double agents? Kovacs was conscious of the necessity of developing and protecting another identity, and as Campbell notes, "That fact is the basis for his sympathy with me." Kovacs reads Howard's daily confessional output and loudly sides with Campbell, "Tell them the things a man does to stay alive! What's so noble about being a briquet?" (*MN*, 22).

But it is the brief portrait of the youngest guard, eighteen-year-old Arnold Marx, which highlights an acculturated schizophrenia ensuring succeeding generational conflicts. The grandson of an Iron Cross medal winner in World War I, Marx knows nothing about the war criminals of World War II. But his interest in archaeology teaches him about the ancient tensions in the Middle East. As a Jew, he very matter-of-factly mentions how the Israelites had burned and conquered Hazor in 1900 B.C., killing all forty thousand inhabitants. Though Solomon rebuilt the city, in 732 B.C. the Assyrian Tiglath-pileser the Third burned it down again (*MN*, 18–19). Arnold overlooks the slaughter committed by the Jews and concentrates on the Arab avengers. He also fails to see that the ancient wars in Palestine almost always attempted cultural genocide, and that Israel's present occupation of land once held by the Palestinians would be viewed as cultural oppression and only encourage more war. The cycle of vengeance is perpetuated by the select reading of *the record*. To paraphrase from Krapptauer's eulogy, "a sort of truth would be with mankind forever, as long as men and women listened to their heart instead of their minds."

As evidenced by Arnold Marx and Howard Campbell, the record is a very shallow truth. Certainly the historical record as passed down to succeeding generations explains the "when" and "what" of specific moments in time, but it will never be able to explain "why." For that, man would need a thorough understanding of his internal chemistry and its symbiosis with all earthly matter. This is obviously beyond reason, and Vonnegut leaves us with the superficiality of *the record* as the only legacy, however unreliable, of life's perceived linearity.

Mother Night is an experiment in recombinant identities. By taking the surface structure of his own ethnicity and his moments at war with the descendants of his ancestral homeland, Vonnegut attempts to read the historical record from a less secure, less confident viewpoint, as Kraft-Potapov assures Howard that

future civilizations—better civilizations than this one—are going to judge all men by the extent to which they've been artists. You and I, if some future archaeologist finds our works miraculously preserved in some city dump, will be judged by the quality of our creations. Nothing else about us will matter. (*MN*, 52–53)

We have to face the possibility that totalitarian regimes, Nazis, may come to hold in high regard such historically significant artifacts as the Gettysburg Address.

Vonnegut's fictional paradox presents us with Hitler admiring Lincoln's appreciation for and explanation of a soldier's supreme sacrifice, while Wirtanen/Sparrow is at a loss to find a meaning for any amount of carnage, "A moral? It's a big enough job just burying the dead, without trying to draw a moral from each death" (*MN*, 137).

What reliable record is left for Campbell? Apparently none outside himself—and he explains that because he feels so compromised by being a negligible player in his own destiny, he decides to commit suicide. But he ends the text with a cryptically punctuated *"Auf wiedersehen?"* Though we later learn in *Slaughterhouse-Five* that Campbell did commit suicide. It is hard to believe his commitment within *this* text. As Vonnegut says in his editor's note to the text, "To say that he was a playwright is to offer an even harsher warning to the reader, for no one is a better liar than a man who has warped lives and passions onto something as grotesquely artificial as a stage" (*MN*, ix). Considering Campbell's schizophrenia, which part of him would be the executioner for crimes against himself?

WORKS CITED

Vonnegut, Kurt. *Mother Night*. Harper and Row, Publishers, 1961, 1966.
———. *Slaughterhouse-Five*. New York: Delacorte Press/Seymour Lawrence, 1969.

Mother Night: **Fiction into Film**

Jerome Klinkowitz

Few popular novelists of his generation are so poorly represented on film as is Kurt Vonnegut. Although his masterwork *Slaughterhouse-Five* had screen success comparable to the excellent films of Joseph Heller's *Catch-22*, Ken Kesey's *One Flew Over the Cuckoo's Nest*, and Jerzy Kosinski's *Being There*, the rest of his canon has until recently suffered from neglect or worse.

Vonnegut himself wrote the movie script for *Happy Birthday, Wanda June*, learning to his dismay that what functions on the legitimate stage is not automatically transferrable to the screen. *Slapstick*, one of his self-confessedly weaker novels, appeared immeasurably worse as a film, thanks to the idiot-savant acting of Jerry Lewis and the self-indulgences of child star Steven Paul, who assumed duties as producer, director, and star. Even director George Roy Hill's deft touch with *Slaughterhouse-Five*, ideal as a film on its own terms, omits the novel's most important character and narrative technique: Kurt Vonnegut struggling to say something intelligible about a massacre and recognizing the deaths of persons, places, and things with the inevitable "so it goes."

Thus, writer-producer Robert B. Weide has the odds against him when setting out to film Vonnegut's *Mother Night*. Were such novels an easy property for cinema, they would have been grabbed up long ago; and look at the difficulties of those who had tried. Moreover, in Hollywood terms *Mother Night* is no *Slaughterhouse-Five*. Though well-known today as are all of his books, *Mother Night* is an early work, written by an unknown author and published as a critically unnoted paperback original. As the author's third novel, it is structured in the matter unique to his initial novels, using a familiar subgeneric format as its justification for existing. Dystopia, space opera, spy-thriller, apocalypse, and rags-riches reversals are the common devices of Kurt Vonnegut's first five novels, with the cloak-and-dagger introduction of *Mother Night* the most obvious Pop culture adaptation. The printed book even looked like a piece of espionage brought to light, Vonnegut signing his own name to a prefatory "Editor's Note" and allowing the protagonist to quite literally write his own story. Only much later, for a hardcover edition in 1966, would the author add an Introduction clarifying his own role in the story. This itself is the first evidence of what from then on would be Vonnegut's most characteristic narrative strategy, the approach taken by his increasingly mature work: that of public spokesmanship within and beyond his fiction. In *Mother Night*, however, it is his character, Howard W. Campbell, Jr., who does the speaking, while Kurt Vonnegut as author stays out of the picture.

In bringing *Mother Night* to the screen, Robert Weide's method is to make it look more like a work of Vonnegut's maturity. This involves dramatizing Howard Campbell's similarities with the author and making Campbell's so-called confessions less an act of soul-searching and more a posture of spokesmanship. One of the film's great successes is how actor Nick Nolte looks and acts like the commonly known image of Kurt Vonnegut. Yet even as a novel, *Mother Night* could be considered to read differently today, given all that its author subsequently contributed to the world. Thus,Weide's reading reflects how this 1961 novel is received by Vonnegut's public in 1996.

Specific challenges are met with this orientation in mind. A cinematic advantage of *Mother Night* over *Slaughterhouse-Five* is how the act of writing becomes part of the plot. It is not Kurt Vonnegut struggling to find what to say about a massacre, but Howard Campbell sitting in a prison cell stripped of virtually everything except a typewriter and a ream of paper. Director Keith Gordon is careful to indicate the present-tense of writing: prison scenes are filmed in black and white, while what Campbell writes about is done in full color. Just as in the novel, the focus shifts back and forth. Yet Weide's film enjoys an obvious advantage, for the crosscutting can be used for great emotional effect. Black and white is perfect for suggesting the prison's sterile, starkly confining atmosphere, and color is ideal for the richness of Campbell's memory. But it becomes an especially heartbreaking contrast when viewers see Campbell receiving the news that his wife has died entertaining troops on the Eastern Front. As pitiful as Nick Nolte can portray grief at hearing the news, it is even more moving as the film cuts to the black and white scene of Campbell at his jail-cell typewriter, overcome by the immensity of having just written the scene that has been shown.

Hence, viewers can appreciate the doubled effect of Howard Campbell's story: not just that he experienced these events, but that he is forced to relive them in writing his memoir. Here again Weide's cinematic choices enhance Vonnegut's theme, for the crosscutting allows not just Campbell's past but his ongoing life to be influenced by the nature of his textual production. Much of the past being recalled from the 1930s and 1940s involves the protagonist's occupation as a writer, first of dreamy romances for the stage, then of virulent propaganda for the Nazi government. Each type of writing involves a code, and each incorporates a facet of its author's beliefs. The playwright's dramas are predicated on the power of love to conquer all, or at the very least to provide a refuge from the world's evils; this is the "nation of two" that he creates, in drama and in life, for himself and his actress wife, Helga. The propagandist's diatribes have a secret, private message, as they are used to convey information of Germany to Allied intelligence forces. Believing there is a good person behind the propagandist's facade,

Campbell sees his phony broadcasts as just that: a sham, nothing that relates to his real identity.

It is the nature of these writerly beliefs that the plot of *Mother Night* throws into question. In his novel, Kurt Vonnegut uses the apparatus of his "Editor's Note" to state the moral, something traditional fiction disallows a conventional author from doing. Even within this scheme Vonnegut as "editor" is careful to note that although Campbell himself wrote the statement, he excised it from the final manuscript. Thus, Vonnegut has to cite it outside the text. Here Campbell sees his crime as having served evil too openly and good too secretly, having done despicable things while taking pride that a better self was hidden inside. For his 1966 Introduction, Vonnegut restates the moral himself, that a person should be careful about pretenses because they so often turn out to be real. By then, Vonnegut was at the point of incorporating himself as author into the body of his narrative fiction. This is just the technique George Roy Hill was unable to portray in his film of *Slaughterhouse-Five*. For *Mother Night* Robert Weide strengthens the writerly nature of Howard Campbell to make such struggle a large part of the movie's action. Campbell struggles, more apparently than he does in the novel version, and in that struggle he comes to reexamine the nature and beliefs of his writer's art, itself a property of Kurt Vonnegut's later work. In doing so, Howard Campbell in the film of *Mother Night* takes on the spokesman's role Kurt Vonnegut has played in the years since the onset of his fame.

Weide achieves this aim not so much by changing Campbell as by strengthening the visual elements in the characterization of Resi Noth. When introduced early in the film as Helga's little sister, Resi is portrayed as a stark, stern nihilist. It is April 1945; her home is about to be overrun by the Russian army, and before she and her mother leave for Cologne (and the more amenable Western front) her pet dog, which cannot be taken along, must be shot. The duty falls to Howard Campbell, but Resi makes it "easy" for him by proclaiming her absolute disbelief in anything other than the finality of death. She even goes so far as to explain the source for this nihilism: that the only life liveable to her was the role Campbell had crafted for his wife, Helga, in their nation of two. As she could not be Helga, what was left for her was something unwritten, something therefore utterly nihilistic.

In this scene the only thing childlike about Resi is her size. Everything else is uncomfortably adult. Her manner is brusk, even harsh. Her posture is stiff and unyielding, and her eyes, which draw much of the camera's attention, stare fixedly with the rigidity of steel. This is no child, the film tells us. This is not a person at all, but rather a character for whom no one has written a role. In a film rich with exceptionally good casting and acting, it is the most effective portrayal of all.

Then, in the film's greatest piece of dramaturgical success, this same characterization is reprised sixteen years later when Resi reappears pretending to be Helga. Howard Campbell accepts her pretense and the plot proceeds this way for twenty-four hours. But viewers, at the very least subliminally, will distrust Helga's presence, and not just for the way it miraculously contradicts history. This unease is triggered by alterations of actress Sheryl Lee's makeup and costuming and in the scene's use of color and lighting. In Campbell's memories from the late 1930s, Helga was all brightness and light; indeed, the view presented of Resi was so contrastive as to shock. Now, as Resi appears in the role of Helga, she is old enough and pretty enough to play the part. But her *look* bears nothing in common with the happy young woman of Campbell's memoir. Instead, her complexion is wan, her dress drab, tinged only with the same blue cast that chilled the depiction of little Resi. Most of all, it is her eyes—not the sparkling visage of Helga, but the icy stare of the nihilistic child in 1945.

Virtually all aspects of filmmaking conspire to form this identity, from writing, directing, and photography to lighting, makeup, wardrobe, and acting. The purpose of these efforts underscores Weide's interpretation not just of Resi but of Resi as a factor in Campbell's art. In her confession of true identity the next day, Resi describes that as a refugee from East Germany she had the choice of remaining the nonperson she was or becoming the fabulously attractive Helga, so attractive because there had been a role written for her. At this point Campbell is able to reembrace his writer's credo from the 1930s, that a nation of two was in fact scriptable as a wholesome way of life—that pretense, in other words, could be quite beneficial. He accepts Resi as Helga, knowing full well that she is not, and even accedes to her wish that he resume writing and craft a play for her. For the first time since before the war, viewers see Howard Campbell writing for art's sake, not history's.

And what a fraud it is. This is what Robert Weide's treatment of Campbell reveals. It is not just that he learns how his presumed friend George Kraft and even Resi herself are Russian spies working to kidnap him to imprisonment in Moscow. Nor is it that he must face this reality as revealed by his continual nemesis, the Office of Strategic Service agent who has consistently pulled the rug out from under all his fabricated identities. The fraud of his own writing must be faced when Resi wilts for lack of characterization, for the lack of a role she has wished Campbell to write for her. Not the play he would compose in Mexico—no, rather the motivation to "die for love" as the competing governments' forces close in to make their capture. Unable to find meaning himself, he fails to provide Resi the motivation she seeks, so she dies by her own hand, for absolutely nothing.

This scene, filmed faithfully from the novel, has been made especially effective by the cinematic identification between Resi the adult, so happily hopeful in her role as Helga, and Resi the child, nihilistic to the point of having no personhood at all. The heart of Howard Campbell's writerly credo has been that pretense is a viable form of refuge from the world. Much of *Mother Night*'s action, both as novel and as film, has been to disabuse him of the notion that pretend-propaganda did no harm; a striking point in both mediums is when his arch-Nazi father-in-law tells him that even as a spy he could never have served the Allies as well as he served Germany, that it was Campbell's speeches that kept the Nazi ideal motivated after all other reasons to continue had failed. But even through the anonymity of his bleak postwar life Campbell had clung to this belief's artistic correlation, that the romance of a nation of two was still workably worthwhile. It is Resi who counters that belief, and her behavior in Greenwich Village of 1961 is all the more effective when so closely related to her more easily accepted nihilism of Berlin in 1945.

What Resi's behavior implies, Howard Campbell's spokesmanship expounds. Robert Weide need not rewrite any of the lines Kurt Vonnegut has provided for Campbell. The only major statement he makes that does not come from the novel is the epigraph Vonnegut chooses for the much later work, *Galápagos*: Anne Frank's ironic conclusion that "In spite of everything, I still believe people are really good at heart." As bitter as these words seem within Frank's *Diary*, they are even more sardonic as a sentiment in *Galápagos*, where in order to escape its habitual inclination for doing evil things humankind must de-evolve into a more simply animal state. As the cinematic Campbell speaks this same line to Resi and Kraft after learning of their perfidy, which is the story's ultimate betrayal, it serves as Weide's salute to Vonnegut's moral spokesmanship—that he knows just how bad people can be and also has some sound advice on how to improve things. Throughout his work, the author has been skeptical of an overly winsome trust in the arts. He himself was directed to a career in science instead, and after studying the actions of biochemistry pursued a graduate career in the human science of anthropology. Beginning in *Breakfast of Champions* and continuing through *Timequake*, he preferred to celebrate not human imagination (in terms of contriving things—beware human contrivance, almost all his fiction warns) but rather simple human awareness, the self-conscious style of knowledge that among all animal life only humankind enjoys. In *Mother Night* his Howard Campbell is a more conventionally aesthetic artist; in fact, it is Campbell's motivation as an aesthete that corrupts his drama and his fascination with playing the ultimately tragic role of hero that damns the world with his propaganda. Thus, when Campbell learns to question the nature of his art, it is Kurt Vonnegut's position being announced.

Except for his reference to Vonnegut's citation of Anne Frank, then, Weide need not write new lines for Campbell. What he does do in defining the role for actor Nick Nolte is to enhance Campbell's physical identity with Vonnegut, especially the Kurt Vonnegut known to millions as a public figure.

From the moment Campbell steps from the Israeli prison van in the scene that runs behind the film's opening credits, it is the image of today's Kurt Vonnegut that he conveys. Stooped forward, mouth hanging a bit open, hair mussed up and clothing rumpled, walking slowly with a shambling gate, it is the most familiar picture of Kurt Vonnegut publicized for the past thirty years. In many scenes Campbell even wears the author's trademark raincoat (on sunny days without a hint of rain). It is the classic look reviewer Robert Scholes described in his April 6, 1969, front-page coverage of *Slaughterhouse-Five* for *The New York Times Book Review*, a look that Scholes compares to the visage of Lot's wife. At Dresden, the reviewer suggests, Vonnegut looked into the abyss, and his sense of shock from that terrifying view has imprinted itself on his writer's personality ever since. In his Bennington College lecture from *Wampeters, Foma & Granfalloons* the author ascribes his shift from optimism to what he saw at Dresden and to the news of Hiroshima and Nagasaki as well. Today as a widely received speaker, that is the image Kurt Vonnegut conveys: careless about his haircut, unmindful of whether his clothes are freshly pressed, and humorously apologetic about his inattention to the finer points of public speaking—all because the shock of the message he needs to convey outweighs these mundane particulars.

For Howard Campbell this transition from optimism to pessimism is underscored by Nick Nolte's appearance. Before the war, he is neatly trimmed and sharply tailored; even as a Nazi broadcaster his look is masterful and imposing, the essence of authority. It is in his postwar life that he assumes the guise of Kurt Vonnegut's public spokesmanship, and the film's constant crosscutting between present and past emphasizes the physical cost this knowledge entails. In his prison cell, as he revisits the scenes of his worldly education to the nature of mankind, the toll becomes even greater. By the film's end, he is quite literally a man at the end of his rope.

A final Weide gesture toward making Howard Campbell a writer-spokesman is having him hang himself not by rope but with a braid made from his used-up typewriter ribbons. The Israelis have provided these as a preliminary to his trial, so that he can draft a memoir of his actions for use by the court. But there will be no judicial sessions, for in writing his story Campbell has tried himself and found himself guilty. In the novel, it is not for crimes against humanity but crimes against himself. In his film Robert Weide stops short of such self-judgment, preferring to let the watching prison guard make sufficient comment with a simple exhalation of smoke, a reminder of his earlier comment of how strapping the legs of the executed Rudolf Hess felt exactly the same as strapping shut his suitcase. In comprehending the error of his art, Campbell has stepped beyond such distinctions.

Weide's emphasis on Howard Campbell's act of writing corresponds to Vonnegut's textual emphasis in the novel. For *Mother Night*, almost all information comes in written, even published form, and the film takes advantage of these plot devices for its exposition. After all, Campbell is being assisted by the entire research staff of the Haifa Institute for the Documentation of War Criminals. Yet there is a higher authority beyond textuality, as indicated by Frank Wirtanen's supposedly liberating letter. Meant to free Campbell, it is the final text that moves him to suicide, the final move of himself as a pawn that ends the chess game of his life.

Other cinematic touches not only credit Weide's faithfulness to the essence of Vonnegut's story but show how so much of that story derives from the popular culture of American life. John Goodman, in a role described as a cameo (he is not listed in the opening credits), melds his own public image with that of the character Kurt Vonnegut created in 1961 (when Goodman himself was a child); both Goodman and Wirtanen are familiar types, their speech and physical manner important for conveying the idea of how Howard Campbell's idyllic German life can be so genially interrupted by just what he does not want to hear from home. Wirtanen makes four appearances, the last in the person of his letter to Campbell in jail, and each time his news disrupts the existence Campbell has so carefully fabricated. Alan Arkin's portrayal of George Kraft is equally adept, world-weariness as a broken widower matching up perfectly with the amorality of a betraying spy. Sheryl Lee's portrayal of both Helga and Resi suggests two entirely different characters, even as one pretends to be the other; her ability to calculate the difference and dissemble it qualifies her as a natural source for Russian espionage, the final issue of Howard Campbell's art.

Weide's neo-Nazis—Dr. Jones, Rev. Keeley, Bundleader Krapptauer, Black Fuehrer Wilson—are ridiculously comic, just as Vonnegut describes them in *Mother Night* (where their ludicrous schizophrenia serves as a model for the totalitarian mind). In one understandable difference from the novel, Weide's real Nazis aren't very funny—there is none of the banality of evil such as table tennis tournaments with Hess and Goebbels and Adolf Hitler rapturing over the Gettysburg Address. In this novel and in *Slaughterhouse-Five* the author has sometimes been criticized for trivializing the Holocaust, and even though the techniques of both novels pierce more directly to the heart of evil (by showing Nazis not as cartoon monsters but as the human beings they were), it is doubtful that today's Hollywood industry could permit a major motion picture to be made that handled the Third Reich's leadership in anything but consistently condemning tones. A hint of Vonnegut's more comprehensive attitude comes in the portrayal of fellow-prisoner Adolf Eichmann: a disembodied voice (spoken by comedian Henry Gibson) whose cautious suggestions to Campbell reveal an utter ignorance of his own culpability.

In all these aspects Robert Weide's *Mother Night* benefits from Kurt Vonnegut's presence. From John Goodman small-talking on a park bench to Henry Gibson's advice, so preposterous that Nick Nolte is given the motivation for the single hearty laugh in the script, almost every nuance is that of the author who restructured the nature of fiction with novels such as *Cat's Cradle* and *Slaughterhouse-Five*. Weide had already immersed himself in Vonnegut's work, spending ten years researching, drafting, and doing the initial filming for a documentary on the subject, and this expertise shows in every frame. Had Kurt Vonnegut himself been trained as a filmmaker, *Mother Night* would not show much differently.

Central to Weide's understanding is how what was implicit in the author's 1961 novel has become a tenet of his public spokesmanship since the onset of fame. To everyone who has seen the physical characteristics of this image, Nick Nolte's portrayal conforms in closely sympathetic replication. Yet even if the viewer has not made the connection, Kurt Vonnegut himself cooperates in forging it near the film's end. After listening to Howard Campbell work his way through to a comprehension of Vonnegut's aesthetic and watching him comport himself with so much of the author's physical manner, the film audience sees this characterization brought to fruition as Nick Nolte, sprung from his last entrapment by the intervention of government intelligence, stands completely immobile on a city sidewalk, lacking the simplest reason to move in any direction at all. He stands here from noon into nighttime, passers-by drifting in and out of telephotoed focus as he remains motionless as a statue. The perspective, timed in very subtle slow-motion, is Howard Campbell's own. And into it, as one of the last pedestrians encountered, comes Kurt Vonnegut himself: shambling, stooped, somewhat rumpled and mouth slightly agape, rather suspiciously but concernedly regarding the person he has created. As their eyes meet, he and Howard Campbell are one, and the film is ready to conclude.

Vonnegut on Film

Jerry Holt

It did not have huge potential, but the thing exists and that's what is wonderful," Kurt Vonnegut said of the 1997 film version of *Mother Night*. "It's rather an old-fashioned movie. It's about something."[1]

Vonnegut's tone, although familiarly low-key, clearly displays enthusiasm for director Keith Gordon's interpretation of the 1961 novel. Gordon did not work from a Vonnegut-written film script, but writer Robert Weide has remained very faithful to the novel's text. This was work Vonnegut seemed happy enough to let Weide do, saying, "I was born in 1922. People who were born that long ago don't think about writing for movies."[2]

As one who comes at this subject as a film historian rather than a Vonnegutian, I find myself in great sympathy with any novelist who commits his work to those who in turn create celluloid. Vonnegut has said that only he and Margaret Mitchell have been served well by the movies, and here he was referencing only George Roy Hill's adaptation of *Slaughterhouse-Five*, scripted by Steve Geller. Thus, with *Mother Night* also drawing good reviews, I hope it will be instructive to look at three Vonnegut novels brought to film as film. Has Vonnegut been served well more often than not? And what are some of the particular problems inherent in bringing this writer, so cinematic in print, to the actual medium?

In purely chronological terms, 1972's *Slaughterhouse-Five* is indeed an auspicious beginning. The director, George Roy Hill, was still riding the crest of popularity he achieved with *Butch Cassidy and the Sundance Kid* in 1969, and he had pretty much his pick of projects. His adaptation of this extremely popular novel could hardly be more respectful, although little is in evidence that would demonstrate why the book was so embraced by the hippie generation only a few years before. Certainly the antiwar statement is clear, but the quirky nature of Vonnegut's approach is just not there. Since Vonnegut himself is such a presence in the novel, his absence on film leaves the point of view almost exclusively to

Billy Pilgrim, and the result is that the film plays as objective clinical history in ways that the novel never does.

What Vonnegut wrote, after all, was very much a work for 1969: an updated *Pilgrim's Progress* that allowed the Vietnam generation, already feeling victimized by government and by their own parents, to see in the suffering Billy a dim mirror image. Here was poor Billy, a decent and simple fellow more than willing to jump through the hoops of the American establishment who, thanks to time and chance, is forced to see more of human cruelty than one should be obliged to see. Such were the sights of Tet and My Lai and the 1968 Chicago Convention. American youth of that era shared that very sense of growing up too soon, if not Billy's stoicism. The electronic, hallucinatory way the Vietnam War came to this country certainly made the feeling of being "unstuck in time" not an unfamiliar one. To understand, as the novel makes clear, that the mistakes of history are repeated and that wars have been and will be fought by children was to understand, war protestors would have said, the quagmire itself of Vietnam. Of course Vonnegut's glibly ironic positing of the wisdom of Tralfamadore—to dwell in good moments and reject bad ones—caught the tempo of the hippie life: a lot of the communal experience was tied to that very philosophy. But Vonnegut's complex approach to these simple truths soared basically as a form to fit the content of 1969. The novel was in the right time and place in the very same way that the Beatles were with *Sgt. Pepper's Lonely Hearts Club Band* two years before.

By 1972, however, some of that popular taste for the absurd had disappeared—or had at least been terribly blunted by the reality of May 4, 1970, at Kent State, the collapse of the South Vietnamese army, and the daily business of the Nixon White House. Thus the literary balancing act that is *Slaughterhouse-Five* in print must have seemed too chancy in terms of box office by this point. Hill's approach is still chancy enough: the film narrative is only semilinear. Nonetheless, and this is partly due to the icy nature of William Atherton's performance as Billy, the film almost asks to be taken as a sort of flower child's *Johnny Got His Gun*: a semidocumentary in which we see how war ravages upon the mind of a simple and gentle man.

There are, certainly, omissions from Steve Geller's screenplay that would deeply offend any Vonnegut lover: Kilgore Trout is referenced once, and then only on the cover of a paperback brandished by Eliot Rosewater. For that matter, there are only about two minutes of Rosewater himself. But it is the first omission that is the more serious: the rich subtext of Kilgore Trout's masterplots is the central joy of the book for many readers. Then there is the problem of depicting Tralfamadore itself: this aspect of the story enters the film relatively late and is so abbreviated that we do not really get the chance to contemplate the bittersweet implications of the Tralfamadorians' finding that "Only on earth is there any talk of free will."

But the film has many glories, and most of them work directly from a Vonnegut blueprint. On film, Paul Lazzaro, Edgar Derby, Wild Bob, and all the British prisoners are wonderful realizations. Howard Campbell appears for the Dresden fire-bombing, given about as much to do as he is in the novel. But he looks wonderfully right, as of course does Billy in his preposterous woman's overcoat and silver boots. The Dresden scenes have great authenticity, particularly in the depiction of the walk from the train to Slaughterhouse-Five, and that aftermath moment when a pile of bodies is burned is filled with chilling authenticity. The sequence in which Billy and Spot wait as the Tralfamadorian light plays over them retains great feeling, and Valencia's death-ride upon learning that Billy's plane has crashed is excessive but arresting nonetheless: there has never been a celluloid smashup of automobiles like it.

Today, the film looks perhaps too portentously mounted for its basic statement of the great paradox about Kurt Vonnegut: that freeform existentialism that says that nothing means anything—but that, damnit, we had better pretend that it does. But the same criticism can and has been made of the novel, in a sense, even by Vonnegut himself, when he told us that artists, like good architects, "give us temples in which something marvelous is obviously going on."[3] To which he adds, "Actually, practically nothing is going on."

Practially nothing is going on in *Slapstick of Another Kind*, Steven Paul's 1983 attempt at depicting another Vonnegut tale of innocents thrust upon an obtuse and vicious world. Paul had tried before with the film adaptation of *Happy Birthday, Wanda June*. It can certainly be argued that both these works, one a novel and the other a play, are inferior Vonnegut; the author himself, in a ploy that has grown increasingly common in recent years, has said, "*Slapstick* may be a very bad book. I am perfectly willing to believe that. Everybody else writes lousy books, so why shouldn't I?"[4]

If *Slapstick* does not stay in the memory as quality Vonnegut, and it doesn't, there really isn't a problem for the author here: he has written plenty that do. The one with the problem would be Steven Paul—at least if he wanted a directing career. After these directorial misadventures, he turned to producing. Too bad, in some ways: Paul's *Slapstick* at least reflects a certain respect for film history, if not for Vonnegut.

This parable of brilliant mutant twins who pretend to be idiots (that's the way, they presume, we want them) really has at its core an interesting argument about salvation through family. Thus, the subtitle: *Lonesome No More*. We follow the twins of the novel into adulthood, but in the film we see them only as children. The family theme is touched—barely, and far too late in the film. The weight of some really bad lines that exhort us to "learn the true language of the universe" are made even worse because they are delivered by the woefully miscast Jerry Lewis and Madeline Kahn.

Interestingly, though, it is Lewis who, as icon, provides the small pleasure of the film: its references to movies and moviemakers who are far better. Lewis, who remains a darling of the French auteurist school, appears onscreen with none other than Samuel Fuller, another favorite of the French. While Fuller has little to do but snort in his brief role as Colonel Sharp, the military school headmaster, his presence is granite for film buffs. Often described as an authentic American primitive, the late Fuller was responsible for 1950's genre-benders like *Shock Corridor*, *The Steel Helmet*, and *The Naked Kiss*, a film so outrageously iconoclastic that it has to be seen to be believed. Seeing Lewis and Fuller together, even though they are doing nothing, constitutes the nicest kind of interior reference to American film. Add to this the brief voiceover by none other than Orson Welles, and *Slapstick of Another Kind* almost backdoors itself into cult status.

Though no one will ever mistake Paul for an auteur, he tries hard in areas beyond the casting as well. There are ghostly appearances in the film from Laurel and Hardy and Charlie Chaplin and the Keystone Kops. Jim Backus, cast as the president of the United States, does, at one point, his Mr. Magoo. Madeline Kahn, hell-bent to rescue her brother from the clutches of Colonel Sharp, lurches toward the barracks like Gort in *The Day the Earth Stood Still*. What is missing from the film is much that has to do with Vonnegut—although he does get lyrics credit for the original song "Lonesome No More." (Yes, at credits' end there is at least one "Hi-Ho!") But those references belong in some other film: this one remains the sort of thing that gives slapstick a bad name.

Mother Night, like *Slaughterhouse-Five* before it, plays as rather too pristine—something of which *Slapstick of Another Kind* will never be accused. It was of this novel that Vonnegut said, "This is the only story of mine whose moral I know. I don't think it's a marvelous moral; I simply happen to know what it is: We are what we pretend to be, so we must be careful what we pretend to be."[5] Keith Gordon's interpretation of this work hammers that point home in every scene. Though the film is clearly made with not only respect but devotion to its source, there are moments in which the message threatens to engulf storytelling. But here is a film whose rewards, nonetheless, are many, and hardly small.

One of the major rewards is the performance of Nick Nolte, an actor who has sometimes been accused of being leaden, who depicts here, and quite successfully, a true stoic. Howard W. Campbell, Jr., the American who, as a young playwright living under the Nazis became both a wildly successful propagandist for the Reich and an American spy, has seen, like Billy Pilgrim, far too much. A lost soul after the war, Campbell settles in Greenwich Village where, a broken widower, he finds himself at the mercy of almost everybody. His nemeses include the wife of the Jewish doctor downstairs who happily turns Campbell in; the American agent who has recruited Campbell and then disavowed knowledge of him; and even the reincarnation of his beloved ex-wife who is, in fact, her younger sister. Nothing is what it seems, a theme of the novel that the film embraces fully, and one whose shockwaves register wonderfully on Nolte's catcher's mitt of a face. He offers a stinging portrait of a man sentenced to life imprisonment with himself.

To gauge how good Nolte's performance really is, note one early scene: the one in which Agent Frank Wirtanen (an amiable John Goodman) recruits Campbell. They are sitting on a park bench, and the goateed Campbell at this point has, though he is young, already drawn inside himself under the pressures of war. Campbell asks why he would want to risk his life as a double agent, and Wirtanen plays to self-absorption: he tells Campbell he knows he would "sacrifice anything in the name of romance."

It works—and how well it works is completely reflected in the actor Nolte's face. He does not admit the truth of what Wirtanen has observed, but his eyes reveal just a slight brightening: his mouth with a phantom of a smile. John Wayne once remarked that good film acting is about reacting, and Nolte proves that in this sequence. His ability to convey the feeling beneath the stoic's mask deepens as the film continues. By the end of the movie the only face we see that is more world-weary and more suffering than Nolte's is the face of Vonnegut himself, who appears on the New York street in a brief and haunting cameo.

The difficulty with the film is that Campbell's romantic soul is just not motivation enough for the life this man has led. While the novel allows Campbell to explain himself, the film, despite its voiceover narration, skimps on this. We see Campbell's enthusiasm for his propaganda and we understand that it contained coded messages to the Allies—but we see only the harm his broadcasts did and not the lives they supposedly saved. How could a human being commit so much evil in the name of good? This is a lived-in theme for Vonnegut and his readers, but Gordon's film never really deals with it. The Campbell we see, though we know he has performed significant action, is one who, like Billy Pilgrim, has been and continues to be acted upon. Thus, the Campbell of the movie remains a fascinating but excessively enigmatic presence, even in view of the theme of the complexity of human nature. Small surprise, though: it is the theme of Hawthorne and Melville as well, and the movies, with far more elapsed time to do it, have never served them well in that regard either. Still, as Vonnegut says, the film is about something. It provokes conversation, and it leads, perhaps, to a potentially wonderful experience: actually reading Vonnegut. There are small pearls within its frames. As fond as most readers of the *Slaughterhouse-Five*'s repeated phrase: "Billy and Valencia nestled like spoons," I was pleased to see it lovingly depicted not in the Hill film but in this one, as Campbell and the woman he believed to be his returned wife actually do so. The autumnal look of the film calls up Vonnegut's recent writing in wonderfully self-reflexive ways. It really does seem to me that this quiet and unpretentious film, whatever its problems, may come closer to getting Vonnegut on film than any other to date.

"In spite of everything," Howard Campbell says (echoing Anne Frank), "I still believe people are really good at heart." The evidence of such in this film is only rarely what we see on screen. Far more, it is reflected in the feelings that the filmmakers, not only Nolte and Gordon but certainly screenwriter Robert Weide, have approached their work. This, certainly, has always been the case with Vonnegut's writing: at the moments he causes us to despair the most for the human condition, he shines a light with the sheer brilliance of his own hopeless hopes. "God damn it, you've got to be kind," Eliot Rosewater says, and you know it's true, just as true as it is in *The Sirens of Titan*, when we are told, "A purpose of human life, no matter who is controlling it, is to love whoever is around to be loved." "Only in superstition is there hope,"[6] Vonnegut writes, and you know good and well he is affirming the Christianity he has debunked. In ways it is difficult to dispute, *Mother Night* on film offers, in its starkness, these very affirmations. If it sets the standard for cinematic interpretations of this author to come, it may even be called a reason to rejoice.

NOTES

1. As quoted in Kirk Miller, "Night Writer," *Total TV* 1997: 1 (Online).
2. Miller, 1.
3. Kurt Vonnegut, *Wampeters, Foma & Granfalloons* (New York, 1974): 124.
4. The Vonnegut Web: *Slapstick* Interview.
5. Kurt Vonnegut, *Mother Night* (New York: Dell, 1961): v.
6. Kurt Vonnegut, *The Sirens of Titan* (New York: Dell, 1959): 126.

WORKS CITED

Miller, Kirk. *Total TV* 1997 (Online).
Vonnegut, Kurt. *Mother Night*. New York: Dell, 1961.
———. *The Sirens of Titan*. New York: Dell, 1959.
———. *Wampeters, Foma & Granfalloons*. New York: Dell, 1974.

The Morning after *Mother Night*

Robert B. Weide

I'm not nearly as well read as I'd like to be and I blame Kurt Vonnegut. I read *Breakfast of Champions* in high school, a little more than twenty years ago, and that was it. I had found my author and I didn't want to know about any others. I gobbled up everything Vonnegut wrote and every word written about him. After I worked my way through his entire library in record time, I started all over again, this time reading all the novels and short stories chronologically. Often, a well-meaning acquaintance would suggest that if I dug Vonnegut so much, I should try Douglas Adams or Tom Robbins or John Irving. I would make occasional sojourns into such foreign territory, but always returned home to my guy.

In the summer of 1996, I was sitting in the back of a limousine with Kurt Vonnegut and Nick Nolte, parked in front of the Place des Arts in Montreal. We had just been ushered through a throng of enthusiastic filmgoers at the world premiere of the movie *Mother Night* starring Nolte and based on the 1961 novel by Vonnegut. Fans were cupping their hands around their eyes, trying to look in through the tinted limo windows. Vonnegut's door was slightly ajar, enough for one woman to peer in and enthuse to the famous novelist, "Thank you for all the books."

"You're welcome" the septuagenarian author replied, casually puffing on one of his ever-present Pall Malls (filterless).

What's wrong with this picture? What was I doing inside the car? Why wasn't I out there with my people? Well, it helped that I had written and produced *Mother Night*.

I produced my first film in 1982, a PBS documentary on the Marx Brothers. After its initial broadcast, I wrote a letter to Vonnegut proposing that I set to work on a documentary about him. He wrote back saying that he had seen my Marx piece and enjoyed it and that he'd be happy to talk with me. I met up with him in New York soon after, and we managed to hit it off. It was another five years before I actually managed to start filming my documentary—a project that continues to this day.

However, back in 1989, I asked him out of the blue about the availability of film rights to *Mother Night*. Within weeks, the rights belonged to me, all based on a handshake and no exchange of money. "You're family," was Vonnegut's reasoning.

It took me three months to write the spec script, after which my friend Keith Gordon and I spent the next five years hunting down the necessary financing. The stock speech we heard from everyone in town was, "I've been in this business for thirty years and this is one of the best scripts I've ever read. I was riveted. I laughed, I cried and I couldn't stop thinking about it for days. It's extremely powerful." (Long, thoughtful pause, then): "It's a shame we could never make it here."

Mother Night chronicles the life of (fictional) ex-patriate Howard W. Campbell, Jr. (played by Nolte), an American-born apolitical playwright living in Germany in the years preceding World War II. One day he is pressed into service by an American operative who convinces him to do some spying for the Allies. His job is to cozy up to the Nazis and join the Propaganda Ministry, making pro-fascist, Jew-baiting, anti-American speeches over the radio. What the Nazis will never know is that Campbell will be broadcasting code throughout his speeches, relaying invaluable information to the Allies. The catch is that Campbell's role will never be made public, so if he survives the war, he will certainly be branded by his native countrymen as the worst kind of traitor.

After the war, Campbell slips back into the United States and lives an anonymous life in New York City until 1961, when word starts to leak out that the notorious Nazi turncoat Howard Campbell is still alive and well. There is no one to bail him out and the only people to offer sanctuary are a motley group of imbecilic neo-Nazis who consider him their guiding light.

The book (and hopefully the movie) captures Vonnegut's unique perspective, walking that fine-line between the tragic and the absurdly comic. (One of the wacky neo-Nazis is a black man, part Malcolm X, part Steppin' Fetchit, known as the Black Fuehrer of Harlem.)

Vonnegut says *Mother Night* is the only book of his whose moral he knows, which is, "Be careful what you pretend to be, because in the end, you are what you pretend to be." Eventually, Campbell turns himself in to Israeli authorities and (in the movie) the day before the commencement of his war crimes trial, he hangs himself in his prison cell, creating a makeshift noose from the typewriter ribbons with which he had been writing his memoirs.

Go figure why no one wanted to finance this movie.

Finally, the executives at Fine Line Features put their money where their mouths were and agreed to fund us. The two caveats were that we had to deliver a "bankable" star and we had to hold to our proposed budget of $5.5 million (the catering bill on the average studio movie). We agreed. Once Nick Nolte signed on for seven percent of his normal fee, we were in business. The cast was rounded out by John Goodman, Alan Arkin, Sheryl Lee, and Kirsten Dunst. My pal and co-producer Keith Gordon directed. The script was preapproved and Fine Line, to their credit, left us alone to make our movie in Montreal, Canada, with minimal creative interference. Ruth Vitale, the president of Fine Line, focused her concerns exclusively on the actress's hairstyles and seemed unfettered by anything else. She even sent up one of the young female studio vice-presidents who bemoaned the fact that she had to fly to Montreal to go on "Hair Patrol."

After reading my final shooting script, Vonnegut sent me a fax, admitting that he wished he could take credit for some of the jokes I had added. He also told me that one critic responded to the novel saying anyone who found anything funny about the Holocaust was very sick. Although it would be a major stretch to classify *Mother Night* as a "Holocaust comedy," the film, like the book, does contain some dark humor. Vonnegut's message was clear: I should anticipate some of the same criticism for the film that he received for the book. (At one point in the film, Campbell, thought to be a genuine Nazi by the Americans and Israelis, is forced into hiding in the dingy basement of a neo-Nazi hangout. When Sheryl Lee's character grouses about those who would force them into such miserable living conditions, Campbell responds, "I don't know. In spite of everything, I still believe that people are basically good at heart." I figured maybe six people would ever get this twisted reference to Anne Frank's heartbreaking epitaph.)

Vonnegut remained extremely supportive throughout production. He even played a cameo in the film and after meeting Nolte declared, "Now I can't imagine any other actor playing Campbell." Regarding box-office prospects, Vonnegut was realistic, as were Keith and I. "Generally, if you produce a show that's about something," he said, "no one will come."

But people did come, at first. *Mother Night* premiered in the same town in which it was filmed, at the Montreal World Film Festival. A capacity audience of more than 2,000 people packed the Place des Arts. The opening scene of the film shows Nolte being escorted to his Israeli prison cell, accompanied by Bing Crosby's rendition of "White Christmas." When I heard Vonnegut chuckle at the juxtaposition, I relaxed. It was a positive review from the only critic I really cared about.

The next morning brought a glowing review in the *Montreal Gazette*. That same day, Keith and I were escorted to a screening at a local public theater, when we came upon a huge line of people winding around three blocks. I asked our escort what the crowd was gathered for. "This is the line for your film," she explained. I shot some photos of the crowd, knowing that lines around the block would be unlikely back in the United States for a film this dark and quirky.

Prior to the U.S. opening, we had a number of advance screenings at colleges, universities, and film festivals. Keith and I would always hold question and answer sessions afterward. I usually made a point to tell our audiences of the importance of word-of-mouth in promoting an independent film. "But be careful," I warned them. "The next few months will see the release of *Twelfth Night, Big Night, The Long Kiss Goodnight, Mother Night, Mother* and *Some Mother's Son*. So if you want to spread the word, please make certain you're recommending the right film."

Preview audiences were consistently supportive and enthusiastic. We started to think that our "controversial" film maybe wasn't so controversial after all. Although we were prepared to defend our movie against those who wished to question its "message," few seemed inclined to do so. Being Jewish, I was curious to see how "my people" would respond to a film that presents an ostensibly sympathetic character who acted as a cheerleader for the Nazi genocide machine. Generally, audience members who identified themselves as Jewish seemed hip to the point of the film (which is essentially a very Jewish notion): You are what you do.

So where were the people Vonnegut warned me about who would miss the point of the film and accuse us of making a Fascist-friendly movie? As it turned out, many of them were members of PEN, the international writer's group. Fine Line had set up a special screening for PEN in New York City, only hours before the official United States premiere. This time, Vonnegut joined Keith and me for the usual postscreening question and answer.

The first audience member to speak up was an outraged veteran who went on about his own wartime experiences as a radio operator in Korea, before finally claiming that only two Jews died in service to the United States during the Second World War, and why was he the only one who was aware of this fact? A murmur arose from a stunned audience. I responded as honestly as I could, saying, "Sir, you are full of crap." The guy stood up and suggested I try to beat it out of him. Others in the audience shouted him down. The evening was off to a roaring start. (Someone later suggested that the veteran's statement was meant to be facetious, implying that this was the obvious point-of-view of the film.)

One man stood up, said he was a Catholic, and wanted to know why Campbell had to commit suicide. "What about the notion of forgiveness?" he asked. A black woman wanted to know why our film didn't address the contribution of Africans to the Second World War and why the film didn't mention that Joseph Goebbels was born in Africa. (He wasn't, but why would she want that advertised if it were true?) She also told us she resented the use of the expression "black humor" (which had been bandied about during the evening), declaring it a racist phrase. I responded, saying, "I'm not particularly offended by the phrase 'white lie,' but to each their own."

Another guy had memorized a page of Campbell's first-person narrative from the book, recited it out loud, and asked why it wasn't duplicated in the film. I told him that I wrote the script for people who hadn't memorized the book. The guy obviously thought he was defending Vonnegut's work. Kurt thought the guy was whacked.

Somebody asked Vonnegut what his credentials were for writing about such a subject. He explained that he was a veteran of the Second World War, had been taken prisoner by the Germans, had directly witnessed the aftermath of the Holocaust, has many friends today who are survivors, and felt he was quite qualified to write about this time in history. One old woman stood up, announced herself as a survivor of Auschwitz, and asked how this film was supposed to help her. Another man suggested that the virulent anti-Semitic rhetoric spouted by Campbell in the film would likely serve to recruit neo-Nazis.

I was struck by the irony that PEN's charter is based on the preservation of artist's rights—protecting the written word, even when it expresses an unpopular viewpoint. The subtext of many of the comments that night were that we had no right to make this film. (What's the old joke about a liberal being someone who will lynch you from a lower branch?) In any event, we finally found the "controversy" that Vonnegut had warned of. In fact, the ugliness of the evening upset Kurt enough that he went home afterward, forgoing the official premiere later that night.

A few weeks later, we held a special screening at the Museum of Tolerance in Los Angeles. As the predominantly Jewish audience filed into the theater, Keith and I meandered through the current exhibits. When we came upon the Anne Frank display I turned to Keith and announced solemnly, "we're dead." This time, I introduced the movie, hoping to give some context to the film's ambiguous nature by quoting Elie Weisel: "I write not so that you'll understand, but so you'll know that you can never understand." Thankfully, they seemed to get the movie. I even heard laughter at the Anne Frank joke. Afterward, one Holocaust survivor told me, "You've made a very important film. It should remind people that evil doesn't always come from the obvious monsters. It lives in everyone."

The plan was to open *Mother Night* on an exclusive "art-house" basis—only eight theaters in Los Angeles and New York. The most theaters we ever played at any one time would be forty. (A major Hollywood studio film may open in 2,300 theaters, and 1,000 theaters would be a moderate release.) Opening day was November 1, 1996. That morning, reviews started to arrive via fax from the studio. I had learned early on in my career not to get emotionally involved with reviews. (I once heard a "critic" defined as someone who walks onto a battlefield after a war has been waged, then shoots the wounded.) However, a small "arty" film such as *Mother Night* would be dependent on positive reviews for its very survival. As they continued to roll out over the next few weeks, I found the rough breakdown to be as follows: 60 percent positive (about half of those, full-fledged "raves"), 25 percent mixed, 15 percent negative (about half of those, "rants").

The most consistent theme I noticed among the critical response was the lack of consistency. For every review that said the script was too slavishly devoted to the novel, another would cite that the screenplay strayed too far from the source material. A few critics loved the rather straightforward dramatic pacing maintained throughout the first half of the film, but felt that it lost its way once it took a comedic turn. Others felt the first half dragged, but the film really picked up once the comedy kicked in. One of my favorite criticisms accused us of perpetuating a racist stereotype with the portrayal of the Negro Nazi. (I had honestly felt that our film put a different spin on the typical Hollywood portrayals of Negro Nazis.)

I was surprised at the number of people who would ask me how Siskel and Ebert responded. I've always thought it sad that people rely so much on critics to help them form their own opinions. I now realized that we had regressed to the next step. Limited attention spans won't make it through an entire review anymore; so inquiring minds want to know, "Where are the thumbs? Show me the thumbs!" In the case of Siskel and Ebert, they were pointed south. Their TV review especially burned up Nolte when Siskel opined that the film was guilty of "romanticizing hate." Nolte actually got on the phone and called Siskel in Chicago, challenging him on this point. Siskel admitted to being wary of a current trend in films that make heroes out of morally ambiguous characters. When Nolte asked for other examples, Siskel offered up *Ransom*, currently in release (and coincidentally featuring Nick's ten-year-old son, Brawley). The following week, Siskel and Ebert gave *Ransom* two thumbs up.

"Can those guys be bought?" Nolte asked me. I reminded him that Siskel and Ebert's show appeared on ABC, which is owned by Cap Cities which is owned by Disney. *Ransom* was released by Touchstone, a distribution arm of Disney. "I don't know if they can be bought," I said. "But I'll bet they've been optioned."

The Jewish press was consistently kind to us, but the winner of the missing-the-point-award went to Philip Berk of the *L.A. Jewish Times*, also a leading figure in the Hollywood Foreign Press Association, sponsor of the Golden Globe awards. Berk accused the film of being anti-Semitic, citing as one example our ironic use of the song "White Christmas" written by Irving Berlin, a Jew. It didn't occur to Berk that we had to license the song from the Berlin estate who granted us the rights on a cut-rate basis after reading the script and voicing their support of the film's message.

The *L.A. Jewish Times* would eventually print my written rebuttal to Berk's attack, the low point being his questioning of Vonnegut's agenda by referring to him as "the son of a German-born American." I informed Berk that Vonnegut's family had emigrated to the United States before the Civil War (not that it should matter). Vonnegut would be less diplomatic in a personal letter to Berk, asking him, "What kind of a twisted monster are you?"

The film actually performed quite respectably during its opening week. However, Fine Line apparently expected bigger things for this dark film about an ambiguous but sympathetic character with Nazi tendencies who eventually kills himself. Literally, after the first night in theaters, a studio will calculate what the product will gross in its theatrical lifetime. After determining that *Mother Night* was not going to be the next *Pulp Fiction*, Fine Line shrunk our newspaper ads down to postage-stamp size for the second weekend. I told Vonnegut that filmgoers would now have to hire a private detective to find where our movie was playing. That weekend saw a fairly precipitous drop at the box office which then made Fine Line's prophecies self-fulfilling. The next week, Vonnegut, Nolte, Keith, and I all made phone calls to the studio's top brass asking them to please replace the rug they had surreptitiously pulled out from under us. The next weekend saw a slight increase in the ad size as well as the box office receipts. Clearly though, without genuine support from the studio, *Mother Night* would have an uphill battle at best. It proved to be a battle that the film would not survive. Fine Line had already placed all their eggs in a basket called *Shine*, an Australian acquisition and Oscar-contending crowd pleaser, which, to their credit, they mined beautifully.

After the question about Siskel and Ebert, the next most-asked question was, "What are your chances for an Oscar?" The answer, of course, was twofold: "Who knows and who cares?" With all the talk of how well independent films are doing at the Oscars, most lay people don't realize the amount of advertising dollars pumped into trade ads that promote academy nominations for the studio's favorite contenders. No ads equal no nominations. Fine Line was betting on *Shine* and took out countless double-truck color ads asking the industry for their Oscar consideration. *Mother Night* received exactly zero ads. Keith and I were still thrilled that the film ever got made, and felt the rest was just so much gravy. Vonnegut said that he felt bad for Nick, who was totally overlooked at Oscar time for what many critics cited as a career-best performance. So it goes.

Well-intentioned friends were insisting that the film would surely do well overseas as, *Mother Night* would obviously appeal to European sensibilities. In England, we had the dubious fortune to open on the same day as *The English Patient*, a similarly themed, big budget, heavily promoted movie that won a slew of Oscars including best picture. The British distributors opened us in all of two theaters, reneged on flying Keith out to London for publicity, then spent nothing on advertising. I was getting e-mail from British Vonnegut fans asking when the film would open in London. "It's playing there NOW," I told them. "Stop looking for ads. There aren't any."

Mother Night was invited to play at the prestigious Berlin Film Festival. We were anxious to see what reaction the Germans would have to our little treatise on guilt and responsibility set in World War II. We'd never get the chance to find out. The German distributors declined the invitation to play the Berlin Festival. They would either go straight to home video or dump the film altogether. When I relayed this news to Vonnegut, his response was pragmatic: "These are still very sensitive issues. No one wants to risk rocking the boat. When are you going to make a commercial film?" he deadpanned. "When John Grisham gives me a free option on one of his books," I answered.

Two weeks later, I would call Vonnegut with more good news: Like their German counterparts, the Israeli distributors had decided to dump the film and eat their investment, rather than put it on public screens. "Do you realize what this means?" I asked Kurt. "Together we've created something that Israel and a reunified Germany can see eye-to-eye on. Talk about a New World Order!"

"Well, Bob. Let's face it," Vonnegut cracked. "You must have made a crummy movie."

I wasn't going to let him get in the last zing. "Hey," I said. "Garbage in—garbage out."

The Boys of *Mother Night*

Nancy Kapitanoff

Robert B. Weide sits opposite Kurt Vonnegut and Nick Nolte in the back of a limousine parked in front of the Place des Arts in Montreal. Slouched in their seats, smoking, the author and the actor look like matching bookends. A few fans mill about the car as it idles on this comfortably warm August evening. "Thanks for all the great books," a woman yells to Vonnegut when the car door opens for another passenger. Weide knows how she feels. He has gone from being a fan to friend to collaborator.

Mother Night, the film starring Nolte based on Vonnegut's 1961 novel, which many consider his most personal book, has just made its world premiere at the Montreal World Film Festival before an enthusiastic audience of over two thousand people, an entry in the festival's official competition. For Weide who wrote the screenplay and coproduced the movie, it is the accomplishment of a dream. Lately, he has taken to carrying a camera around, he says, to provide evidence that he isn't just dreaming, that he really did make a movie based on a book by one of his childhood idols.

When he was a seventeen-year-old high school senior in 1977, Weide taught a class on Vonnegut. Sunny Hills High School in Southern California's Orange County ran an alternative education program called "Open School," in which students with exceptional knowledge of a subject could teach their peers. A year earlier he had picked up Vonnegut's novel, *Breakfast of Champions*.

"Like many people that I talk to who are Vonnegut fans, after reading that I said, that's it, I found my author, and just went back and read every single thing that he had written and everything I could about Vonnegut—press going back to the beginning of his career," Weide (pronounced why-dee) said. "If you go back and read my high school yearbook my senior year, the autographs will say, 'To the biggest Marx Brothers, Lenny Bruce, Kurt Vonnegut, Woody Allen fan.' My personal Mount Rushmore."

Weide's Vonnegut course was a credited literature class; students got grades. Part way through the semester, the skinny, bespectacled professor with the big hair caught on that one of his best friends wasn't reading the books, he was reading the Cliff Notes. "Here I was having to tell my friend I know you're cheating in my class and I'll have none of it," Weide recalls with a good laugh. "I confronted him and he got very embarrassed and dropped out of the class. And it didn't affect our friendship at all. I couldn't care less as far as our friendship was concerned." Twenty years later, after his friend saw *Mother Night* at a screening Weide had invited him to attend, he wrote to Weide: "Loved the film. Much better than the Cliff Notes." Weide knows how to make friends and keep them.

"We happen to be very close friends," Vonnegut says of Weide during a press conference in Montreal. His remark was in response to a reporter's comment that the film was unusually faithful to its source.

Vonnegut, author of over twenty books including *Slaughterhouse-Five*, the celebrated 1969 novel that made him one of the most famous writers in America, marked his seventy-fourth birthday on November 11. Weide is exactly half his age. Brothers under the skin, their age difference never got in the way of an ever-evolving, vibrant friendship. During the past fourteen years, they've shared a lot of laughs and jokes (some of them pretty bad), much about their lives, even a crush on ABC news correspondent Cynthia McFadden.

"Of course he has lots of friends," says Nanny Prior, Vonnegut's daughter, about her father. "But this one, Weide, has really dug in deep. I love seeing my father having this pleasure of friendship in his life."

"When they're together they have a tremendous by-play of humor that goes back and forth," says Nick Nolte of Vonnegut and Weide. "Kurt views the world with a sense of irony and humor and he enjoys people that get that too. That's what the connection is.

"I think Kurt is looking back in his life a bit and Bob is looking forward a bit. And so there's this—I don't suppose it's a father-son, but it's a mentorship kind of thing. And it's really refreshing to see. It's developed into a wonderful relationship, a friendship, that's delightful to be around."

In Hollywood, friendship is rarely at the core of a movie deal as it was with *Mother Night*, the fictional tale of Howard W. Campbell, Jr. (Nolte), an American playwright living in Berlin before World War II who is recruited to spy for the Americans by playing the role of a Nazi propagandist. On a handshake, Vonnegut gave Weide, a seasoned documentary filmmaker but neophyte screenwriter, the rights to adapt the novel *Mother Night*. That was in 1990. Nobody including Vonnegut got paid until the first day of principal photography on the $5.5 million film, five years later. It is not the way Don Farber, Vonnegut's New York attorney/agent for over twenty-five years, prefers to do business.

"I don't believe in free options," says Farber, adding that Vonnegut always asks his advice on such matters and usually listens to him. "I believe if someone wants to do a film or a play, if they can't come up with some money, they don't have an investment and it just doesn't happen. Kurt and Bob Weide became very friendly, and Kurt, because of this friendship, wanted to see what he could come in with. He believed in him."

"It was [this] basis of trust that enabled us to make this film in an unusual way," Weide says. "I didn't have to face that dilemma of having a studio own a film and possibly asking for major changes or putting on another writer—which would have been their right—or not making it at all, which could have been the worst thing. By writing the script on spec[ulation], it enabled us to say, 'This is the script we want to do; yes or no?' Ultimately Fine Line [Features] stepped to the plate and said yes. . . and the friendship survived, which is the other nice thing."

Surely in 1982 when Los Angeles-based Weide, then twenty-three, wrote his second letter to Vonnegut in care of his attorney (his first, written in high school, was not answered), he could not have imagined where it would lead him. But from their lengthy correspondence over the years, it's obvious he'd been preparing for that night in Montreal since he taught his Vonnegut class.

June 29, 1982

Dear Mr. Vonnegut:

Earlier this year I produced [*The Marx Brothers in a Nutshell*] for PBS. . . . I am currently developing a number of other film projects, all of them dealing with subjects that are of a personal interest to me. The films of the Marx Brothers, for instance, were among two things that kept me going through my high school years. The other thing that kept me going was the writing of Kurt Vonnegut, Jr. The Marx Brothers now have their definitive documentary. How about allowing Kurt Vonnegut, Jr. to have his? . . . I'm certain that funding for such a project would be no problem. If the documentary had your authorization, I'm confident that I could arrange for financing immediately. . . . Thank you for getting me through high school. I hope to hear from you soon.

Sincerely,

Robert B. Weide

"The first book I read was not *Slaughterhouse* but *Breakfast of Champions*," Weide says. "I just really dug his humor and I think that's still a big part of it. He's just so bright and so damn clever. What I came to love about all of his books is this combination of how hysterically funny Vonnegut was and how full of humanity he was. Like I've told people before, for all of his philosophical musings in his books, I think the bottom line is he considers himself a humorist—sees himself as a joke teller."

Vonnegut replied to Weide's letter on July 27, 1982:

Dear Robert Weide—

I've been out of town for most of this summer and so read your friendly letter of a month ago only this morning. It turns out that I already know something of your work. I saw the Marx Brothers tribute, and liked it a lot. Who wouldn't?

I am honored by your interest in my work, and I will talk to you some, if you like, about making some sort of film based on it. But there is sure no great footage to start with. *Slaughterhouse-Five* is the only good movie having anything to do with me. . . . Anything that is any good of mine is on a printed page, not film. Maybe you have some ideas as to what to do about that. I don't. . . . Give me a ring, if you like. . . .

Cheers—

Kurt Vonnegut

Since the enormous success of *Slaughterhouse-Five*—based on his World War II experiences in which he was captured by German troops at the Battle of the Bulge and survived the Allied bombing of Dresden in 1945—Vonnegut has received a lot of correspondence from young fans. Weide's letter stood out for more than the obvious reason that he wanted to chronicle the author's life.

"When he got in touch with me, he was already an accomplished artist. He was a colleague," Vonnegut says. "He'd already done good work about comics and I think that I was flattered to be treated as a comical person, which I've always tried to be. He thought I was funny and he was into funny men, and most people don't approach me that way. They don't usually comment on how hard I work to be funny. And he had read everything I've ever written, which is very nice."

Like the financing for most documentary films, it did not come immediately for a Vonnegut documentary either. Since that first exchange of letters, Vonnegut has written four novels and is working on another. Weide has produced and directed several documentaries on comedians including *W. C. Fields Straight Up*, and *Mort Sahl: The Loyal Opposition*. Nine years in the making, he is just finishing *Lenny Bruce: Swear to Tell the Truth*.

"Little did I know it'd be six years before I could even start," Weide says, referring to a small amount of money he got for the Vonnegut project in 1988 from PBS's American Masters series. "Now it's 14 years later and it's still unfinished. It might be interesting for a documentary profiling someone to actually follow his life for ten years, although certainly if I had my druthers. I would have wrapped the thing up already."

When Weide received that first letter from Vonnegut, he was hesitant to call him. "I really didn't want to bother him," Weide says," but "Farber said, 'Oh no, you should call him otherwise he'll feel hurt that you didn't or that you changed your mind.'"

"I remember that initial phone call, that I every now and then would try to say something about how meaningful his work was. And he wouldn't have any of that. All he wanted to do was talk about the Marx Brothers. There is a scene in *Animal Crackers*, which is in the documentary, where Harpo is basically beating up on Margaret Dumont. There's a bell that goes off as if they're fighting in a ring and Chico is acting as the referee. When Harpo punches her in the stomach, she actually lifts up in the air—they must have had her hooked up on a wire or something. I'm trying to say something to Vonnegut about the importance of his work and all he kept saying was, 'God that was funny when Harpo was fighting Margaret Dumont. I thought I was gonna split a gut,' or something like that. He broke into one of his typical laughs which starts off as a laugh and then goes into this cough from smoking Pall Malls since he was sixteen. You're wondering if you're going to have to call 911."

Shortly after the phone call, Weide visited Vonnegut in New York. "You hear that it's not always good to meet your heroes because they can be disappointing in real life," Weide says. "You know, Vonnegut was basically everything I had hoped him to be. Because of his personality, it took a while to really feel comfortable around him. It was a combination of his personality being a bit reclusive, but more than that I had worshiped him so out of any reasonable proportion. I'm still somewhat deferential around him, but now it's become almost like a father-son thing where I'm almost protective of him around other people.

"The first trip I made to his house, I remember just trying to act calm but inside being a wreck. And it stayed like that for a while until finally I became what I pretended to be. Eventually I did get calm around him. What I relied on initially, conversationally, to keep things comfortable is this love of old movies and W. C. Fields and Laurel and Hardy. The first few times we got together, most of our conversations revolved around those topics 'cause I knew it was common ground that we could both feel comfortable with."

During that first visit, Vonnegut suggested possible interview subjects for the documentary. One former colleague had gone on to head the Eagle Shirt Manufacturing Company. "I remember [Vonnegut] saying to me that up to that time, basically a man's shirt was just white, or light blue like [mine]," Weide says. "And then when he got into the business, suddenly there were all kinds of colors and patterns and different designs.

"There was this pause and Vonnegut said, 'God it was an exciting time to be a man.' And that struck me as very funny. That's his Indiana roots coming through. It's heartland humor, but with an ironic eye. There's an intellectual element observing the fact that he knows he's just a Hoosier from Indiana."

In search of his author, Weide trekked to the heartland before 1982 was out to meet with Vonnegut expert Jerry Klinkowitz, professor of English at the University of Northern Iowa in Cedar Falls. In the mid-1960s, Klinkowitz was in graduate school in the middle of a seminar on Chaucer when a philosophy student gave him a shabby little paperback by a guy named Kurt Vonnegut. He read the book, which happened to be *Mother Night*, gave up Chaucer for life, and decided to study Vonnegut's work. "At the time there weren't a lot of market opportunities for Vonnegut experts," he says. That changed after *Slaughterhouse-Five*'s publication. He is currently working on his seventh book on Vonnegut.

Weide arrived in Iowa with a book Klinkowitz had just finished called *Kurt Vonnegut* which Vonnegut had given him. "He was still in his Boy Wonder phase," Klinkowitz says of Weide, a college dropout. Enrolled at USC, he had tried three times to get into the university's respected film school. Three strikes and USC was out. He took a job in the film business. "It was his first trip to the Midwest and he'd never been in cold weather. He had gone to the Salvation Army or something to buy the most ridiculous overcoat. I mean this guy was dressed for the North Pole because the overcoat came down to his shoe tops. He looked like some immigrant off the boat at Ellis Island a hundred years ago. But beneath this shabby, moth-eaten overcoat was this very hip, L.A. guy, so I brought him home.

"The mere fact that he was trailing this résumé behind him with the Marx Brothers, which I'd seen myself on public TV, I knew this guy was accomplished. And I could see he was very enthusiastic about Vonnegut. People who are enthusiastic about Vonnegut are a dime a dozen. Bob seemed to be someone who could channel this enthusiasm into something that was gonna happen."

November 16, 1983

Dear Bob—

I thank you for your Armistice Day greeting. I trust that you joined me in one minute of silence as the second hand ticked off the eleventh minute of the eleventh hour of the eleventh month. . . . I hack away at a new novel called *Galápagos*.

Cheers,

Kurt Vonnegut

December 20, 1984

Dear Kurt:

You've been on my mind lately because there's a new woman in my life, and during that early exploratory period where you're sharing significant influences on your respective lives, I've introduced her to your work. Started her out with *Cat's Cradle*, then on to *Breakfast*, figuring if that didn't scare her off nothing would. Her favorite line from *Breakfast* was also my own favorite: "Make me young! Make me young!". . . I've had some guilt about the slow pace with which I've progressed on the film we've discussed. . . . Having recently reread my past correspondence to you regarding this project, I realize this has been going on so long that its' starting to sound like a joke. All I can say at this point is that I'm still working on it and I still desperately want to do it. I've also had a few exploratory conversations regarding a feature film based on one of your books. I've developed something of a game plan which I'd like to discuss with you next time I'm in New York . . . (I promise I won't direct.). . . .

Best wishes,

Bob Weide

November 3, 1986

Dear Kurt:

. . . Well, I spent three days in Cedar Falls and I imagine your ears must have been burning. Loree [Rackstraw, English professor at the University of Northern Iowa and a Vonnegut scholar] was a sweetheart and she showed me your impressive drawings and the Requiem which was inspiring. [A secular, humanist requiem written by Vonnegut, it is his antidote to the venomous source of Andrew Lloyd Webber's "Requiem," the fifteenth-century Council of Trent.] Let it be a lesson for those who label you a pessimist. You are a "wimp" by true pessimist's standards. Now the Council of Trent, there's a group of guys with an attitude problem! Good for you for making a stab at correcting something so boneheaded. I would like to see the premiere. . . .

December 27, 1987

Dear Bob—

How can I not be touched and flattered by your continued interest in my work? I now have a videotape, by the way, of the only visible thing I've done worth watching, an onstage performance at a fundraiser for PEN a couple of years ago. . . . As for Laurel and Hardy: to find yet another excuse to televise their perfect works has to be OK, like doing the *Nutcracker* yet again at Christmastime. . . . Two other comedians who are in the first rank with Laurel and Hardy: Jack Benny and Buster Keaton. All humanity is the audience they were able to keep in mind. Almost nobody can do that, so I tell writing students of mine not to try. . . .

Cheers,

Kurt Vonnegut

January 11, 1988

Dear Kurt:

Nice talking to you the other day. I'm thrilled that we'll be able to film the Requiem and the speech. . . . Once you know how you'll travel to Buffalo (train, plane, etc.), please advise. I might like to shoot a little film of you on your way up there, provided you don't feel your privacy would be invaded or that we'd be in your way. . . . My girlfriend of the past three years and I have sort of thrown in the towel on our romance but we remain great friends. I got her reading your books when we first started dating. . . . I'm really looking forward to March. I'll speak to you before long. Thanks. Regards to Jill [Krementz, Vonnegut's wife] and little Lily [their adopted daughter].

Best,

Bob Weide

In March 1988, with the PBS funds, Weide and a film crew accompanied Vonnegut by train to Buffalo, New York, where a Unitarian church choir would perform Vonnegut's requiem. Written in English, Vonnegut had it translated into Latin and hired a composer to score it. Weide interviewed Vonnegut and his older brother, Bernard, on the train as well as covered a speech by Vonnegut in Buffalo and the requiem performance.

"It was the trip to Buffalo where things entered a new phase. That was a point where I felt, O.K., we really are friends now. It's not about fan and idol or filmmaker and subject so much as we really are good friends," Weide says. "A lot of it was just the amount of time that we spent and the fact that we were in this town together and had the evenings too. There is this guy thing about sitting around at night and having a couple of drinks and opening up. We'd reveal things about ourselves and I'd talk about women stuff I was going through and a lost love at the time, and he would counsel me about that. We talked about the highlights and the disappointments in our lives and just really talked like two friends opening up to each other.

"After close to a week, we were almost like college dorm mates. Even the difference in ages started to fade away, and then we just started to hang out. At this point, it had been five years that we had an acquaintanceship and over this five years I didn't do anything to betray his trust. In fact I haven't until now," he says referring to this interview.

Vonnegut has a theory that it is the youngest member of a family that usually turns out to be the funny one, the joker. "It was the only way you could get attention," Vonnegut says. "My brother is nine years older than I am. When I was six he was fifteen, so he had all kinds of exciting things to talk about. My sister was five years older than me. She had really exciting stuff to talk about and I had little crap."

Weide graduated high school having been voted not only the most likely in his class to be famous, but class clown. He is also the youngest of three children. "That might be part of our bond," Weide says. "Everyone in my family is sort of funny in their own way, but I certainly exploited it more than anybody."

"It seems like a complicated relationship," says Keith Gordon, thirty-five, *Mother Night*'s director and co-producer and a close friend of Weide's since Gordon moved to Los Angeles in 1982. An actor turned director, he had leading roles in John Carpenter's *Christine*, Brian De Palma's *Dressed To Kill*, and in *Back to School*. He first met Vonnegut when the author came to the set of this Rodney Dangerfield movie to do a cameo appearance. Gordon took a small acting job on the Nick Nolte film, *I Love Trouble*, just to get the *Mother Night* script to the actor. Nolte's agents had turned down the project years earlier.

"When Bob's passionate about somebody," Gordon says, "he's very communicative, but he's not like, let me kiss your feet, let me treat you like God, which I think would probably scare Kurt off. I think in Bob he probably found someone who could really talk about a lot of things he cared about without feeling everything [he says] is being taken like it's gospel. They both have very wry senses of humor. They both enjoy the weird juxtapositions of existence in life. Even in [Bob's] documentaries, what he focuses on about people is the contradictions in their lives. And I imagine that there is a connection there too in that I think there's probably more sadness than either of them is very [willing] to let on to other people."

January 16, 1989

Dear Roberto—

On the reverse side find a copy of a note from Bob Elliott. I wrote him saying that my best Christmas present came from you those PBS tapes [of comedy duo Bob and Ray], all of which I've played twice. . . . The Bob and Ray stuff is one part of an adventure in Jungian synchronicity which has enabled me at last to get going on another book with some enthusiasm. For two years I wasn't getting anywhere and then those tapes gave me permission to be, like them, intelligently ridiculous. . . .

Cheers,

Kurt Vonnegut

November 13, 1989

Dearest Whyaduck [Weide's production company name]—

Where indeed is your *Slaughterhouse-5*? Have you considered cutting off an ear and sending it to a prostitute?

These things take time. Remember Herman Melville. Remember F. Scott Fitzgerald, who was completely out-of-print when he died so young. . . . It seems to me that your permanent contributions to civilization have been substantial, although the paymasters, being thugs, may never come to see that. Or care. . . .

Love as always,

Kurt Vonnegut

August 22, 1990

Dear Kurt:

Well, I'm sorry that we weren't able to hook up in New York, but I'm especially glad that we got to see each other in L.A. . . . I've been giving a lot of thought to something that I'd like you to consider: I'd really like to get a great movie made from *Mother Night*. No glitzy special effect, no 20-million dollar budgets, no overpaid stars just a great script and the right director. Keep it small and stay true to the book. . . . Keith Gordon and I would like to write it for Keith to direct. . . . He's a big fan of yours and his sensibilities are perfect for this piece.

(I'm including a few reviews of his film, *The Chocolate War* which he adapted from Robert Cormier's novel). . . . Now there's a favor involved for which I call on your trust. . . . I want to ask you for a very brief option. The idea being that once we have a script, we could set up financing for the, film within four months' time. We can negotiate in advance what sort of payment you would want for the rights with the understanding that such payment would be made once our financing becomes available. . . . Give it some thought Kurt. . . .

As always,

Bob

November 15, 1990

Dear Kurt—

I am so thrilled about *Mother Night*, the truth is I found myself too embarrassed to call you for fear I'll gush all over myself thanking you. I was going to call on the 11th to tell you that my birthday present was the promise of a first class film. . . . I've already started on a first draft script. I intend to keep as close to the book as possible because it's already so cinematic. . . . Again, my deepest thanks for the trust you've placed in me. I'll do good by you.

Love,

Whyaduck

"Anybody who adapts a work of mine—like Stephen Geller, who did *Slaughterhouse-Five*, did a wonderful job—I just told him and I told other people who are doing adaptations, just think of my book as a friendly ghost around the house and make a new work of art for God sakes, or it won't be any good," Vonnegut says.

Gordon was an impressionable eleven-year-old when he attended the New York City premiere of *Slaughterhouse-Five* with his father, acting coach Mark Gordon. The lead actor in *Slaughterhouse*, Michael Sacks, was one of the elder Gordon's students.

"I was floored by the movie, and also this was probably the first R-rated movie I'd seen, so Valerie Perrine's breasts were also a big moment in life, but beyond seeing a half-naked woman and that being a thrill, it was also a movie that even at eleven was very powerful to me and very moving," Gordon says. "I don't think it was long after that that I determined I wanted to read the book it was based on. I was probably about twelve or thirteen. I think the next thing I read was *Cat's Cradle* and then I started working my way through all of them."

At the end of 1990, Gordon was preparing to go into production on *A Midnight Clear*, based on William Wharton's autobiographical novel about his World War II experiences. So Weide started to write the script on his own.

"I think somewhere I had—to be honest—an attitude of well, he'll write the first draft and then I'll rewrite it," Gordon says, "because I'd done two films where I had written the scripts and I assumed in some self aggrandizing way that I would of course need to fix Bob's script." I read it and went, "Oh, there's really not much I'd do to this. This is pretty terrific. At that point, my biggest contribution really became more of an editor than a re-writer."

March 8, 1991
To Bob Weide
From Kurt Vonnegut

It looks like a good script to me. I didn't realize that you yourself were going to write it. Comment:
Hoess and Hess were two different guys. . . . Campbell's broadcast, still to be written, should be worth listening to. . . . Maybe somebody out there can dig up transcripts of Lord Haw Haws' broadcasts. His real name was William Joyce and he really was entertaining in an awful way. . . .

"When I first wrote *Mother Night* and submitted the script to Kurt was when I started to realize that he's just not very effusive about his opinions," Weide says. "He will tell you in a few words what he thinks. From his initial comment on the script, I thought gee, maybe he was just saying that to be polite, 'cause he never got into much detail with me. Part of how I learn about how he really feels is through third parties. It's the same way perhaps my own father won't pay me too big a compliment, but then I hear from somebody else at a dinner party he went on and on about something."

"We had the script and we started sending it out and that became our five-year strange trip through the halls of money in Hollywood," Gordon says. "We had all sorts of interesting adventures and misadventures and deals that weren't deals and deals with people who didn't really have money and deals with people who had money but backed out of the deals. The usual rollercoaster."

In March 1994, while they were still experiencing whiplash from their *Mother Night* merry-go-round, Weide spent his own money to continue the Vonnegut documentary, meeting Vonnegut and a film crew in the author's hometown, Indianapolis. Vonnegut reminisced as he walked around his elementary school and high school, and Weide conducted interviews with him at his boyhood home and inside the house where his mother committed suicide on Mother's Day when he was twenty-one.

Vonnegut invited his daughter, Nanny Prior, to join them. Then thirty-nine, the artist, wife and mother of three had not traveled alone with her father since she was fifteen. When she accepted her father's invitation to meet him in Indianapolis, she didn't know a documentary filmmaker was coming along too. "Dad sort of left out that little detail," she says. "I didn't want to go in that case because it suddenly struck me as being part of his celebrity life. I'm very shy and I didn't want to have to meet a lot of people and I really wanted him all to myself."

When she first met Weide, she says, "I told him, 'I don't trust you people.' I had to get that out of the way when I first met him, 'cause there are a lot of scumbuckets out there. I'm a little too mistrustful, but that's what happens to us kids of famous people. He sort of laughed.

"When I saw how they were together, it totally put me at ease. I really hate seeing people fawn over my father or be scared of him or that whole bigger-than-life thing. I realized this is somebody who has some depth, who really loves my father, who really knows him and cares for him."

Nanny Prior's time in Indianapolis with her dad and Weide turned out to he fun. "I have a twelve-year-old son and I would say maybe they were in the range of between twelve and fifteen in [that] they were really good together. They would bop each other over the head with a newspaper, have stupid little disagreements," Prior says. "This was an especially poignant part of the documentary because these are my father's roots. There was a lot of joking and I think that really does put my father at ease. You can't ask him too many serious questions, so there was this balance of being funny and then the next minute, talking about taking bodies out of rubble in Dresden or his mother's suicide.

"Also it was funny to me to see Weide tell him to do things over and over again. I don't know that much about filmmaking, but he had him keep walking down this corridor or throw this paper airplane, and Dad was like putty in his hands. Now Dad can sometimes get a little grumpy and I didn't see any of that. I think Dad was having a great time and somehow I saw Weide working magic with him."

When Weide had received the letter from Vonnegut saying the Bob and Ray tapes had gotten him writing again, Weide felt that if he does nothing else in his life, he had contributed something because he helped get Vonnegut unstuck on a hook that eventually came out (*Hocus Pocus*). "Conversely," Weide says, "if he's done nothing else, he got me started drinking martinis."

Ambling around Indiana, they got to talking about their different generation's drinking habits and Vonnegut said, "In my day the big thing was martinis." Weide told him he'd never had a martini in his life. Vonnegut made him promise that that would come to an end while they were still in Indiana.

"There was a night in Indianapolis where there was a reunion of the surviving Vonneguts still in Indianapolis. It was at this very Gentile country club called The Woodstock Club," says Weide, who is Jewish. "When the waitress came by and asked, 'What would you like to drink?' Vonnegut answered for me and said 'He'll have a martini.' I took a few sips and Vonnegut leaned in and said, 'What do you think?' I said, 'This is really nice.' It also made the evening go a lot smoother too.

"There was one point at dinner, I think Cousin Richard, who's in his eighties, started going on about Jews not to imply that it was an anti-Semitic tract necessarily, but he was talking about The Jews. I think Richard's wife suddenly looked at me and then looked at Richard and started nudging him and telling him to shift. Nanny [Prior] was there, sitting across the table, and we were exchanging glances. When the waitress came around again, Vonnegut ordered Weide another martini. Now I really love martinis. I told him, 'Now I understand your generation.'"

They drove back to New York together in Vonnegut's Honda in one long shot, taking turns driving and snoozing. The gee whiz side of Weide is still there: "It was a lot of fun being on the road and talking with him and listening to the radio," he says. Weide had the final shift into the city and took Vonnegut's instructions to follow a bus. The next thing they knew, he was driving up a ramp in a municipal bus parking lot, surrounded by rows of buses. "We both started to crack up. I kept saying, 'another fine mess you've gotten us into.' It took me about twenty minutes to figure out how the hell to get out of there."

The next day in New York, they tried to make a date with Cynthia McFadden. Weide had discovered her on Court TV covering the Lyle and Eric Menendez trial. "I would always tune in to watch her. I didn't care about the Menendezes," he says.

Before their Indiana trip, he met her at the Cable ACE Awards ceremony. McFadden had been nominated for an ACE award for her trial coverage. Weide had produced Larry Gelbart's political satire *Mastergate* and stand-up comedian Rick Reynolds' one-man show, *Only the Truth Is Funny*, both for Showtime, and was nominated for two awards.

At the awards ceremony, Weide went up to McFadden, introduced himself. In conversation, she told him that someone recently told her that Kurt Vonnegut has a big crush on her. "I got real jealous," he says. She suggested the three of them get together for lunch in New York and told Weide she was in the phone book. He promised to call.

Within hours Weide was on the phone to Vonnegut. "The first thing I said was, 'Well Kurt, it's pistols at dawn, we're both after the same woman.' To which he said, 'Cynthia McFadden?' So that confirmed things. I told him about the lunch invitation. He said, 'Sounds great. We'll have to do that when we come back [from Indiana].'"

Weide looked up McFadden in the phone book and called her from his hotel room. A man answered who "sounded like he had been napping on the couch," Weide says, and begrudgingly took the message that Bob Weide and Kurt Vonnegut were in town and wanna have lunch.

The next day when Weide arrived at Vonnegut's home, the first thing he wanted to know was if he'd reached McFadden. Use my phone, call her again, Vonnegut said. "I got the same guy again," Weide says. "This was on a Saturday and she had left Court TV to go to ABC. He said she was at work. I said, 'Boy, they really got her busy over there at ABC, huh?' He said, 'What are you talking about?' I said, 'Isn't she at ABC now?' and he goes, 'She works in a toll booth.' Well, I got the wrong Cynthia McFadden out of the phone book.

"When I told Kurt, he got hysterical. We were both laughing. Coming into the city we probably saw her cause we went through every toll booth on the Eastern Seaboard. I was telling Kurt, 'You may be famous and have all the money, but I'm closer to her age.' We were like fighting over her." *The* Cynthia McFadden was out of town on assignment. They have yet to have lunch with her.

September 1995

Bob Weide

The final script is a knockout. There are a lot of funny lines I wish I'd written but didn't. One reviewer said she didn't think there was anything funny about concentration camps, and something was seriously wrong with anybody who did.

KV

Last fall (1997), *Mother Night* was shot entirely on location in Montreal. Vonnegut visited the set just once to shoot his cameo appearance. Leaving the film to the filmmakers, he was still interested in being informed about the progression of the project. "He was like a little kid calling me up every week and [asking questions like], 'What's going on?' and 'How's Nolte in the role?' and 'Are the studio people behaving themselves?'" Weide says. "He was thrilled with Nolte. He says he cannot imagine anybody else besides Nolte playing the role, which is the ultimate compliment."

"He is a wonderful actor," says Vonnegut, "and what he did to get up for this part was very smart. He thought of it himself. He got a whole bunch of tapes of Arthur Godfrey broadcasts."

After the Montreal premiere, says Nolte, "[Vonnegut] said to me, and Bob was with us, 'It's unsettling, it's rather disturbing.' And I said, 'yes.' He said, 'That's good.' Rather than the normal reaction you get, 'Oh, that's a great ending of a film, I feel so great.' He saw that to be disturbed, to be perplexed, to be moved is important.

"It's a very nervous proposition to sit there and watch work that we've all done. I feel very good about the film, about grasping the spirit of Kurt's work and putting it on film. So I felt really good just to be sitting with those guys. The difficulty is when the lights come up because now you fall out of the story that was being told and now you're kind of naked and people are staring at you. Kurt and I immediately—he went for his Pall Malls and I went for my Marlboros."

Though Vonnegut had seen an early cut of the film on video, he had not seen the finished film until the Montreal premiere. Invited to earlier screenings in New York, he didn't want to go, he says. "It was just too scary. I finally went to Montreal because that was my responsibility. You feel responsible for what the actors are saying and doing. Very guilt inspiring; my God, did I do this to these people?"

Nanny Prior did attend one of the early screenings of *Mother Night*. "There's so much in that movie, and so much of my father, of his essence and his humor," she says. "It's incredibly romantic and incredibly dark and that's how I could describe my father in a nutshell in growing up with him. This movie really captures what my father meant to put across in his books. I think *Mother Night* is really the most personal of any of his books."

"I think there's an awful lot of Kurt Vonnegut in that character, Campbell—someone who appreciates the paradox of language and the accidents of race and the horror of war and who feels it so deeply," says Loree Rackstraw, a student of Vonnegut's at the University of Iowa's Writers' Workshop in 1965 who became an authority on Vonnegut's work. She retired this year as professor of English at the University of Northern Iowa.

"He lives the paradox of life so close to the surface, and by that I mean the contradiction that is true," she says. "His whole life he's had to face that in one way or another—the paradox of being a German American during World War II and the accident of being captured in the Battle of the Bulge and ending up in prison and getting blasted by your own air force. I think there have been crazy accidents in his life that have put him in a position of almost being two persons at the same time—having to face his mother's suicide on Mother's Day. One irony after another. I think his vision is quite dark. To keep yourself alive by having a way of laughing when you're at your very lowest point requires an enormous amount of energy and intelligence."

March 3, 1996

Dear Bob

Home from Sacramento to find your FAX awaiting. I have no illusions about the prospects for *Mother Night* as a money-maker, nor about the attractiveness of properties of mine written so long ago. My life at this point is a garage sale on the edge of a high speed superhighway. . . . I will be the luckiest man in the world again if you write a script for *Sirens*, and you are crazy enough to do that. . . .

Love as always,

K

Vonnegut refers to Weide's next project, adapting Vonnegut's *Sirens of Titan*. He wants the same deal: a handshake and the opportunity to write a spec script faithful to the book, without interference from Hollywood executives.

March 3, 1996

Dear K—

I just stepped in at 1:30 A.M. Saturday night (Sunday morning) and found your very moving fax which has left me a bit choked up on several counts. . . . By writing *Sirens* now, I'm only attempting to keep the illusion going a little longer before people find out that I have no original ideas of my own. Fuck Hollywood. The fact that all your books are still in print means a lot more than whether some asshole studio executive knows the difference between *Mother Night* and "Night, Mother." If I had a dollar for every college kid who flips out when he learns I know you and swears to have read everything you've ever written, I could finance these movies myself. . . . So, in fact, it is I who am the luckiest man in the world. Secondly, for the opportunity to collaborate with you and throw our bastard children out into the cosmos in an attempt to warp yet more minds. . . . but primarily for our friendship. . . .

As ever,

Whyaduck

"The amazing thing now is he acts as though he's indebted to me for putting in the time and effort [to get] *Mother Night* made into a film," Weide says. "I could never write anything like that from scratch. I feel like he allowed me to use his genius to leapfrog myself into the feature film business." Since *Mother Night*, Weide has written the screen version of Lois Lowry's *The Giver* for Jeff Bridges. "[Vonnegut's] always writing me and telling me just how grateful he is to me, and I just think that's the funniest joke in the world."

Pilgrim's Process

Eric Simenson

A while ago, Steppenwolf Theatre of Chicago asked me to write and direct an adaptation of *Slaughterhouse-Five*. After we secured the rights and agreed on an approach, I thought it would be wise to phone Kurt Vonnegut and ask him for some advice. The first thing he said to me was "I don't know how the hell you're going to stage it." I told him that's what everyone said, but I wasn't going to worry about that now. The second thing he told me was I should make sure the American soldiers were filthy. "They didn't care about their appearance," he told me. "They were miserable, disgusting, and all the soldiers from the other countries hated them. That's all I have to say. Good luck."

I knew I could take care of the filthy soldier part. That was easy: just tell the costume designer. But as to how I was going to adapt this lightning-fast, labyrinthine book to the stage, I hadn't quite figured that one out. I knew what my goals were: I wanted to create a stage version of what I felt was an objective representation of the book. In other words, very simply, I wanted to put the book in stage form. As obvious as that sounds, it has to be said, because the fashion these days is for director/adaptors to create personal and highly subjective interpretations of their source material. Just read Edward Albee's adaptation of Nabokov's *Lolita*, and you'll see what I mean. It's no more Nabokov than *West Side Story* is Shakespeare. A novel can take on a whole new personality if adapted by an overly zealous, or overly ambitious writer.

Part of my interest in adapting *Slaughterhouse-Five* was my fascination with its popularity. I'm amazed by how many people have not only read *Slaughterhouse-Five*, but continue to read it and remember it as one of their favorite works of literature. So, for those who had read and loved the novel, I wanted to give a rich, objective, and satisfying rendering of the story. For those who hadn't read the novel, I wanted to, simply, present the story; show them why this novel and the character of Billy Pilgrim seem to have become a part of the nation's collective subconscious. I began to think of the project not so much as an adaptation, but as a translation.

Slaughterhouse-Five is very cinematic, which is why the 1968 film works so well. The tempo and pace of the novel are dictated by frequent and sudden leaps through time and space: one second Billy Pilgrim is on a golf course in 1963, the next second he's in a German boxcar in 1944. Scenes last sometimes the length of a sentence, and most are no more than two or three minutes in length. It's very easy, while reading the book, for the mind to flip back and forth from place to place, but try to manifest that in real time on a stage and you start running into trouble. It takes effort and time to move actors on and off stage. Where the mind can move instantly from one scene to the next, it takes twenty actors and a stage crew real time (seconds, though they seem like minutes) to get from on place to another.

A familiar convention in creating epic dramas is for the playwright to consciously alternate scenes in which a character appears. For instance, if Hamlet and Ophelia finish a scene in the castle hall, they'll rarely appear at the top of the next scene on the battlements. This way, the action of the play continues unabated as one group of actors essentially passes the baton to another. Shakespeare was an expert at this type of transition. That's why his plays, which often have as many as forty scenes, are able to maintain a certain energy. They're as close to "cinematic" as a play can get.

If I could employ this device in *Slaughterhouse-Five*, half my problems would be solved. But in the novel, Billy Pilgrim appears in every scene, so there's no "other character" to "pass the baton" to. So I create one. Initially, I called him "Vonnegut," but later I changed his name to "Man." He wasn't a narrator, although his only relationship was exclusively with the audience. His lines were Vonnegut's narration from the book (the play would start with Man saying "All this happened, more or less. . . "), but I thought of him as a character with a real history; a person who had a pressing need to tell us about his experiences during the war. In creating him, I could keep all the great lines I loved from the book ("Listen. Billy Pilgrim has become unstuck in time."), as well as the running mantra, "So it goes."

Then I came up with what I thought was a pretty good idea. I would have several actors playing Billy at different ages. Scenes could be as short or as long as I wanted, and the "Billys" would switch off playing from one scene to the next. I would have three "Billys": Billy as a boy, a young Billy (age eighteen) appearing mostly in the war scenes, and an older Billy (early forties) for the scenes in Ilium.

This solution seemed so simple I wondered why I hadn't thought of it before, and the more I thought about it, the better I liked it. Billy could literally "look at himself" in the past, or the future. The gesture would resonate as a suggestion that the two mature Billys are different people living in distinctly separate, but equally absurd, lives. Or, all three Billys on stage would reenforce the Tralfamadorian notion that past, present, and future are one. Most important, it would free me up, as director, to express the story exactly as it was written.

I finished the first draft, and then I phoned Kurt Vonnegut to tell him I was sending him a copy. Three days later (far sooner than I expected) he called me back to tell me he had read the script and that he liked it, and if I had any questions

I shouldn't hesitate to call. He added, "I still don't know how the hell you're going to stage it."

The experience of creating something new for the theater is exhilarating, particularly when an artistic team comes together and finds a common language. The collaboration of production design, when it is working, can be just as rewarding as the collaboration of an acting ensemble. I felt by the time I put together my design team (which included Neil Patel on sets, Karin Kopischke on costumes, John Bosche on slides, and Rob Milburn and Michael Bodean on sound), the script was in good enough shape to create the visual world of *Slaughterhouse-Five*. The set would be spare, while minimal props, costumes, slides, and sound established time and place. Neil Patel came up with an ideal set that looked like a cross between a real live slaughterhouse and an empty theater. It was simple, elegant, and efficient.

About the time I approved the sets and costumes, but before I had cast the show, I started hearing some rumblings of concern from the Steppenwolf Theatre artistic staff. Some Steppenwolf company members (there's a group of thirty of us, including myself) were confused about the use of "multiple Billys." There were no objections with the adaptation, which most everyone liked, but some wondered why I couldn't use one actor in the central role. They thought, understandably, that the audience would become emotionally disengaged if they had to invest in three actors playing one character, and they argued that one actor playing Billy would be a much more exciting challenge for the audience and for the actor cast.

I saw their point, but I wasn't sure I wanted to rethink the test at this point and time. To demonstrate how three Billys would work, I directed a staged reading that went very well, but the blocking was minimal and my colleagues weren't persuaded. For the sake of experimentation and to prove I was indeed on the right track (for myself as much as anyone else), I agreed to write a draft using one actor playing Billy. It nearly killed me. The frustrations of manipulating scene after scene to fit the limitations of the conceit taxed my creative impulse. I felt like I was trying to solve a Rubic's cube. But the results weren't as bad as I thought. In the one-Billy version, the part of the narrator grew to about twice its size. This was not part of my original intention, but it turned out to be beneficial for the piece overall. In the three-Billy draft there were problems with Man being too elusive and vague, so giving him more dialogue to cover scene shifts forced me to find some great lines I'd overlooked the first time around.

I sought advice from people I respected. They read both versions; we had a reading of the one-Billy draft that went resoundingly well. The feedback was very clear, and my own opinion began to shift. One-Billy was winning out. Eventually, I decided to go into rehearsal using one actor playing the role Billy Pilgrim, and it was a mistake.

When we went to the one-Billy approach, the part of the narrator, however engaging (or not), grew beyond all expectations, and the inherent structure of my original draft, which was inspired by the book, was forever changed. During rehearsals, I found myself adding gratuitous speeches to cover complicated scene shifts that required Rick Snyder (the actor playing Billy) to get from one side of the stage to the other. Technical wizardry was introduced into what started out as a very simple, uncomplicated design concept: cool-sounding and extended effects, extra music and fancy lights that threw focus away from an actor getting into place, became an essential part of the production.

I was tinkering with the text and design all the way up to opening. By the time we'd reached our eleventh and final preview, I'd lost all objectivity of the production but knew in my heart that the tempo and pace were off. I was hobbled in my efforts to do anything about it because I didn't have the tools necessary to make adjustments. But that's theater; that's the creative (and collaborative) process.

The results weren't all bad. For starters, we succeeded by satisfying the country's love of, or obsession with, the book itself by merely presenting it on stage. As I said before, one of the reasons I took on this challenge was because everywhere I went I found fans (in the truest sense of the root of the word: fanatic). People from all over recalled they "grew up with the book . . . read it five times . . . loved the part about." To me the greatest thing a theater artist can do is express the otherwise inexpressible. Somehow, *Slaughterhouse-Five* has expressed something over the years, over the generations, that is truly a part of who we are as a culture—something about the irreconcilable urges to be simultaneously individuals and upstanding members of a community. The writing style is spare, full of dry wit and recognizable archetypical characters—it is very American. No matter how many ways it has been expressed (the book itself, the movie), the live experience of theatre forces a communal—even religious—experience when the story is known and popular especially if it has attained mythic status. *Slaughterhouse-Five* has done just that. This is a story to be told by live performers in the presence of large groups of people night after night. This is a story for the stage.

I haven't spoken to Kurt Vonnegut in a while, though we correspond. He continues to send encouraging words about my adaptation, and perhaps I'll get a chance to do it again someday. If nothing else, he must be happy I got the soldiers' costumes right, because they were very disgusting.

In Search of Slaughterhouse-Five

Julie A. Hibbard

When I was first offered the opportunity to spend a year on exchange at the Technische Universität in Dresden, my first thought was, *Slaughterhouse-Five*. I replied to the offer, without much further consideration: "Yes, I will go. Thank you."

I am sure I would know very little—if anything at all—about what happened to Dresden in February 1945 if I had not read Kurt Vonnegut's *Slaughterhouse-Five*, which impelled me to learn more about Dresden. It seems that the topic of fire-bombing in World War II was rather neglected in public high-school history courses, and as geography is not a strong element of the standard American public education curriculum, and history in the culture of western Europe is nonexistent, it seems that many Americans of all ages have never even heard of Dresden. Unless, of course, they collect Dresden China.[1] Or, unless, of course, they have read *Slaughterhouse-Five*. I have met a few Americans, at various times throughout the years, who have actually been to Dresden. I would always ask them, "Did you go to Slaughterhouse-Five?" Some would say, "Yes, of course."

I wonder now, just what these people were looking at when they thought they were looking at Slaughterhouse-Five. It is not easy to find.

It was lucky that the first time I set out to explore the Slaughterhouse district happened to be a holiday. My friend Alex had explained to me just how to get to the area. I had been telling him about the strange coincidence of having recently read a passage in *Mother Night* in which Vonnegut referred to the cigarette factory in Dresden, and also having seen, earlier that same day, a picture labeled "Zigarettenfabrik" in a book of old Dresden postcards. I paged through this book again, and there it was: "Die Zigarettenfabrik Yenidze in ihrer orientalischen Pracht, im Vordergrund die Marienbrücke."[2] The factory is Byzantine in style and there is a sign on the roof that says "Salem Aleikum."

Alex told me that the Zigarettenfabrik of the postcard book is still in existence and is now some sort of cultural center.[3] I dug out my Dresden map so he could show me where it is and the location of the Slaughterhouse District. Alex tells me that the entire District was principally designed by the Dresden architect Erlwein,[4] who had wanted to break up standard rectangular forms. I think that this is what I heard someone talking about at a gathering a couple of weeks earlier: the style of Slaughterhouse-Five—the building, not the book. As I was a bit jet-lagged at that time, I had not quite understood.

Soon thereafter, I set out to find Slaughterhouse-Five. Since it was a holiday, I didn't have to work. All of the offices with which I still had unfinished business—visa, green card, contract, etc.—were closed. A good day for exploring Dresden. The bus that runs close to the Slaughterhouse District was not running. I did not know this until I checked the schedule. We were at a stop close to the Zigarettenfabrik, which is where the tram I took intersects with the bus I wanted to take. This made sense to me, as I already seemed to be experiencing a strange interconnectedness in the elements of Dresden I associate with Kurt Vonnegut. The Zigarettenfabrik has recently been refurbished. It is beautiful. The roof no longer says "Salem Aleikum," as depicted on the postcard.

I walked from there. When I reached the Schlachthofring, the first buildings I saw were obviously not slaughterhouses, never had been. I could take the Ring—the road that entirely encircles the Slaughterhouse District—either around to the north side, or around to the south. I opted for the north. Soon I was accompanied on my left by a very thick, very tall, uninterrupted stone wall. This wall surrounds the entire Slaughterhouse District, excluding those few buildings I first saw when I reached the Ring. I kept walking, looking for an entrance. I walked a very long way and thought, "What a perfect place to keep prisoners." I was also thinking, "Maybe I should have gone to the south."

I finally came to a break in the wall, a driveway-width entrance with a small security shack. No one is in the shack and I see no sign of anyone, anywhere, so I enter. On the left are woods; on the right, a building that is being used as a warehouse for a frozen seafood company. As I walk along, the woods are displaced by a group of buildings surrounded by a tall fence pieced together from scraps. These buildings have an obvious, abandoned look to them. The frozen foods company gives way to a generator company that currently occupies a group of buildings that all look alike. They look *slaughterhousy* to me, so—as I am hearing voices every once in a while, but have seen no one—I begin wandering up and down the alleys in between, weaving my way through generators. I am looking for signs, though I am not sure what to look for. The buildings are white, single story concrete block. I look to see if they are numbered, but they are not. I find that these buildings are fenced off from the rest of the district and that the drive I walked in on does not go through, so I head back to the entrance. Walking back, I see that the piecemeal fence protecting the abandoned buildings begins with the building nearest the woods. I walk into the woods and around to the back. No fence. No door on the back entrance of the building, either—it is missing. I go in.

There is a lot of junk one would have to maneuver through or climb over in the first room. I wonder about rats. I am not afraid of rats—I just don't want to inadvertently step on the home of one and get bitten. I climb through anyway. The inner rooms are empty and dark. There are a couple of shower rooms and several rooms with lockers. Gym lockers, not meat lockers. There are a few posters on the walls in the locker rooms, and magazine cut-outs and such pasted on the locker doors. There are many images of bare-breasted women that remind me of calendars I used to see in garages or workshops. RAM TOOLS, or some such name, with a bare-breasted woman posed "seductively" among pneumatic hammers. I don't see these sorts of advertising freebies so often anymore in America.

I find my way back out to the sunshine and head for the next building, but it has been more efficiently closed off. I make my way around to the north and discover a small-gauge rail and a small, depotlike structure. Its doors are also missing. I am able to walk through to the forbidden area. There is a large, concrete yard, grown up with weeds. There are bones scattered among the weeds. There seem to be only two buildings here, but they are much more complex, with legs and arms growing off of them in an unnatural manner. These buildings, along with the rat-employee house and the depot, are all in the same style. I think they must be Erlwein, because—though much smaller—they remind me of the gargantuan warehouse near the river and the mill-like building that towers up from the center of the Slaughterhouse District, both of which I have been told were built by Erlwein. I go in the first open door and I find myself in a network of rooms and halls, mostly empty. There are meat hooks affixed to walls in many rooms, a pulley system in the center room, and a few scattered articles here or there—broken tools, work gloves. I find a slew of black, plastic sixes scattered on the floor, each about one-inch tall. I exit a door that takes me to a relatively hidden part of the yard, as it is protected by contorted arms and legs. There is a broken imprint in the stucco next to a large, double-door that is near the door I just exited. It very definitely looks like the remnants of a large number six. Hm. Well, if this is building number six, maybe the other one is five.

It is not easy to find a way into the other building, as the doors are all blocked. I am not finding any fives labeling the doors, either, but the fence adjoins this building, so I cannot see the east side. I finally find a window I can get through. It is quite dark and hard to see. The roof has collapsed in on what seems to be a single, large interior room. I think I might be able to work my way through, but it doesn't look safe for exploration. I hear voices nearby and get nervous. I suspect, considering the circumstances, that if anyone saw me, I could be in big trouble. I climb out the same way I got in and head toward the depot, sticking close to the wall for protection. I spot another door, open, at the back of this unexplored building, so I quickly duck inside. It is one, relatively small and separate room. The roof is intact. Sunshine is pouring through the windows, casting geometrically skewed patches of yellow on the floor all around a large hole in the middle of the room. The hole is filled with shadow and debris. I see glimpses of a stone stairwell. I study this scene for a moment, then leave. Quickly.

Due to the fire-bombing, Dresden looks like no other European city I have seen. The architectural designs and construction methods of the German Democratic Republic (GDR) made for an interesting approach, to say the least, to rebuilding this city. I guess I should say, to building up this city, as the rebuilding of Dresden was not begun until the 1970s. This approach produced acres and acres of buildings made from preformed, concrete slabs and structures that were simply pieced together like Lincoln logs, often used in combination with corrugated steel or fiberglass. These buildings, typically five to fifteen stories high, occupy most of the center of the city known as the Altstadt—the area that suffered the worst in the bombing. As one travels out in any direction from here, the modern architecture is interspersed with older architecture, much of which dates from the late nineteenth century, with the older buildings dominating the farther one travels. Still, one may find oneself suddenly confronted by a grove of Plattenbauten[5] after having just walked through a pleasant, old neighborhood, far from the city center.

In the Altstadt itself, one is struck by the contrast these new buildings create in juxtaposition with the historic area of the Altstadt along the south side of the river Elbe. Here one finds the buildings that were deemed historically worthy enough to actually rebuild after the original design, such as the Zwinger[6] and Albertinum[7] museums, the Semperoper,[8] the Schloß,[9] and the katholische Hofkirche.[10] This rebuilding is ongoing, as there is yet much work to be done on the palace, and the reconstruction of the Frauenkirche[11] only just began in 1993 and is progressing slowly—I find it hard to believe they will finish by 2006, as is their goal.

There is a huge pedestrian mall in the area between the Hauptbahnhof—the main train station of Dresden—and the rebuilt, historic Altstadt. The first time I walked through there, which was my first day in Dresden, I felt as if I was walking over the twice-buried dead. Being my first day in Dresden, I did not know that I was walking through the area that had been the center of the bombing: ashes mixed in rubble and earth, then covered in concrete and steel.

I told a west German friend who is studying in Dresden about this. She replied, "*Ja*, but one gets used to it."

I realized that there was no way I could know if the abandoned building next to building number six was Slaughterhouse-Five. It was obvious that the Slaughterhouse District is made up of distinct groups of buildings, any or all of which could have had a building number five. I simply needed more information. I decided to talk to the man I once heard talking about the style of *Slaughterhouse-Five*. He is a Dresdner, Demola, who teaches in the English department of TU Dresden—language, not literature. Demola tells me that he is not sure exactly where Slaughterhouse-Five is, but that we should be able to find out if we ask around in the Schlachthof district, so we plan a trip that included two others, Helen and Lauren. We three—Helen, Lauren, and I—are all Americans who are all interested in finding Slaughterhouse-Five. We three are all here on exchange from the same department at the same university in Cedar Falls, Iowa. The three of us had not all known each other before coming to Dresden. I had never even met Helen before. I had to come all the way to Dresden to meet and develop a close friendship with a woman I should have met a hundred times over in the previous five years I had been living in Cedar Falls. This makes sense to me, too.

Demola takes us to the south side of the Slaughterhouse District. There is a larger break in the wall here, through which one can see between the bars of an iron fence. However, there is a small security building through which one must pass in order to actually get inside. We go in and Demola begins to explain to the security guard just what we are looking for. The guard tells him, yes, lots of people come here and ask to see Slaughterhouse-Five, but there is no building to see. He explains that this particular little group of buildings in this area of the district were collectively known as Slaughterhouse-Five during World War II. As the buildings are presently operating as a slaughterhouse, we cannot go in and just look around. Demola tells us this, then continues to chat with the guard. Demola speaks Saxon, being a Dresdner, as does the guard; thus, they recognize each other as east Germans. I am thinking that this is to our advantage. However, Demola does not look Saxon, as he is half Nigerian, and the guard is eyeing him—as well as us Americans—suspiciously. I am thinking that this is not to our advantage. Demola is told that the guards never let in the foreigners (Americans) who come looking for Slaughterhouse-Five. This guard once turned away a woman who cried when she explained that her father had been held here as a prisoner of war. The guard figured if there is no building to see, there is no building to see.

Demola and the guard begin to talk about the currently operating slaughterhouse. It seems that it will not be operating much longer, as it has gone bankrupt. They discuss how this has come about, slowly but surely, as a result of various economic considerations of the German reunification. By the end of this rather lengthy conversation, the guard has warmed up a bit to Demola. He tells him that he supposes there is no harm in letting us walk around a little, even if there is nothing to see. After all, there is already hardly any work going on here, in light of the imminent closure.

We thank him and walk through to the door that opens into the protected group of buildings we were told had been collectively known as Slaughterhouse-Five. We walk to the west down a long row of buildings that are already deserted. When we get to the end and begin to go north, the guard calls us back. He has been watching us. He explains that there is nothing to see up there. We walk back toward the guard house and continue past to the east end of the row of buildings. The one on the end is still being used. As we head around the corner to go north from there, I look for the guard again, waiting for him to call us back another time. He is still watching us, but he lets us be. As it turns out, there is a store at the north end of this leg of buildings where one can buy meat. If we had told the guard we wanted to buy meat, we would have been immediately admitted. It seems they only deny entrance to those who come asking about Slaughterhouse-Five.

There is a man standing in an open doorway. He is wearing white clothes and an apron, smoking a cigarette and watching us. Demola asks him if he knows anything about Slaughterhouse-Five. The man has never heard of *Slaughterhouse-Five*. Demola explains what *Slaughterhouse-Five* is. The man says that he has worked at this slaughterhouse for twenty-five years and that he has never heard anything about prisoners of war being held in the Slaughterhouse District. He seems rather intrigued. I suppose this would be an interesting thing to learn, at the end of one's career, about the place where one has worked for twenty-five years.

We go into the store and Demola buys some meat. None of we three Americans are very interested in eating meat, but we thoroughly explore the place as if we might buy meat. Helen buys cheese. We thank the guard again on our way out.

In the car, Helen tells us that she is not surprised that the slaughterhouse worker had never heard about the prisoners of war who were kept in the Slaughterhouse District. She tells us about a former student from our university who once tried to find Slaughterhouse-Five when she was in Dresden. This person went to the tourist information bureau and asked where she could find Slaughterhouse-Five. The helpful information clerk told her that Slaughterhouse-Five did not exist and that prisoners of war were never kept in Dresden, as the book, *Slaughterhouse-Five*, is nothing more than absolute and complete fiction. Demola confirmed that, yes, many Dresdeners seem to believe that this never happened. I wonder if what appeared to me as interest on the part of the worker was nothing more than amusement.

I knew the tourist information bureau Helen was referring to. It is on Prager Strasse, which is the name of the pedestrian mall cemetery. It just so happens that I had recently been there to buy tickets for David Liebman, who would be playing at the Jazz Club Tonne the following night.

The Jazz Club Tonne was in the basement of a bombed-out building across from the east end of the rebuilt Albertinum. There are only a handful of these bombed, shells of buildings still standing in Dresden. In many cases, the basements are intact and are being used for some purpose, though the Jazz Club has since moved, and no other business has yet moved into this particular building. It is a special place. The fifty-two-year-old ruins above offer no clue that they rest upon huge, stone chambers of Romanesque vaults below. From the time I first entered these chambers on the following night, I was struck by the beauty of this hidden sanctuary. During the concert, I suddenly realized that this place would have been considered an excellent bomb shelter and surely must have been used as such. A good bomb shelter, yes, but the fire would have baked them through. Much too close to the center.

I was musing over this very thought when David Liebman announced the next tune. It was called, "Crimes of Our Fathers." A chill ran through me.

After my second visit to the Slaughterhouse District, I realized that the place I should be looking for clues to finding Slaughterhouse-Five was *Slaughterhouse-Five*, the book. It had been years since I read it. I checked it out of the library. I had obviously been struck with the book from the beginning, but it all meant much more to me this time, now that I was living in Dresden. When I read about the prisoners being marched from the train station to the Slaughterhouse District, I thought about the position of the Hauptbahnhof, southeast of the district, with the Zigarettenfabrik in between, and of the road that links the Zigarettenfabrik and the district. When I read the description of the building the prisoners were kept in, I thought about the generator company. When I read the description of the basement the prisoners took shelter in while the bombs walked overhead, I thought about the debris-filled hole in a floor. When I read about the prisoners opening the ovens that had protected tens of thousands of people from the bombs but not the fires, I thought of the Jazz Club Tonne.

In the same vein, when I met a man a couple of weeks later who told me the story of how his city burned, I thought of the prisoners climbing out of the hole and over the rubble to the outskirts of the city in search of survivors who might have food and water. Survivors like Tom.

Tom is a rarity. He was fifteen years old when he watched his city burn, which is how he remembers the destruction of Dresden, after the noise stopped. "I watched my city burn," he said several times.

He is a rarity because not many survivors of the bombing of Dresden will talk about their experience.

"I watched my city burn."

He never so much as alluded to death at all.

I realize that people deal with horrors of history and with their own horrifying experiences in different ways.

"I watched my city burn."

I find it very interesting that this man who is willing to talk about his experience with the destruction of Dresden leaves out the people. I find it interesting that 35,000 is the death toll figure commonly believed by Germans, both eastern and western, to represent the numbers lost in the destruction of Dresden.[12] This is 100,000 less than the figure I have commonly heard and read in America. I find it interesting that there are Dresdeners who refuse to believe that prisoners of war were at one time kept in the Slaughterhouse District of Dresden. I find it interesting that so much of the public art of the GDR that contained obvious and specific GDR-era imagery has been removed from this city.

One can certainly not change history by adjusting figures, ignoring facts, or removing statues, but it would appear that denial, to some degree or another, is a common device people use in order to deal with history.

I also find it interesting what is chosen to acknowledge, or represent, history. At the same time that the destruction of Dresden is down-played in the low, death-toll figure propagated in Germany, the ongoing project to rebuild Dresden's Frauenkirche has increased, on a worldwide scale, the awareness and acknowledgment of the destruction of Dresden. I find it interesting that foreign investors will step over a recently fallen wall to come to Dresden and launch this project to rebuild a church from absolute ruins. I find it interesting that millions of dollars worth of worldwide currencies can be amassed for the raising of this church, but that the economic burden of the reunification process, which seems to become heavier every year, has basically fallen on the German government. The German people of both sides of this fallen wall are left to bear the economic burden. I find it interesting that many people seem to be more interested in the rows upon rows of sorted, categorized, and shelved remnants of the Frauenkirche, than in the actual rebuilding of the church itself. I, myself, find these categorized ruins much more interesting than the prospect of a wholly rebuilt Frauenkirche; but then, I am of the opinion that the Frauenkirche was a hideous atrocity of architecture to begin with.

As I said, I find it interesting what is chosen to acknowledge history. One might choose all sorts of numbers, all of which may represent people, living or lost; or one might choose to support the re-establishment of one former element of a city burned. It depends on how one deals with the horrors of history.

Thankfully, some people deal with the horrors of history by writing books.

When I first came to the Technische Universität of Dresden in the fall of 1996, I learned that the English department had discussed the possibility of granting an honorary doctoral degree to Kurt Vonnegut. The English department here is as new as the current Germany, and this would be the first honorary degree to come out of the department. Considering the significance of Kurt Vonnegut's connection to Dresden through literature, he is considered to be the most appropriate candidate to whom this department could extend such an honor. In February 1997, the faculty officially sanctioned the go-ahead to pursue this project. A letter has since been sent, but as of yet, there is no definitive news. It seems that everyone here understands that Mr. Vonnegut may choose not to accept their offer, but we all hope that he will.

On March 26, 1997, a bomb was unearthed at a construction site on the north side of the Hauptbahnhof. They are building a tunnel there that will link Prager Strasse to the Hauptbahnhof, eliminating the heavy pedestrian traffic across a busy street and tram line. I saved a copy of the *Dresdner Morgenpost* of the following day. The *Morgenpost* is a sensationalist daily newspaper that seems to enjoy quite a popularity. The front page of this day's paper features a large picture of the explosion with the headline in red, "Bomb crippled city."[13] There are many photographs and headlines found throughout the paper regarding this historical event. My personal favorites are a picture of the man who unearthed the bomb next to a picture of his backhoe. An American equivalent to the headline would read: "Excavator Olaf—the man with nerves of steel."[14] Near the center of the newspaper, there is a picture of a bare-breasted woman,[15] but that is a regular feature, unrelated to the story of the bomb found at the construction site by Olaf.

This is what actually happened: A strange looking metallic object was uncovered at the construction site. Experts were called in. It was determined that the object was a World War II–era bomb of British manufacture with a chemical detonation system. The area within a 1,000-meter radius of the site was evacuated. This included the Hauptbahnhof. The bomb was rigged with explosives by the bomb experts, as they were unsure how to go about detonating it. The bomb was then packed with cardboard and paper. It was blown up at 5:10 P.M., Middle European Time.

When I passed through the Hauptbahnhof about four hours later, the train schedule was not yet back on track. As I walked along the east wall of the fence that encloses this construction site, the only indication that anything out of the ordinary had happened was the inordinate amount of trash that was scattered about—reams of remnants of paper and cardboard. I was walking the route I usually take on my way home to the Plattenbau in which I live. It is a student dormitory Plattenbau, on St. Petersburger Strasse, about 1,500 meters from the site where the bomb was found. On a map of Dresden that could be considered accurate, but that is over eight years old, one will find that St. Petersburger Strasse is called Leningrader Strasse. It is the street that runs next to Prager Strasse on the east side.

I thought that the most interesting aspect of the *Sächsische Zeitung* report was a quote from the bomb expert. Apparently, he is the top man in his field in all of Saxony. He said, "I believe that this should be the last bomb we find in Saxony."

Well, it certainly should be. One can only hope.

After I reread *Slaughterhouse-Five*, I had every intention of returning to the Slaughterhouse District. I thought the descriptions of the buildings were important clues that would help me end my search for Slaughterhouse-Five. I have not yet returned, and at this point, I do not intend to return.

I have grown to love Dresden as I got used to it. *Ja*, I got used to the haunting feelings Dresden instills in one. But I have grown to love Dresden because, even though I got used to it, Dresden has never stopped instilling these feelings in me.

The most important thing I have learned since coming to Dresden and searching for Slaughterhouse-Five is this:

You never know what you are going to find when you go live in another country. Sometimes what you find makes you happy because it makes you feel at home somehow. But even at home you had been missing it, only without knowing you were missing it. Then you realize that the real reason you are happy is because what you have found is actually a part of yourself.

This makes sense to me.

NOTES

1. Dresden China is actually the English name for Meißner Porzellan, the porcelain invented in Meissen and produced there since 1710. The fact that this is an English name is found in *Das Große Duden-Lexikon in acht Bänden*, ed. Lexikonredaktion des Bibliographischen Instituts, vol. 2, s.v. "Dresden China" (Mannheim: Lexikonverlag, 1967), 480. (Hereafter I will cite *Duden-Lexikon* with the title of the entry, volume number: page number.)

2. *Dresden in alten Ansichtskarten*, ed. Brigitte Weidlich (Frankfurt/Main: Gondrom Verlag, 1994), 97.

3. The term "Zigarettenfabrik" is a misnomer in translation here, as the Yenidze Zigarettenfabrik was never actually used as a cigarette factory. It was originally built (1907–1912) by the Dresden "Tabakkönig" Hugo Zeitz to serve as the brokerage house and

offices for the Yenidze tobacco company. The building was designed by the architect Adolf Hammitzsch, who purposely used Byzantine architectural features in order to create a "Turkish" look. Various architectural elements, such as the minarets and a great, colorful, glass onion dome, caused a great deal of controversy and the building came to be referred to as the Tobacco Mosque. From *Baedeker Allianz Reiseführer: Dresden*, 4th ed., s.v. "Tabakkontor Yenidze" (Stuttgart: Verlag Karl Baedeker, 1995), 190.

4. Hans Jakob Erlwein (1872–1914) was a Bavarian born architect who served as the Stadtbaurat (city architect) in Dresden from 1905–1914 ("Erlwein: 2. Hans Jakob," 2:755).

5. The word "Plattenbauten" is the plural form of "Plattenbau," meaning "slab building." It is a distinctly East German term that specifically refers to apartment buildings of this modern, concrete slab design. Since reunification, the word has increasingly been used in a derogatory manner, as is associated with the GDR-era.

6. The Baroque Zwinger was first erected between 1711 and 1728 ("Zwinger," 8:779) and was originally designed by the architect Matthäus Daniel Pöppelmann (1662–1736) ("Pöppelmann," 6:505f.).

7. The Albertinum was originally built in 1559–1563 (Caspar Voigt von Wierandt, architect) as an armory; thus, it was known as the "Zeughaus." It was converted into a museum by Carl Adolf Canzler in 1884–1887 and was named the Albertinum after King Albert (1828–1902), who ruled Saxony from 1873 until his death (*Baedeker*, "Albertinum," 63).

8. The original opera house (first erected 1837–1841) was designed by the world famous architect Gottfried Semper (1803–1879), who tended to favor Baroque architectural elements. He also designed and built (1847–1854) the Gemäldegalerie wing of the Zwinger ("Semper: 1.," 7:338). The Semperoper of today is the second reconstruction of the original, which was called the Hoftheater. The original burned down in 1869 and was rebuilt in 1871–1878, again, as the Hoftheater. The present building (reconstructed 1979–1985) is the first to be called the Semperoper (*Baedeker*, "Berühmte Persönlichkeiten," 40).

9. The history of the Schloß (palace) is rather complex. Suffice it to say that the roots of the Schloß date to the 13th century, but most of it was built in the 16th century, with a few additions in later centuries (*Baedeker*, "Schloß," 181f.).

10. August der Starke (the Strong) had the catholic Hofkirche (court church) specially designed and built by the Italian Baroque architect Gaetano Chiaveri (1689–1770). Construction began in 1738 ("Chiaveri," 2:140). August der Starke (1670–1733) ruled as the elector of Saxony under the name Friedrich August I and also ruled as the king of Poland from 1697 until his death. In order to be eligible for the kingship of Poland, August converted to catholicism in 1697 ("August: 5. A. II.," 1:385).

11. The Frauenkirche was designed by George Bähr and built in 1727–1743. It replaced a church that had stood at the same site since the 11th century, which was known as the "Kirche zu unseren lieben Frauen" (*Baedeker*, "Frauenkirche," 87f.).

12. There has been much dispute over the death toll of the bombing of Dresden, a short discussion of which can be found in: "Der Streit um die Toten," chapter in Carl-Ludwig Paeschke and Dieter Zimmer, *Dresden: Geschichten einer Stadt* (Berlin: Brandenburgisches Verlagshaus, 1994), 170–173. Various reports based on varying factors have stated death tolls ranging between 2,000 and 300,000 people. The German government had already officially stated the Dresden death toll to be 35,000 by the time Germany was divided into East and West in 1949 (Paeschke and Zimmer, 173). I suspect that the American figure of 135,000 is based on the report compiled by David Irving for the British government, released in 1963 (Paeschke and Zimmer, 171).

13. "Bombe legte City lahm," *Dresdner Morgenpost*, 27 March 1997, photo by Jörn Haufe, 1.

14. "Baggerfahrer Olaf—der Mann, der die Nerven behielt," *Dresdner Morgenpost*. Kerstin Merdel, Jörn Haufe, and Mattias Rietschel, photographers, 4.

15. "Baggerfahrer Olaf," photo by Ove Lagraf, 11.

Unstuck in Time

Simultaneity as a Foundation for Vonnegut's Chrono-Synclastic Infundibula and other Nonlinear Time Structures

Sharon Sieber

Kurt Vonnegut's *The Sirens of Titan* introduces to the literary world an aspect of simultaneity known as *chrono-synclastic infundibula*, which somehow means to be everywhere at once and yet nowhere in particular, a mode of being and perception similar to the *aleph* in Jorge Luis Borges's short story by the same name. The very nature of chrono-synclastic infundibula is to curve back upon itself in a circular if not reflective way, as defined by Vonnegut citing the children's encyclopedic authority, Cyril Vance: "Chrono (kroh-no) means time. Synclastic (sin-class-tick) means curved toward the same side in all directions, like the skin of an orange. Infundibulum (in-fun-dib-u-lum) is what the ancient Romans like Julius Caesar and Nero called a funnel" (*Sirens*, 15). These kinds of time warps are hidden or concealed within linear time structures as small pockets or "leaks," as they are referred to in *Breakfast of Champions*, converting linear time into something like a minefield, with fractures and ruptures that perfectly normal people can fall through on any ordinary day.

Slaughterhouse-Five's Billy Pilgrim is a seasoned time-traveler, yet there is a naivete about him which experience can't change, and knowing the secrets of past and future, life and death, does not and cannot give Billy the power to change the present. The prayer framed on Billy Pilgrim's office wall, and which is worn simultaneously by his kidnapped mate on the planet Tralfamadore, the one-time earthling pornography star Montana Wildhack, is the famous "Serenity Prayer," which calls for acceptance and courage. Ironically, the reader is immediately told in juxtaposition to this prayer that "among the things Billy Pilgrim could not change were the past, the present, and the future" (*Slaughterhouse*, 60). There are profound contradictions in this powerlessness, such as the main character's being compelled to stand back and watch his own life from a distance, knowing that the outcome cannot change. Separated from that outcome by the certain foreknowledge of what is about to happen, belying the surface assertions of what is really happening, Billy gets on the plane in spite of the fact that he knows it's going to crash. The haunting and lyrical explanation of the event, "The moment was structured in that way" (*Slaughterhouse*, 154), suggests an ineluctable quality of that moment with a predestination built into the defining character of the moment itself. There is a circular nature to the events, a fatalism of time that is structured to bear the genetic imprint of these moments to always express themselves in the same way. Clearly, Billy's reflection on the nature of these events changes his perception as he goes into them: the fact that he can't prevent them from happening seems to be almost a form of *hamartia*, a fatal flaw in his character that defines the quality of hopelessness that comes from being condemned to human life on the planet. He is condemned not to existential freedom but to reliving the rigid demands of linear time without the possibility of change, since his knowledge of the future is useless in terms of its application to the present.

Yet Billy is able to change the very nature of the present moment so that he is aware of all moments of his life, past and future, from whatever point he begins his time travels. In *simultaneity*, everything occurs at once in the now of the moment point of the present, and everything endures. As Marc Leeds observes in "Beyond the Slaughterhouse: Tralfamadorian Reading Theory in the Novels of Kurt Vonnegut," "Implicit in this theory and as illustrated by the narrative structure and events of *Slaughterhouse-Five*, all history awaits repetition in the future: All existence is-as-it-was-and-is-supposed-to become; all moments exist simultaneously" (Leeds, 1996: 91). What has been liberated in this context is Billy's imagination; no longer subject to the serial constraints of time and space, Billy is free to create a kind of dream landscape in his imagination where anything is possible. His dizzying travels through and beyond any present moment introduce into the novel the modern fragmentation of perspective, perception, storyline, character, rhythm, and sequence, which is repaired by coincidence or *synchronicity*, the structuring of thought and experience along associative patterns.

In *Breakfast of Champions*, we are informed of the symbolic importance of mirrors and their connections to other universes (hence the universe is not a closed, hermetically sealed, or circular system), and essentially mirrors change the nature of reality by their ability to reflect and interact with the viewer, causing the viewer to reflect upon himself, and imposing what Vonnegut terms a "leak," or fracture in the hermetic system. The mirror held up to reality is supposed to reflect, through mimesis, things as they are, yet in Vonnegut's novel, mirrors interfere with reality in a way that Octavio Paz has described as follows: "If art mirrors the world, then the mirror is magical; it changes the world" (Paz, 60). The symbolic importance of mirrors as they relate to literature and to reality lies not only in their ability to reflect, then, but also in their ability to fragment or interrupt the continuous flow of sequential reality so as to impose a self-conscious perception (or self-reflexive reality) that places the viewer outside of time, or in Borgesian terms, to introduce the paradox of a concept like eternity within a temporal context. Readers are likewise outside of time as they read the text, which in Paz's terms is another mirror. Seeing oneself in a mirror, then, is to be transformed immediately into the other, a means of creating narrative confusion or fusion that becomes layered, distant, alienated, without clear boundaries, and like all symbols, stands for something other than itself, like the poetic image converting itself into more than what it seems to be.

The intrinsic distance emanating from the pessimism of the implied author is maintained throughout between the narrator and the protagonist and heightens the irony and comedic nature of Billy's tragic life. However, this ironic distance also obstructs and obscures the reader's sympathies so that the reader takes on the aspect of the voyeur, motivated by curiosity to find out what happens rather than because of identification with or attachment to the main character. The pathetic nature of Billy Pilgrim's life resonates whether he is a victim of war or a victim of life; he is an anti-hero who the narrator tells us is "unenthusiastic about living" (*Slaughterhouse*, 60), and that in this "light opera . . . Billy Pilgrim was the star" (*Slaughterhouse*, 150). There is a curious symmetry running through Billy's life in both the military and civilian guise: while Billy is in Dresden, his father is the victim of the same kind of random and arbitrary violence in another, entirely unrelated and senseless incident—he is killed by friendly fire in a hunting accident.

Thus, in Billy's life, there is what Carl Jung has referred to as a "failure to understand" the images of the unconscious, which "imposes a painful fragmentariness on his life" (Jung, 193). In the twentieth century, chaos theory has reorganized time into nonlinear structures. James Gleick points out that chaos and arbitrary or random events, characterized by a lack of any perceivable pattern, often involve the perception of yet a larger circle. Simultaneity involves an understanding of time that surpasses causality and serial perception in favor of synchronicity, which Jung defines as the fusion of simultaneity and meaning, creating a sense of Baudelarian correspondences or coincidences between seemingly unconnected events.[1] That intuition underlies our understanding of time has long been the subject of contention by literary critics and philosophers. As Agnes Arber asserts in *The Manifold and the One*, "The recognition of sequence implies time. We may hence regard reasoning as intuitive understanding made finite and patterned into discursive thought by the introduction of the time element" (62).

Unk, in *The Sirens of Titan*, otherwise known as Malachi Constant and whose name according to Vonnegut means "faithful messenger," is also a "space wanderer"—a journeyer, wayfarer, or pilgrim. Like Billy Pilgrim, Unk is on an open-ended pilgrimage; he is also the victim of, as he puts it, "a series of accidents." Of course, a pilgrimage is also a symbol of renewal or rebirth, a renaissance, and both Billy and Unk have been reduced to something less than human through their military activities. Billy has been stripped of his humanism through the devastation of war, yet he is out of place. Neither Billy nor the reader ever seems to make sense of this pilgrim's journey, of why Billy has gone to fight in a war, of what has been accomplished other than devastation and destruction. It is clear, however, that he has become someone else, that he has been transformed into the other, and that the renewal of Billy Pilgrim insists on the destruction of the old. Similarly, Unk is forced to participate in a battle in a very mechanical way, since the device implanted in his forehead is used to control him for purposes other than his own. The reader's sympathies are with him, however, as he strives to come back from nothingness, from having his memory wiped clean yet another time. We see him carrying on with hope, rising up on the bed of Phoenician ashes, to be "reborn" as he attempts to make sense of his life. Unk's particular pilgrimage involves a journey to a sacred place, the carrying of a sacred message, in this case to turn around the McLuhan phrase, the medium is not the message, the messengers are the message. There is a confluence of meaningful symmetries or coincidences not only within each discrete novel, but also between the characters as they relate to one another outside of the novel, and within other Vonnegut novels.

We learn that Billy first came unstuck in time during the time that "World War Two was in progress" (*Slaughterhouse*, 30), yet clearly there is the sensation that Billy Pilgrim has died in this war, and his insane time-travels are the traditional hallucinations of the dying, similar to what happens to the protagonists in the modern feature film directed by Adrian Lyne, *Jacob's Ladder*, and in Ambrose Bierce's short story, "Hanging at Owl Creek Bridge."[2] There is a poignancy in both *The Sirens of Titan* and *Slaughterhouse-Five* concerning the ineluctable and suffocating stability of the nature of time, that in spite of chrono-synclastic infundibula and becoming "unstuck" in time, things are as they always will be, and that death, in this context, is meaningless. This seeming validation of the death experience as an integral part of what it means to be alive also highlights the level of desperation and despair of Billy's pilgrimage through the meaninglessness of life, the randomness of existence, the chaos that symbolizes the unknown, and which becomes solidified as the known through the unveiling of the message from Tralfamadore. It is important to read *The Sirens of Titan* and *Slaughterhouse-Five* in juxtaposition to each other because each work elucidates the other. In *Slaughterhouse-Five*, we learn that Tralfamadorians think all humans are machines. This makes more sense as we read in *The Sirens of Titan* that all Tralfamadorians *are* machines. Curiously, however, Salo, the Tralfamadorian messenger stranded on Titan, becomes much more human in an idealized way, almost sentimental in his friendship with Winston Niles Rumfoord. In *Slaughterhouse-Five*, by contrast, Billy Pilgrim's human daughter, Barbara, becomes more machinelike. She is given pills so that she can "function," as the narrator explains, "in spite of the fact that her father was broken and her mother was dead." We learn that the all-important message carried by Salo, whose integrity must be protected at all costs—even at the expense of entire Earthling civilizations manipulated by the Tralfamadorian UWIB (Universal Will to Become) to spell out trite messages to Salo (Stonehenge, for example, built by humans, meant simply "Replacement part being rushed with all possible speed" [271])—is the single dot that in the Tralfamadorian language means "Greetings." Apparently machines can't differentiate the importance of their messages. They do, however, come closer to an understanding of time as the "enigma which escapes measurement" than do their human counterparts.

Billy's letters to the Ilium newspaper describing life on Tralfamadore sum up the postwar existential sense of alienation as well as the simultaneous validation of life and death as aspects of different kinds of time:

The most important thing I learned on Tralfamadore was that when a person dies he only *appears* to die. He is still very much alive in the past, so it is very silly for people to cry at his funeral. All moments, past, present, and future, always have existed, always will exist. The Tralfamadorians can look at all the different moments just the way we can look at a stretch of the Rocky Mountains, for instance. They can see how permanent all the moments are, and they can look at any moment that interests them. It is just an illusion we have here on Earth that one moment follows another one, like beads on a string, and that once a moment is gone it is gone forever.

When a Tralfamadorian sees a corpse, all he thinks is that the dead person is in bad condition in that particular moment, but that the same person is just fine in plenty of other moments. (*Sirens*, 26–27)

The intricacy of such vision allows Tralfamadorians to see patterns and rhythms of moments that human beings cannot see about their own lives. There is a simultaneity of space as well as time; Billy's simultaneous existence on Tralfamadore and Earth is easily explained by the fact that years on Tralfamadore can take place in an earthling microsecond.

On the surface, Billy Pilgrim's unpredictable pilgrimage through time would seem to be a traditional manifestation and affirmation of prevailing contemporary theological beliefs: that life events are preordained and there is no changing them. In spite of the fact that Billy Pilgrim journeys through life with the foreknowledge of future events, such as his plane crash, he is powerless to change them or to exercise his free will. There is, interestingly, a deep cynicism on the part of the narrator in *Slaughterhouse-Five*. It seems to correspond to that of the author, who intervenes behind the narrator at moments that are clearly intended to startle the momentary "suspension of disbelief" of the reader. For example, the narrator reports that as Billy gets off the train in Dresden, "Somebody behind him in the boxcar said, 'Oz.' That was I. That was me. The only other city I'd ever seen was Indianapolis, Indiana" (*Slaughterhouse*, 148). Such intrusions in the novel are not limited, however, to only the authorial kind. There is also clear interference from characters from other Vonnegut novels. Eliot Rosewater shares a room with Billy after his first nervous breakdown and introduces him to yet another Vonnegut character from another book, Kilgore Trout. There Bertram Copeland Rumfoord (clearly a representative stand-in from *The Sirens of Titan*), who shares Billy's hospital room after his plane crash and who cannot tolerate Billy's presence nor his purported experience of what really happened in Dresden's fire-bombing.[3]

So Billy's time travel does not limit him to investigating the nature of the events in his own life, rearranging them in an order that is anything but chronological. It introduces Billy in a Derridean way that deconstructs through the difference of play—involving not language, but the characters from the larger body of the Vonnegut opus. Their context clearly shifts in relationship to one another, or perhaps they can be likened to variations of musical themes, where the melodic refrain serves not only to unite the works into a larger integration, but also to introduce the various levels of the works that come into deconstructionist play against each other, causing a constant shift or redefinition through a haunting desperation that has been described as having a simultaneous "leveling" or planing effect. That is, at the metafictional level on which the characters interact with one another, the narrator and the author causes a constant shifting or a gestalt relationship on the part of the implied reader and the unstable relationships between the magnified characters of Vonnegut's entire corpus.

The allegorical nature of the work culminates in *Slaughterhouse-Five* when Billy steals Cinderella's silver boots from beneath a makeshift stage prop throne. The narrator tells us "the boots fit perfectly. Billy Pilgrim was Cinderella, and Cinderella was Billy Pilgrim" (145). Billy is renewed through putting on Cinderella's silver boots, and in times of war, we see that boots are a serious matter and can mean the difference between living or dying, as in the case of Roland Weary, Billy's doomed companion on the way to Dresden. The serious nature of these boots is made ridiculous by the fact that they are Cinderella's and by the fact that they are silver, hardly a striking military uniform. Yet the origin of Cinderella's name does not escape us here in this identification. Clearly, the little girl who gets her name from sweeping cinders is a reference to the incineration of Jews as well as to the Allied incineration of Dresden. It also refers to the complete and utter destruction of the individual, to the collective psyche of Billy Pilgrim, which, more than being renewed, has been replaced. The resulting alienation from what mankind has done transforms Billy and his noble purpose: his humanity is reduced to the ridiculous, the metaphorical, and the gallant soldier is no more than a tragi-comedic waif waiting for help from his fairy godmother, powerless to do anything more than obey the orders of his captors. Likewise, in terms of alienation, the Tralfamadorians cannot imagine what time looks like to Billy. Their metaphor to describe this sense of time is imagining a human with his head encased in steel, with only one eyehole to peek through, "and welded to that eyehole were six feet of pipe" (*Slaughterhouse*, 115). The narrator tells us that "this was only the beginning of Billy's miseries in the metaphor" (*Slaughterhouse*, 115). Billy has been transformed into a metaphor, an analogy for a lack of human understanding. Yet Billy's task is to inform humans of the true nature of time; he had been trapped in time but now he is unstuck across time. In fact, he is simultaneous. He is the text of time, has always been and always will be. As Vonnegut says, "the moment is structured in that way" (*Slaughterhouse*, 117).

NOTES

1. See James Gleick's book, *Chaos: Making a New Science*, for an explanation of Chaos Theory, "the Butterfly Effect," and its relationship to non-Aristotelian time structures.

2. Conversation with Judith Hutton Levenson, March 1997 at Idaho State University, regarding the similarity between Billy Pilgrim's becoming "unstuck" in time and the traditional images of the dying.

3. See Marc Leeds's *The Vonnegut Encyclopedia* for a complete treatment of Bertram Copeland Rumfoord's contrapuntal relationship to Billy Pilgrim.

WORKS CITED

Arber, Agnes. *The Manifold and the One*. Wheaton, IL: Theosophical, 1967.

Gleick, James. *Chaos: Making a New Science*. New York: Penguin, 1987.

Jung, C. G. *Memories, Dreams, Reflections*. Trans. Richard Winston and Clara Winston. New York: Vintage.

Leeds, Marc. "Beyond the Slaughterhouse: Tralfamadorian Reading Theory in the Novels of Kurt Vonnegut." In *The Vonnegut Chronicles: Interviews and Essays*, Peter J. Reed and Marc Leeds, eds. Westport, CT: Greenwood, 1996.

———. *The Vonnegut Encyclopedia: An Authorized Compendium.* Westport, CT: Greenwood, 1995.

Paz, Octavio. *Children of the Mire.* Trans. Rachel Phillips. Cambridge: Harvard University Press, 1974.

Vonnegut, Kurt, Jr. *The Sirens of Titan.* New York: Dell, 1959.

———. *Slaughterhouse-Five.* New York: Dell, 1968.

The Apotheosis of Philanthropy

Kurt Vonnegut's *God Bless You, Mr. Rosewater*

Donald E. Morse

[I]t strikes me as gruesome and comical that in our culture we have an expectation that a man can always solve his problems.
—Kurt Vonnegut (Standish, 91)

When the *Mayflower* set sail, that original colonizing ship contained not only the Pilgrim Separatists with their dream of a New World where they could establish a New Jerusalem and practice their religion in peace and freedom, but also the "strangers," those in the majority who joined the company not for religious reasons but to seek their fortune on the new continent. The division between the two groups became so strong that it occasioned the colonists' first political document, the Mayflower Compact. The dreams of America held by each group: a land of peace and individual freedom of conscience and a land of plenty and individual accumulation of wealth thus coexisted as uneasily on the *Mayflower* as they have throughout American history. For there are, and always have been, not one but two American Dreams: one rooted in the dream of freedom and the other in the dream of riches. It is the collision of these conflicting dreams that centuries later becomes the matter out of which Kurt Vonnegut creates his satiric portrait of greed and uncritical love, inherited wealth and philanthropy in *God Bless You, Mr. Rosewater* (1965).

American philanthropy itself derives from contradictory impulses of generosity and greed: Greed is necessary for the accumulation of wealth, without which there can be no philanthropy, while generosity is necessary for the dispersal of wealth which is the essence of philanthropy. The happy meeting ground of these twin impulses is the nonprofit foundation, such as the Rosewater Foundation in *God Bless You, Mr. Rosewater*. Typically, the model for the mid-twentieth-century Rosewater Foundation, whose ostensible purpose is to give away money while paying its officers handsome stipends and safely hiding the principle from the Internal Revenue Service, is the various foundations established by either the descendants of or the original nineteenth-century robber barons; twentieth-century American philanthropy is based by-and-large upon nineteenth-century accumulated wealth:

> Like so many great American fortunes, the Rosewater pile was accumulated in the beginning by a humorless, constipated Christian farm boy [Noah Rosewater] turned speculator and briber during and after the Civil War. . . . Abraham Lincoln declared that no amount of money was too much to pay for the restoration of the Union, so Noah priced his merchandise in scale with the national tragedy. (*Rosewater*, 11)

Samuel, Noah's successor, in his turn "bought newspapers, and preachers, too" to spread the gospel of hard work for low pay as the American way (*Rosewater*, 13). Thus the accumulated fortune comes down to Lister Rosewater who "never was in business . . . [but] spent nearly the whole of his adult life in the Congress of the United States, teaching morals" (*Rosewater*, 14). As a way of saving the fortune from taxes and keeping it intact, the senator establishes the Rosewater Foundation with his son, Eliot Rosewater, a self-described "drunkard, a Utopian dreamer, a tinhorn saint, an aimless fool" (*Rosewater*, 14), ensconced as president of the foundation able to draw an unlimited salary and do whatever he wants.[1]

The Rosewater fortune accumulates because, claims Eliot, of "the folly of the Founding Fathers in one respect: those . . . ancestors had not made it the law of the Utopia that the wealth of each citizen should be limited" (*Rosewater*, 12). Yet Thomas Jefferson, for one, fought long and hard against what he called, "an artificial aristocracy, founded on wealth and birth without either virtue or talents." To Jefferson this was "a mischievous ingredient in government, and provision should be made to prevent its ascendancy." Jefferson led the fight to pass legislation noting, "abolishing entails . . . abolishing the privilege of primogeniture, and dividing the lands of intestates equally among all their children, or other representatives." These laws, he believed, would effectively abolish or at least radically limit inherited wealth as the basis for the pseudo-aristocracy of wealth and birth by preventing the accumulation of wealth in the forced break-up of large estates. Since no individual or family would enjoy an advantage, a new "natural aristocracy . . . [whose] grounds . . . are virtue and talents" would be free to emerge in each new generation (Jefferson, 484, 485).

Historically, things worked out quite differently from what Jefferson planned as the Rosewaters and their ilk circumvented the laws and/or made their fortunes not from land (which Jefferson's laws were designed to prevent) but from natural resources, inventions, slaves, technology, and so forth. As a result, such families did amass great wealth, which they then secreted in foundations so that their heirs, regardless of their virtue or talents, could indeed become an aristocracy—an aristocracy founded upon greed. Some critics of *God Bless You, Mr. Rosewater*, such as Robert Uphaus emphasize this negative phenomenon:

> the United States was founded on a highly imaginative (if not utopian) ideal of "life, liberty, and the pursuit of happiness." This ideal, regrettably, is easily transformed into a pageant of

winners and losers, for without money an American is only "free" to lose. . . . Eliot is thus a winner who wishes to share his wealth with losers, but the drama of his efforts is played out against the resistant backdrop of American history—a history which says that "all men are equal" but which also implies "some men are more equal than others." (169)

Eliot, therefore, inherits not only a great deal of money but also the family guilt (Godshalk, 100). Realizing that his ancestors and others like them had thwarted the promise that was America, "which was meant to be a Utopia for all," and replaced it with Jefferson's pseudo aristocracy within an "entirely inappropriate and unnecessary and humorless American class system" (*Rosewater*, 12) based upon inherited wealth, Eliot, in effect, exclaims *mea culpa* and sets out to atone for the loss of Utopia though giving away money—since "money is dehydrated Utopia" (*Rosewater*, 121). Attempting to assuage his guilt through philanthropy, he spends huge sums buying paintings for museums, supporting starving artists and writers, staging operas, and so forth, but all with little success. He still feels much like Ralph Waldo Emerson's "foolish philanthropist" in "Self-Reliance" giving money "to such men as do not belong to me and to whom I do not belong" (Emerson, 1321), so he switches to Emerson's wise form of philanthropy: personal service to "a class of persons to whom by all spiritual affinity I am bought and sold; for them I will go to prison if need be" (Emerson, 1321). Thus he visits the sick, comforts the lonely, feeds the hungry, gives drink to the thirsty, helps those in trouble through the Volunteer Fire Department. He becomes the one who listens to those who have no listener and who comforts those who are the outcasts of society. "I'm going to love these discarded Americans, even though they're useless and unattractive," he declares (*Rosewater*, 36). As Diana Moon Glampers tells him at the end of a telephone conversation in the middle of the night where Eliot treats her like a human being, taking her fears seriously, with never a trace of sarcasm: "You gave up everything a man is supposed to want, just to help the little people, and the little people know it. God Bless You, Mr. Rosewater" (*Rosewater*, 61).

In addition, Eliot realizes that money's prime function in this form of philanthropy lies in its symbolic value which shows that someone cares, so he "gave them love and trifling sums of money" (*Rosewater*, 40).[2] But it takes huge quantities of emotional energy to "[treasure] human beings because they are human beings" (*Rosewater*, 183), which is what Eliot is attempting to do. His beautiful wife divorces him not because she hates what he does or because she does not approve or understand, but because she does not have the stamina to keep on doing it with him (*Rosewater*, 53–54). A typical caller to the Rosewater Foundation, for example, will begin talking to Eliot by saying "I'm nothing" (*Rosewater*, 74) and believe it. Realizing that wealth will not help such folk, nor the "arts and sciences," he offers them his time and a prescription against most minor aches and pains both physical and emotional, "take an aspirin with a glass of wine." Beyond this he also invents useful things for them to do, such as fly hunts:

the fly hunts were actually rituals, and were ritualized to such an extent that conventional fly-swatters were not used, and men and women hunted flies in very different ways. (78)

The purpose of the fly hunts became fulfilled when participants felt needed and believed that they were rendering a useful service, rather than receiving one.

These "useless" people Eliot Rosewater helps find themselves in similar circumstances to those who were battered by the Great Depression. Brought up in the faith that God blesses those who truly believe and work hard, many Americans, found themselves in the Great Depression with no work, with no means to support their families, and, therefore, with no value. They were integers in a simple but harrowing equation: no job = no income = no worth. Tossed aside by society, like so many empty husks, men began wandering across the country—useless men with no job, no family, no one to care for and no one to care for them. The legacy, for Vonnegut's generation, was devastating, and so he concludes that "part of the trick for people my age, I'm certain, is to crawl out of the envying, life-hating mood of the Great Depression at last" (*Wampeters*, 285). Near the end of *God Bless You, Mr. Rosewater*, in answer to Senator Rosewater's contention that: "A poor man with gumption can still elevate himself out of the mire . . . and that will continue to be true a thousand years from now," another character asserts: "Poverty is a relatively mild disease for even a very flimsy American soul, but uselessness will kill strong and weak souls alike, and kill every time" (*Rosewater*, 184). This is as close as anybody in *God Bless You, Mr. Rosewater* or in any of Vonnegut's early novels comes to preaching. Undercutting the sentiment is, however, the character of the preacher himself: for the words are put into the mouth of Kilgore Trout, a hack science fiction writer who works at a Green Stamp redemption center! An amusing minor character, Kilgore Trout shows us first, Eliot's limitations as a reader—he reads only for plot since, as he says, "writers [such as Trout] couldn't write for sour apples" (*Rosewater*, 18), and, second, through his fiction Trout does for readers what Eliot attempts to do with his money which is to provide people "with fantasies of an impossibly hospitable world" (*Rosewater*, 20). Finally, at the end of the novel, Trout is brought on stage to give his sermon on the dangers of soul-rot and the uselessness of human beings.[3] Trout's *2BR02B*, which appears in plot outline in *God Bless You, Mr. Rosewater*, also vividly highlights the uselessness of human beings who, as work becomes automated and the earth of the very near future becomes more and more crowded, face the moral categorical imperative of committing suicide so as to provide room for others (*Rosewater*, 20–21).

Although "people can use all the uncritical love they can get" (*Rosewater*, 186), many have a vested interest in seeing that people do not receive it. One of those is the unscrupulous young lawyer, Norman Mushari, who is determined to rid Eliot of his fortune and in the process siphon off a sizable chunk of it into his own safekeeping. Mushari pictures himself as David doing battle against Goliath (*Rosewater*, 10), but Eliot is anything but Goliath being called by Mushari's colleagues "The Nut," "The Saint," or "John the Baptist." David and Goliath are present in *God Bless You, Mr. Rosewater* but David is clearly Eliot Rosewater, while Goliath is the Rosewater fortune, "A leading character in this tale about people" (*Rosewater*, 7). Eliot responds to Mushari's attack by refusing to do battle; he retains no lawyers, files no countersuit. Rather than making an opposing argument in court, he "turns the other cheek" and, in what may well be the ultimate philanthropic act, gives away his fortune through inheriting the fifty-seven or more children of Rosewater County who fraudulently claim him as their father. Hence, the Rosewater fortune, which is a "leading character" in the book and which has proven to be an impotent force for alleviating pain and suffering and has proved "a force aligned with inhumanity" (Leff, 31), leaves the Rosewater family forever, never to burden another with the responsibility of caring for it. Eliot feels only relief and happiness in practicing this third form of philanthropy as the family fortune disappears.

All three forms of Rosewater's philanthropy—giving away large sums of money, giving away small sums along with uncritical love, and giving away the entire fortune—are linked significantly through moral questions and personal guilt to events in World War II. To citizens of the United States, this war appeared to eliminate ambiguity from national and private morality because the enemy was portrayed as so terrible, so inhuman, so evil. But moral ambiguity resurfaced when those who participated in the war, such as Eliot, found themselves in predicaments that forced them to ask difficult questions about their own or their country's actions. For Vonnegut, these questions usually focus on the Allies' bombing the "open," undefended city of Dresden where the resulting firestorm incinerated 135,000 people within a few hours. Such actions led to an ethical dilemma: what happens if the "good" side uses inhuman, evil means (firestorms in Dresden or the atomic bomb on Hiroshima or Nagasaki) in order to achieve a good end (the defeat of Germany or Japan)? Is the result good or evil? Or is it perhaps morally neutral? These questions were part of what I described earlier as the "moral hangover" left by the war.

In *God Bless You, Mr. Rosewater* the "hangover" is appallingly and personally present in Eliot Rosewater's terrible memory of the tragedy that occurred when he did his duty and obeyed what appeared to be legitimate orders given "under fire." He had been told to take an objective and hold it. So he heroically led his troops in an assault on a building, and personally killed three of the enemy before someone realized that these "enemy" were unarmed, and what was especially tragic were unarmed firemen "engaged in the brave and uncontroversial business of trying to keep a building from combining with oxygen" (*Rosewater*, 64). To make matters even worse, Eliot discovers that of his three unarmed victims the two he killed with a grenade were old men, while the one he bayoneted was a teenaged boy! So it goes. It was, of course, no one's fault—"mistakes" are bound to happen in war, but Eliot now has to live the rest of his life with the memory of killing three unarmed people who were acting selflessly to save the property and lives of others, hence his enthusiasm for volunteer fire departments and, in part, his engaging in philanthropy. Yet, like Dr. Schlichter von Koenigswald in *Cat's Cradle* also working to overcome a moral deficit (126–127), the prospect of his ever clearing his debt is doubtful, at best.[4]

"Vonnegut goes well out of his way to show the validity of Eliot's viewpoint, making him perhaps one of the most endearing of his protagonists" (Mustazza, 1990: 99). Nevertheless, Vonnegut also avoids treating either his ghastly "mistake" in killing three unarmed firemen or the many instances of Eliot's "good deeds" sentimentally—always a danger in a novel with a "good hero"—in part by showing his main character's considerable limitations both in themselves and in contrast with those of other characters.

Eliot dramatically contrasts Henry Pena with, for example, the robust, healthy fisherman who with his sons works hard for a living, is in constant danger of bankruptcy, and maintains a clear sense of what is "real" and what is unreal, fantasy, or phony whether it is a fish, woman, or man. Eliot enjoys none of these positive virtues, attributes, or abilities. Instead, he is alcoholic, fat, mentally disturbed, suffers from a bad conscience, and is enormously rich. Yet he does what he can to alleviate pain and suffering in the little town of Rosewater, Indiana, while his unknown nemesis, Mushari, plots to steal his inherited fortune by proving him mentally incompetent. His father also emphasizes his son's limits when he hires a psychiatrist who says Eliot is bringing his sexual energies "to Utopia," and "has the potential for a samaritrophic collapse" (*Rosewater*, 73, 43). Eliot, himself, helps dampen sanctimony by comically reducing the radical thrust of Christianity's New Commandment that "you love your enemies, bless them that curse you, do good to them that hate you, and pray for them which despitefully use you, and persecute you" (Matthew 5:44) to, "God damn it, you've got to be kind" (*Rosewater*, 93).

Eliot is clearly a good person unlike, say, the evil Howard W. Campbell, Jr. in *Mother Night*. As Mustazza maintains, "Vonnegut deliberately places his protagonist within a milieu where no one is morally superior to him, however troubled he might be" (Mustazza, 1990: 99). In many ways he is as naive as Paul Proteus in *Player Piano*, as misguided as Malachi Constant in *The Sirens of Titan*, and as removed from life as Jonah/John in *Cat's Cradle*. His ultimate philanthropic gesture, while judged "insane" or at least highly eccentric by others in positions of power or responsibility when looked at in light of either its limited but positive results or its ethical implications, appears eminently sane and even highly commendable. Although Vonnegut is a rational atheist who rejects all forms of institutional religion (see *Wampeters*, 240; Standish, 78), in this novel he appears to advocate what might be loosely described as "Christian ethics" based upon the Sermon on the Mount (Matthew 5–6) in which Jesus admonished his listeners to follow a discipline of radical love, even to loving one's enemies and "doing good to them that hate you." In *God Bless You, Mr. Rosewater* Eliot's life comes to reflect the Sermon on the Mount in that he becomes one of the "meek," who, Jesus says, will inherit not riches, such as the Rosewater fortune, but "the earth"—his true inheritance.

Vonnegut once claimed in a private conversation that, "There's no better way to understand people than by looking at the stories that shaped their cultures" (quoted in Mustazza, 1990: 198n). One of his own best stories about his early life in Indianapolis illustrates the power of New Testament texts as motives for philanthropic actions. In it he tells of a luncheon meeting between his father, the wealthy, successful architect whose fortune was wiped out in the Great Depression and who by this time found himself "in full retreat from life" (*Jailbird*, xiii), his Uncle Alex, who was puzzled by, though sympathetic with, his young nephew, and

Powers Hapgood, the Harvard-educated labor organizer. Hapgood arrived straight from court where he had been "testifying about violence on a picket line some months before. . . . The judge was fascinated. . . . 'Mr. Hapgood,' he said, 'why would a man from such a distinguished family and with such a fine education choose to live as you do?' 'Why?' said Hapgood. . . . 'Because of the Sermon on the Mount, sir.'" Apparently unable to frame an appropriate reply, the judge declared a recess for lunch (*Jailbird*, xviii–xix).

At the end of *God Bless You, Mr. Rosewater*, Eliot believes he has found a solution "for settling everything instantly, beautifully, and fairly" (*Rosewater*, 188) in what for him is the ultimate philanthropic act—giving away totally his inheritance to strangers—the world in which he lives will view it as simply "crazy." His three criteria, "instantly, beautifully, and fairly," are naively utopian, although perfectly consistent with his life. Eliot's efforts may be doomed, because as Clark Mayo contends, "*God Bless You, Mr. Rosewater* deals with the confusions of money, power and love in a 'Free Enterprise System,' which provides a hostile environment for 'uncritical love' in midtwentieth century America" (Mayo, 37). "Eliot is a man crying in the wilderness, crying against the tide of greed and hypocrisy that has swept over America, crying the only message he finds worth hearing: "'God damn it, you've got to be kind'" (Mustazza, 1990: 98). In giving away all he has to strangers regardless of their worth or lack of it, he uses formal, sacramental language to assure these dozens of unnamed children of his uncritical, forgiving love: "Let their names be Rosewater from this moment on. And tell them that their father loves them, no matter what they may turn out to be" (*Rosewater*, 190). A majestic figure in snowy tennis whites, he "raised his tennis racket as though it were a magic wand"—as if it were Prospero's wand or perhaps God's hand—to add his blessing concluding with God's admonition, "And tell them to be fruitful and multiply" (190).

Knowing that it is harder for a rich man to enter heaven than for a camel to pass through the eye of a needle, Eliot stops being a "rich man" and becomes poorer than the poor. Although dissuaded by lawyers from selling all he has and giving it to the poor, as Jesus admonished the young rich man to do, in the end he does manage to distribute his fortune to innocent strangers. In another memorable sermon Jesus divides people into those who do such good works and those who do not; between those who "when I was an hungred . . . gave me meat; I was thirsty . . . gave me drink; I was a stranger, . . . took me in; Naked . . . clothed me; . . . sick . . . visited me; . . . in prison . . . came unto me. Then shall the righteous answer him, saying, Lord, when saw we thee an hungred, and fed thee? or thirsty, and gave thee drink? . . . And [He] the King shall answer and say unto them. Verily I say unto you, Inasmuch as ye have done it unto one of the least of these my brethren, ye have done it unto me" (Matthew 25:35–40).

Readers surely hope that having so quickly cut the Gordian Knot created by Mushari, Eliot will be able to return to peaceful Rosewater County, Indiana, and take up his old life, but judging from earlier events, his prospects may not be that good. When the greedy lawyer forces him to leave Rosewater to defend his way of life, he becomes catatonic. Subsequently, he has a vision of the destruction of the earth in a firestorm—similar to the one that destroyed Dresden—where the firestorm appears directly over Indianapolis "at least eight miles in diameter and fifty miles high" (*Rosewater*, 176). In much the same way his own world of Rosewater County at that moment appears about to be destroyed by lawyers, courts, and what the world calls "obligations," Eliot's efforts may, therefore, be doomed.

At the end of *God Bless You, Mr. Rosewater* ambiguities and doubts remain: Imitating God in the Garden of Eden blessing His creation[5] hardly guarantees an increase in the amount of generosity or a decrease in the amount of greed in the world, although it may momentarily distract some of those bent on seizing all they can get while the "getting is good." Clearly, Kilgore Trout's assessment is based on wishful thinking and viewing the world and people through rose-colored or perhaps deeply shaded glasses: "Thanks to the example of Eliot Rosewater," he gushes, "millions upon millions of people may learn to love and help whomever they see" (*Rosewater*, 187)—an extravagant pronouncement in its assurance of change and grandiose effect. Eliot's example was enacted out of the limelight in an obscure corner of Indiana away from the harsh lights of the media. The most that may happen is a fleeting, momentary notice before the world moves on to another distraction somewhere else. Millions will neither know nor care. Nor does Vonnegut believe it matters very much if they do. All politics is local as is all morality. Eliot does the right thing at the right time.

At the opposite extreme, as exemplified in the criticism of Robert Uphaus, Eliot's act may be viewed as futile and empty:

in the face of American history his [Eliot's] gestures amount to nothing more than noble posturing . . . the tennis racket represents a concrete activity and serves as a historical remainder of Eliot's upper-class position; the magic wand is what Eliot would sincerely like to have, what millions of Americans in fact need, but what they will never get. (Uphaus, 169)

But Eliot is not simply posturing since in this act he does give away completely the Rosewater fortune. The importance of his act lies not in any external changes that may or may not occur in others or in the United States as a whole or in American history, nor in whether others acquire a "magic wand" or not, but in the change in status of the Rosewater fortune and in the internal change within himself. He is not, however, attempting to rectify any "damage" he may or may not have done to those he tried to help, as maintained by Stanley Schatt:

It is unclear whether Eliot is a saint replete with magic wand and Madonna's smile, a madman still recuperating in a hospital after a complete nervous breakdown, or a sane, repentant man who see the damage [*sic*] he has done his "clients" and seeks to rectify it by one last, completely unselfish act. (64)

The fortune is now gone: never to be reconstituted, never to control another's life. David has indeed slain Goliath. Moreover, Eliot's principle of uncritical love inherited from the "saints" on the *Mayflower* has carried the day against the fortune-seeking "strangers" and brought him peace without guilt at last.[6] As

Emerson wisely said at the end of "Self-Reliance": "Nothing can bring you peace but yourself. Nothing can bring you peace but the triumph of principles" (1338), which is exactly what occurs in Eliot Rosewater's gesture.

Thus, if the novel's conclusion is ambiguous about Eliot's ultimate success, it is not ambiguous about his immediate triumph. Rather than emphasize Uphaus's "pageant of winners and losers" in American history, readers of *God Bless You, Mr. Rosewater* might more profitably reflect on the "saints" and "strangers" on the *Mayflower* and their very different conflicting dreams of the New World. No victory has ever been final for either side, no defeat has been lasting. Eliot Rosewater, through the medium of philanthropy based upon uncritical love, stands in the company of the saints having defeated, if only momentarily, the strangers and in that moment he also joins the ranks of Thomas Jefferson's natural aristocracy possessed of virtue and talents.

NOTES

1. Vonnegut described in an interview how he once shared an office with the man who became his model for the philanthropist, Eliot Rosewater:

there really is a man who is that kind. Except he's poor, an accountant over a liquor store. We shared an office, and I could hear him comforting people who had very little income, calling everybody "dear" and giving love and understanding instead of money. . . . I took this very sweet man and in a book gave him millions and millions to play with. ("Interview" with Bellamy and Casey, 160)

Richard Giannone suggests that "Rosewater seems modeled after his nineteenth century namesake Frank Rosewater who in 1894 wrote *'96: A Romance of Utopia: Presenting a Solution of the Babor Problem, a New God and a New Religion* (Giannone, 64), but offers no evidence other than the suggestive book title.

2. Broer's description of these acts appears particularly obtuse and ill-founded: "In truth [*sic*], Eliot's cajolings and bribes can be seen as a form of moral prostitution, trading money for peace of mind" (76). Shades of Senator Rosewater teaching morals. Mustazza's usually sharp critical perspective fails here as well: "An artist whose tools are uncritical love and vast wealth, Eliot comes to effect change, to undo the damage done by his forebears' greed and pride, as well as to set time moving again and thus provide hope to the hopeless" (95), but the one thing Eliot does not do is give away vast sums of money. In fact Senator Rosewater complains about how little Eliot gives away each year while living in Rosewater, Indiana.

3. Some critics of Vonnegut become so preoccupied with Trout that they attach more importance to him than his actual place in this particular novel deserves. Later, he will become a major character in *Slaughterhouse-Five*, *Breakfast of Champions*, and *Jailbird*, while making an appearance in *Galápagos*.

4. Eliot's belief that he was responsible, at least in part, for the death by drowning during a boating accident of his beloved mother reinforces his feeling of guilt.

5. Uphaus unaccountably substitutes Christ for God, the Creator, as he describes Eliot's blessing as "his last Christ-like words" (166). Nowhere in the Bible does Jesus ask anyone to "multiply."

6. Broer attributes all of Eliot's problems, guilt, and "insanity" to his "lifelong unwillingness to deal with the . . . painful and immediate hostilities between himself and his father" (78), which severely oversimplifies the novel.

WORKS CITED

Allen, William Rodney, ed. *Conversations with Kurt Vonnegut.* Jackson, MS: University Press of Mississippi, 1988.

Bellamy, Joe David and John Casey. "Kurt Vonnegut." In Allen, *Conversations with Kurt Vonnegut,* 156–167.

Bradford, William. "Of Plymouth Plantation." In McMichael, *Anthology of American Literature,* 33–50.

Broer, Lawrence R. *Sanity Plea: Schizophrenia in the Novels of Kurt Vonnegut.* Ann Arbor: University of Michigan Research Press, 1989.

Emerson, Ralph Waldo. "Self-Reliance." In McMichael, *Anthology of American Literature,* 1318–1338.

Giannone, Richard. "Violence in the Fiction of Kurt Vonnegut." *Thought* 56 (1981):58–76.

Godshalk, William L. "Vonnegut and Shakespeare: Rosewater at Elsinore." *Critique: Studies in Modern Fiction* 15 (1973):37–48. In Mustazza, *Response,* 99–106.

Hume, Kathryn. "Vonnegut's Self-Projections: Symbolic Characters and Symbolic Fiction." *The Journal of Narrative Technique* 12 (Fall 1982):177–190. In Mustazza, *Response,* 231–243.

Jefferson, Thomas. "Letter to John Adams." In McMichael, *Anthology of American Literature,* 483–487.

Leff, Leonard. "Utopia Reconstructed: Alienation in Vonnegut's *God Bless You, Mr. Rosewater.*" *Critique: Studies in Modern Fiction* 12 (3):29–37.

Mayo, Clark. *Kurt Vonnegut: The Gospel from Outer Space.* San Bernardino: Borgo Press, 1977.

McMichael, George, ed. *Anthology of American Literature: Colonial Through Romantic.* New York: Macmillan, 1974.

Morse, Donald E. *A Readers' Guide to Kurt Vonnegut.* San Bernardino: Borgo Press, 1992.

Mustazza, Leonard, ed. *The Critical Response to Kurt Vonnegut.* Westport, CT: Greenwood Press, 1994.

———. *Forever Pursuing Genesis: The Myth of Eden in the Novels of Kurt Vonnegut.* Lewisburg: Bucknell University Press, 1990.

Schatt, Stanley. "The World of Kurt Vonnegut, Jr." *Critique: Studies in Modern Fiction* 12 (3):54–69.

Standish, David. "*Playboy* Interview." In Allen, *Conversations with Kurt Vonnegut,* 76–110.

Uphaus, Robert W. "Expected Meaning in Vonnegut's Dead-End Fiction." *NOVEL: A Forum on Fiction* 8.2 (1975). In Mustazza, *Response,* 165–174.

Vonnegut, Kurt. *Cat's Cradle.* New York: Holt, Rinehart & Winston, 1963; Dell, 1963.

———. *God Bless You, Mr. Rosewater.* New York: Holt, Rinehart & Winston, 1965; Dell, 1966.

———. *Jailbird.* New York: Delacorte Press, 1979; Dell, 1980.

———. *Mother Night.* Greenwich, CT: Fawcett, 1961; New York: Harper & Row, 1966 (includes the now standard introduction); Dell, 1974.

———. *The Sirens of Titan.* New York: Dell, 1959.

———. *Wampeters, Foma & Granfalloons.* New York: Delacorte Press, 1974; Dell 1976.

Kurt and Joe

The Artistic Collaboration of Kurt Vonnegut and Joe Petro III

John Dinsmore and Ollie Lyon

I first met Ollie Lyon in Lexington, Kentucky, in the late 1980s, when we were members of a business consulting team. One noon while having lunch with Ollie at Suggins' Bar & Grill, a favorite lunching spot in our neighborhood, I brought up Kurt Vonnegut's name in reference to something, quite by accident. Ollie glanced over at me and replied that he'd known Kurt for years, was an old friend of Kurt's. My jaw dropped.

This was, to say the least, quite a revelation to me. I'd read Kurt's first book, *Player Piano*, in 1961, as a University of Minnesota undergraduate, got hooked on Vonnegut, and remained an enthusiastic reader and collector of Kurt's books since then. Ollie went on to mention how he and Kurt first met at General Electric (GE) in Schenectady, New York, in the late 1940s, following their military service with the U.S. army in World War II, in the European theater. Long story short, they became fast friends during their tenure at GE, and have remained in touch with each other ever since that time.

Ollie Lyon turned out to be one of the most engaging gentlemen I've been privileged to meet during my (now fifty-eight) years on the planet, and it was my good fortune that we became frequent lunchin' buddies, often returning to Suggins' for good food and talk. In 1991, I made a decision to engage in the modern first editions book-selling business. I brought it up with Ollie, highly knowledgeable about a lot of things, who discussed the pros and cons as he knew them from a friend who'd been in the book business. Full steam ahead, I created my first catalog of books for sale in July 1991, and advertised its availability in *Firsts*, an extraordinary book collectors' magazine that had just begun publication in January 1991. In fact, it was the appearance of *Firsts* that eliminated any hesitation I'd had about getting into the modern first editions business. Then another shoe dropped.

I can still recall that sunny afternoon in summer 1991 when I got a local phone call from a man who said he'd seen a copy of my new catalog in a local book store, and was calling to inquire about what Kurt Vonnegut books I might still have available. The caller turned out to be Joe Petro III (long "e"); he wanted to get together ASAP. I agreed, and a few hours later a tall, friendly, thirty-something chap wearing shorts walked into our home. He told me he was an artist and showed me some of the projects he'd completed, including dazzling, multicolored silkscreens and posters for Greenpeace. We talked for some time about art, books, and, inevitably, Kurt Vonnegut, whose books Joe had collected for over twenty years—collected seriously. Joe and I became fast friends and colleagues and engaged in some swapping/selling of Vonnegut books, art books, all kinds of stuff.

I'd already written two articles for *Firsts*, one on author bibliographies, the other on book collectors and computers (the latter became quite popular with *Firsts* readers, and I continue to create an annual update for the magazine). I decided that it might be interesting to interview Ollie Lyon about his early career days at GE, where he first met Kurt, and talk about how it was back then. Ollie agreed, so did the editors, and they published the interview as an article called "Kurt and Ollie," which appeared in the October 1992 issue of *Firsts*. Ollie dug up an old, previously unpublished snapshot of Kurt, and one of himself. The article garnered substantial interest in bookselling and book collecting circles, but little did we realize the amazing story that would unfold as a result.

After the *Firsts* issue appeared, I gave copies to both Ollie and Joe. It didn't take long for Joe to mention that he'd like to meet Ollie. I thought it might be fun, and set up a lunch for the three of us at Suggins' Bar & Grill. Ollie and Joe hit it off from the very first. We recalled how Kurt had traveled to Lexington in 1991 to give his entertaining lecture-performance, "How to Get a Job Like Mine," at Transylvania University. It was a sellout crowd. Joe's artist father, also named Joe Petro, was on the art faculty at Transy, so Joe III got a ticket for the event and was able to meet Kurt for the first time. During lunch, Ollie mentioned, as a member of the Development Council of Midway College (a few miles outside of Lexington), that he was considering inviting Kurt to come back to Lexington sometime in 1993 for another performance, as a fundraiser for a new library building at Midway.

Joe brought up his idea of doing some sort of artistic collaboration with Kurt and showed Ollie some of his work. Ollie took the idea and Joe's posters to the Midway Development Council. They agreed, after a discussion or two, that it might be interesting to have Kurt and Joe do some self-portraits of Kurt, to be offered for sale to raise additional funds for the Midway library. Ollie discussed it with Kurt off and on, and by summer 1993, most of the plans for Kurt's appearance and involvement with the artistic project were under way. In New York, Kurt (who donated his time for the project) would design the self-portrait images on acetate sheets furnished by Joe and ship them back to Lexington. Joe, an accomplished silkscreen artist, would pull proofs of the silkscreen images and send them to Kurt for his examination and approval. Then Joe (who also donated his time) would be responsible for pulling each set of the silkscreens.

As the self-portrait collaboration project took off in the summer of 1993, Kurt and Joe developed an easy rapport during their nearly daily telephone conversations between New York and the Bluegrass. I visited Joe's studio in downtown

Lexington on numerous occasions to see how things were moving along and recall arriving one morning to find Joe in a tizzy.

"Kurt just called," he yelled. "He wants the background for the large self-portrait pulled in battleship gray. What the hell is battleship gray?" Joe was standing at his silkscreen table, stirring a plastic quart container with some gray ink in it.

"Where's your black ink?" I asked. "Add some." Joe opened a can, poured in a healthy dollop, stirred a bit, pulled out the stir stick. "More black," I demanded. Joe added more black, checked the stir stick. "That's battleship gray," I said.

"How do you know?" he asked.

"Trust me," I replied, with conviction. When Joe sent the proof to New York, Kurt agreed, and that color became "battleship gray" in the large "Self-Portrait No. 1," one of three self-portrait silkscreens executed by Kurt and Joe for Midway College.

Federal Express got real busy during summer and fall, shuttling large cartons of silkscreen prints back and forth between Lexington and New York. The two collaborators ("conspirators" is perhaps the better term) laid an enigmatic handle on this stage of their efforts: "The Origami Express Project." Many of the large shipping cartons were hand-lettered thus, and decorated, often humorously, with additional drawings and messages. Final prints went to Kurt for signing, then came back to Joe for embossing. Here's the result:

LIMITED EDITION SILKSCREENS, CREATED, AND SIGNED BY KURT VONNEGUT

Kurt Vonnegut's first-time artistic use of the silkscreen process: His personal, quintessential self-portrait profile drawing, created by the author/artist and transformed into original silkscreen impressions by Lexington, Kentucky, artist Joe Petro III.

SELF-PORTRAIT NO. 1. Limited, numbered edition of 235 impressions, signed in pencil by Kurt Vonnegut. Silkscreen executed in four colors: Red, blue, two shades of gray. On Rives paper with deckled edges. 30" H x 22" W.

SELF-PORTRAIT NO. 2. Limited, numbered edition of 100 impressions, signed in pencil by Kurt Vonnegut. Silkscreen executed in three colors: Red, two shades of gray. On Lenox paper with hand-torn edges. 28" H x 22" W.

SELF-PORTRAIT NO. 3. Limited, numbered edition of 100 impressions, signed in pencil by Kurt Vonnegut. Silkscreen executed in two colors: Red and gray. On Lenox paper with hand-torn edges. 18" H x 12.5" W.

SELF-PORTRAIT NO. 2. Limited, unnumbered edition of 200 impressions, unsigned. Silkscreen executed in five colors: Two shades of red, blue, two shades of gray. On Lenox paper with cut edges. 40" H x 26" W. A poster commemorating Mr. Vonnegut's November 1993 lecture appearance to assist the Development Council of Midway College, located at Midway, Kentucky, in their quest to fund a new Library building ("Noodle Factory"[1]) for the College.

Ollie asked Kurt to stay with him and his wife, Billie, at their home during Kurt's visit. His performance was scheduled for 8:00 p.m. on Monday, November 1, 1993, at a large meeting hall in downtown Lexington. Ollie met him at the airport Sunday evening and shuttled him to the house to rest up. At 6:00 p.m. Monday there was a by-invitation reception for Kurt at a private club downtown. Many people associated with Midway College were in attendance, a very pleasant and low-key event. Kurt and Joe's framed silkscreens were displayed on easels, their first "public" showing. The silkscreens were then moved to the meeting hall lobby, where they were offered for sale along with Vonnegut T-shirts. The meeting hall was full by 8:00, with a large number of high school and college students present. Ollie drove Kurt around back to a private entrance, and Kurt came out to a great round of applause. His performance was a huge success. Afterward, Ollie and Billie entertained a small gathering at their home with a buffet and drinks.

There was quite an agenda for Kurt during his visit. He met with Peter Reed, a Vonnegut scholar from the University of Minnesota who has written extensively on Kurt's work. Also in town for the occasion were Marc Leeds, who wrote *The Vonnegut Encyclopedia* (published by Greenwood Press in November 1995), and Asa Pieratt, Kurt's bibliographer for well over two decades. On the morning before Kurt's performance, a small group met at Joe's downtown Lexington studio where photos and videotape were taken while Kurt and Joe talked. Then Kurt left with Ollie and Joe to get to a local television studio where Kurt was interviewed. Kurt also met later with some World War II veterans who had been with him in the slaughterhouse at Dresden, Germany, during the fire-bombing, which he had described in his great novel, *Slaughterhouse-Five*.

During Kurt's visit, it became apparent that his and Joe's artistic collaboration with the Midway silkscreen project was only the tip of the iceberg. Kurt had told Joe earlier that he had some other artistic projects in mind, and he invited Joe to continue with the collaboration. Since then, they have produced around twenty original silkscreens in signed, limited editions, based on designs Kurt had created over the years, with titles such as "Sphincter," "Wasp Waist," "One-Eyed Jack," "Egyptian Architect," "Nostalgia," and "Cheops."

"Sphincter" is a very large image of Kurt's asterisk ("asshole") signature, produced in a tiny limited edition of thirty-six signed impressions. This image was later retitled "Asterisk" and assembled as a deluxe set of ten prints, each a different color asterisk, and presented in a handcrafted, black cloth portfolio box. Only ten sets were created. A similar deluxe edition was completed for "Wasp Waist."

In 1995, Kurt asked Joe to transform some of his designs into sculptures, which was done. Joe had earlier created a national advertisement for Absolut Vodka, and asked Kurt if he'd like to get involved. The result was "Absolut Vonnegut," a large color art piece that appeared for the first time in the *New Yorker* magazine, in the June 26/July 3 double issue, and also in the August 1995 issue of *Harper's* and other quality magazines. The advertisement is based on an original design by Kurt, using his fifth book, *Cat's Cradle*, as basis for the graphic motif.

What other projects will emerge from this collaboration is conjecture. Kurt and Joe's relationship is genuine, and established. They have only their creative imaginations, and their time, to come up with new productions that will satisfy both of them while continuing to amaze and delight the collectors of these editions.

NOTE

1. See Vonnegut's essay, "The Noodle Factory," concerning the dedication of a new university library, in his *Palm Sunday* (1981).

More Graphics by Kurt Vonnegut

Peter J. Reed

The Appendix of the present editors' *The Vonnegut Chronicles* describes Kurt Vonnegut's increasing interest in working in the visual arts in recent years. It recounts how this interest led in 1993 to his working relationship with Joe Petro III, the artist from Lexington, Kentucky, who silkscreens what Vonnegut has painted on acetate sheets. This partnership has continued, and by 1998 the catalog of Vonnegut's art contained fifty-one items.

The small selection that follows illustrates some of the more recent work. It exhibits the same characteristics evident in the earlier selection in *Chronicles*, viz, whimsical humor, wit, abstraction of facial features, bold lines, sparing color, and architectural structure. The combination of heavy framing, over which the subject sometimes protrudes, receding lines, and open white spaces often accentuates perspective and depth, as in "Prozac." If anything, the later graphics seem more spare and more abstract than their predecessors. Human physiognomy still often provides the starting point for abstraction, as can be seen in "Strings."

There was a time when Vonnegut was quite emphatic about keeping his visual art separate from his writing (despite having brought his drawing into his writing in *Slaughterhouse-Five* and *Breakfast of Champions*). In "Absolut Vonnegut," the 1995 painting commissioned by Absolut Vodka as part of a series of works by famous figures, there are obviously allusions to his novel *Cat's Cradle*. More recently he has taken familiar subjects from the fiction as the subjects for artworks. One in particular, "Trout in Cohoes," depicts the science-fiction writing alter-ego with eleven eyes, with the birdcage of Bill, Trout's parakeet, standing open in the background. Readers will remember that story from *Breakfast of Champions*. Tralfamadore, the planet from whence aliens come in *The Sirens of Titan* and *Slaughterhouse-Five*, becomes the subject of two other graphics.

Kurt Vonnegut would wish his readers and viewers to make what they will of these works. But one further note. Most people today do not remember that November 11, 1918, marked the end of the First World War. Vonnegut's birthday is also on November 11. He remembers how in his younger days it was a holiday called Armistice Day, commemorated by a minute's silence at the eleventh hour of the eleventh day of the eleventh month, marking the moment all hostilities ceased. "November 11, 1918" was originally to be titled "Peace Monument."

"Absolut Vonnegut"
1995. 22 x 30 inches. Edition of 30. Each monotype is hand-printed in nineteen colors. All artwork courtesy of Kurt Vonnegut and Joe Petro III. Reproduced with kind permission.

"Astronomy"
1996. 10^5/$_8$ x 5^1/$_2$ inches. Edition of 30. Light blue eye, dark red and green eyebag, orange between the
two bottom frame lines.

"Tralfamadore #1"
1996. 22 x 30 inches. Edition of 30. Six colors, predominantly green and red.

"Tralfamadore #2"
1996. 22 x 30 inches. Edition of 30. Seven colors and black.

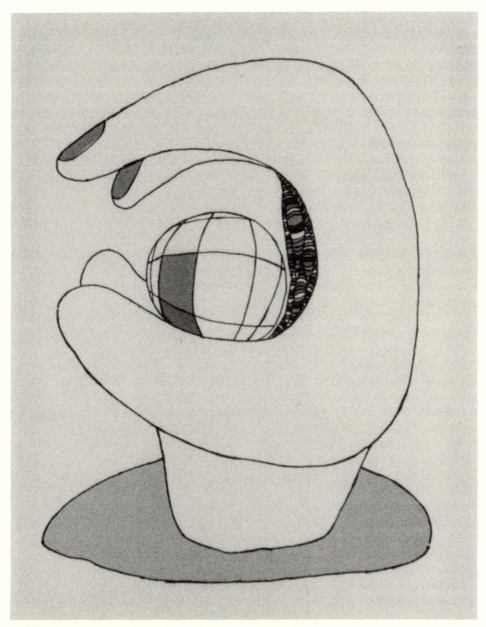

"November 11, 1918"
1996. 22 x 30 inches. Edition of 30. Gray base, red finger nails, blue and red panels in the globe.

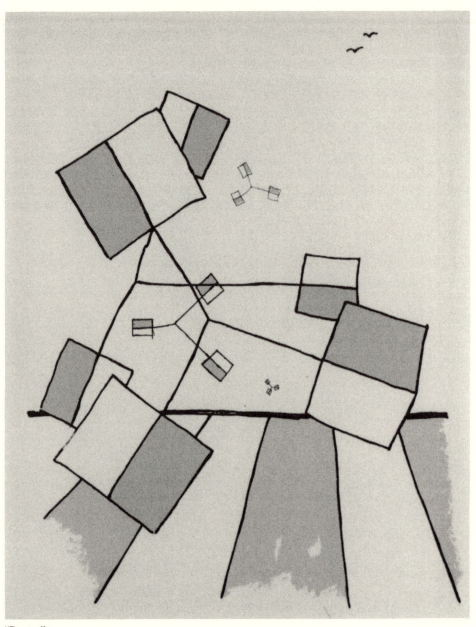

"Prozac"
1996. 22 x 15 inches. Edition of 30. Yellow panels on the figures, light blue in the lower strips.

"Trout in Cohoes"
1997. 22 x 30 inches. Edition of 77. Medium green and medium blue in sweater and eyes. There are also a deluxe edition and a special edition of 18 and 6, respectively, in eight colors and on different papers. These are signed by Kurt Vonnegut and "Kilgore Trout in Cohoes, 1975," in pencil. Each also has a self-portrait remarque in pencil by Vonnegut.

"Strings"

1996. 15 x 22 inches. Edition of 30. Blue background, yellow balls. Hand-printed in four colors. Yellow, medium blue, tan, and black, on white Coventry paper. The upper two-thirds background is blue; the small circles are yellow and tan, centered.

Selected Bibliography

Allen, William Rodney, ed. *Conversations with Kurt Vonnegut*. Jackson: University Press of Mississippi, 1988.

Arber, Agnes. *The Manifold and the One*. Wheaton, IL: Theosophical, 1967.

Baedeker Allianz Reiseführer: Dresden. 4th ed., s.v. "Tabakkontor Yenidze." Stuttgart, Germany: Verlag Karl Baedeker, 1995.

Borges, Jorge Luis. *Labyrinths: Selected Stories and Other Writings*. 1962. Ed. Donald D. Yates and James E. Erby. New York: New Directions, 1964.

Bradford, William. "Of Plymouth Plantation." In *Anthology of American Literature*, ed. George McMichael, 33–50. New York: Macmillan, 1974.

Broer, Lawrence R. *Sanity Plea: Schizophrenia in the Novels of Kurt Vonnegut*. Ann Arbor, MI: UMI Research Press, 1989.

Dällenbach, Lucien. *The Mirror in the Text*. 1971. Trans. Jeremy Whitley and Emma Hughes. Chicago: University of Chicago Press, 1989.

Farmer, Philip Jose. *Venus on the Half-Shell*. New York: Dell/A Laurel Edition, 1974.

Flaubert, Gustave. *The Temptation of Saint Anthony*. Trans. Kitty Mrosobsky. Ithaca, NY: Cornell University Press, 1981.

Freese, Peter. "Surviving the End: Apocalypse, Evolution, and Entropy in Bernard Malamud, Kurt Vonnegut, and Thomas Pynchon." *Critique: Studies in Contemporary Fiction* 36.3 (1995).

Frye, Northrop. "The Argument of Comedy." In *Shakespeare: Modern Essays in Criticism*, ed. Leonard F. Dean. New York: Oxford University Press/A Galaxy Book, 1967.

Giannone, Richard. "Violence in the Fiction of Kurt Vonnegut." *Thought* 56 (1981).

Gleick, James. *Chaos: Making a New Science*. New York: Penguin, 1987.

Goethe, Johann Wolfgang von. *Faust: Part One and Part Two*. Trans. Charles E. Passage. Indianapolis: Library of Liberal Arts/Bobbs-Merrill Company, Inc., 1965.

Das Große Duden-Lexikon in acht Bänden. Ed. Lexikonredaktion des Bibliographischen Instituts, vol. 2, s.v. "Dresden China." Mannheim, Germany: Lexikonverlag, 1967.

Hall, James. *The Tragic Comedians*. Bloomington: Indiana University Press, 1967.

Hayles, N. Katherine. *Chaos and Order: Complex Dynamics in Literature and Science*. Chicago: University of Chicago Press, 1991.

Hume, Kathryn. "The Heraclitean Cosmos of Kurt Vonnegut." *Papers on Language and Literature* 18.2 (spring 1982): 208–224.

Jung, C. G. *Memories, Dreams, Reflections.* Trans. Richard Winston and Clara Winston. New York: Vintage.

Jung, C. G. *Psychological Reflections.* Ed. Jolande Jacobi and R.F.C. Hull. New York: Bollingen Foundation, 1953. Princeton: Princeton University Press, 1970.

Leeds, Marc. *The Vonnegut Encyclopedia: An Authorized Compendium.* Westport, CT: Greenwood Press, 1995.

Leff, Leonard. "Utopia Reconstructed: Alienation in Vonnegut's *God Bless You, Mr. Rosewater.*" *Critique: Studies in Modern Fiction* 12.3: 29–37.

Mayo, Clark. *Kurt Vonnegut: The Gospel from Outer Space.* San Bernardino: Borgo Press, 1977.

McMichael, George, ed. *Anthology of American Literature: Colonial Through Romantic.* New York: Macmillan, 1974.

Melville, Herman. *Moby-Dick; or The Whale.* New York: Heritage Press, 1943.

Morse, Donald E. *A Readers' Guide to Kurt Vonnegut.* San Bernardino: Borgo Press, 1992.

Mustazza, Leonard, ed. *The Critical Response to Kurt Vonnegut.* Westport, CT: Greenwood Press, 1994.

Mustazza, Leonard. *Forever Pursuing Genesis: The Myth of Eden in the Novels of Kurt Vonnegut.* Lewisburg, PA: Bucknell University Press, 1990.

Paeschke, Carl-Ludwig, and Dieter Zimmer. *Dresden: Geschichten einer Stadt.* Berlin: Brandenburgisches Verlagshaus, 1994.

Paz, Octavio. *Children of the Mire.* Trans. Rachel Phillips. Cambridge: Harvard University Press, 1974.

Prigogine, Ilya. "Man's New Dialogue with Nature," *Perkins Journal* (summer 1983): 4–14.

Reed, Peter J. *Kurt Vonnegut, Jr.* New York: Thomas Y. Crowell/Warner Books, Inc., 1972.

Reed, Peter J. *The Short Fiction of Kurt Vonnegut.* Westport, CT: Greenwood Press, 1997.

Reed, Peter J., and Marc Leeds, eds. *The Vonnegut Chronicles.* Westport, CT: Greenwood Press, 1996.

Rose, William, ed. *The Historie of the Damnable Life and Deserved Death of Doctor John Faustus.* 1592. Notre Dame, IN: University of Notre Dame Press, 1963.

Schatt, Stanley. "The World of Kurt Vonnegut, Jr." *Critique: Studies in Modern Fiction* 12.3: 54–69.

Weidlich, Brigitte, ed. *Dresden in alten Ansichtskarten.* Frankfurt/Main: Gondrom Verlag, 1994.

NOVELS AND COLLECTED WORKS BY KURT VONNEGUT (*in order of publication*)

Player Piano. New York: Charles Scribner's Sons, 1952.

The Sirens of Titan. New York: Dell, 1959.

Canary in a Cat House. Greenwich, CT: Gold Medal/Fawcett, 1961.

Mother Night. New York: Harper and Row, Publishers, 1961, 1966.

Cat's Cradle. New York: Holt, Rinehart and Winston, 1963.

God Bless You, Mr. Rosewater. New York: Holt, Rinehart and Winston, 1965.

Welcome to the Monkey House. New York: Delacorte Press/Seymour Lawrence, 1968.

Slaughterhouse-Five. New York: Delacorte Press/Seymour Lawrence, 1969.

Happy Birthday, Wanda June. New York: Delacorte Press/Seymour Lawrence, 1970.

Breakfast of Champions. New York: Delacorte Press/Seymour Lawrence, 1973.

Wampeters, Foma & Granfalloons. New York: Delacorte Press, 1974; Dell, 1976.

Slapstick. New York: Delacorte Press/Seymour Lawrence, 1976.
Jailbird. New York: Delacorte Press/Seymour Lawrence, 1979.
Palm Sunday. New York: Dell, 1981.
Deadeye Dick. New York: Delacorte Press/Seymour Lawrence, 1982.
Galápagos. New York: Delacorte Press/Seymour Lawrence, 1985.
Bluebeard. New York: Delacorte Press, 1987.
Hocus Pocus. New York: Putnam, 1990.
Fates Worse Than Death: An Autobiographical Collage of the 1980s. New York: Putnam, 1991.
Timequake. New York: Putnam, 1997.

SHORT STORIES BY KURT VONNEGUT

"Custom-Made Bride." *The Saturday Evening Post*, March 24, 1951, 30, 86–87.
"EPICAC." *Collier's*, November 25, 1950, 36–37.
"The Foster Portfolio." *Collier's*, September 8, 1951, 18–19, 72–73.
"Go Back to Your Precious Wife and Son." *Ladies' Home Journal*, July 1962, 54–55, 110.
"Lovers Anonymous." *Redbook*, October 1963, 70, 146–148.
"Miss Temptation." *The Saturday Evening Post*, April 21, 1956, 30, 64.
"More Stately Mansions." *Collier's*, December 22, 1951, 24–25, 62–63.
"The Powder Blue Dragon." *Cosmopolitan*, November 1954, 46–48, 50–53.
"Report on the Barnhouse Effect." *Collier's*, February 11, 1950, 18–19, 63–65.
"Unpaid Consultant." *Cosmopolitan*, March 1955, 52–57.
"Unready to Wear." *Galaxy Science Fiction*, April 1953, 98–111.

Index

About the Editors and Contributors

JOHN DINSMORE, a former teacher of English and foreign languages and a university librarian, is currently a dealer of rare first-edition books and fine art prints in Lexington, Kentucky.

LESLIE A. FIEDLER, Ph.D., Samuel Clemens Professor of English and State University of New York Distinguished Professor at the University at Buffalo, did post-doctoral work at Harvard after receiving his Ph.D. from the University of Wisconsin. He is famous for his provocative views and passionate devotion to a nonelitist look at popular culture. The author of more than twenty-five books, including his most famous *Love and Death in the American Novel* and his most recent *The Tyranny of the Normal*, Fiedler has earned numerous awards and prizes for his criticism and fiction. He has lectured all over the world and many of his writings have been translated into other languages.

JULIE A. HIBBARD, a Wisconsin native, studied liberal arts and music at Coe College in Cedar Rapids, Iowa, completed a Master of Music degree at Miami University of Oxford, Ohio, and is currently finishing work for a Master's of Philosophy degree from the University of Northern Iowa. Hibbard has been living in Dresden since August 1996, teaching in the English department of the Technische Universität Dresden. She has published in *The Triangle of Mu Phi Epsilon* and *Carmina Philosophiae*, the journal of the International Boethius Society. Hibbard served as coauthor and editor of the English translation of the *Guide to Castle and Museum Nöthnitz* and of the proceedings of the annual German Anglistentag Conference, *Anglistentagsband* (1997), and her poetry has appeared in *Litspeak*, the journal of international creative writing in English, published by the Institut für Anglistik und Amerikanistik of Technische Universität Dresden.

JERRY HOLT, Ph.D., is Professor of English and Dean of the College of Arts and Sciences at Shawnee State University in Portsmouth, Ohio. He is also the author of the play *Rickey*, a one-person show based on the life of the legendary Branch Rickey, the man responsible for bringing Jackie Robinson into the major leagues and thereby integrating major league baseball. The play has been performed across the United States in venues which include the Baseball Hall of Fame in Cooperstown, New York. His article on the films of Paul Robeson is featured in the upcoming *Robeson Memorial Collection*, and his novel *The Killing of Strangers* was a finalist in the 1999 St. Martin's First Mystery Contest.

NANCY KAPITANOFF is a freelance writer living in Los Angeles. She is the contributing editor for American independent and foreign films for Tower Records's *Pulse!* magazine. A regular writer about art for the *Los Angeles Times* and a curator of photography exhibitions, Kapitanoff's essay in this collection appeared in a shortened form in *Written By*, the Journal of the Writers Guild of America.

JEROME KLINKOWITZ, Ph.D., Professor of English and Distinguished Scholar at the University of Northern Iowa, has authored over thirty books on literature, art, music, philosophy, sports, military history, and other aspects of contemporary culture. His seven volumes on Kurt Vonnegut reach from *The Vonnegut Statement* (1973) through *Vonnegut in Fact* (1998). He is also an editor of *The Norton Anthology of American Literature*, fifth edition (1998).

MARC LEEDS, Ph.D., authored *The Vonnegut Encyclopedia: An Authorized Compendium* and together with Peter J. Reed coedited and contributed to *The Vonnegut Chronicles: Interviews and Essays* (Greenwood, 1996). Leeds has also written a number of articles on computer-assisted instruction. He is currently a freelance writer and research analyst for an investment banking firm in Boca Raton, Florida. Leeds directed computer-assisted writing programs at Shawnee State University in Ohio and East Tennessee State University.

OLLIE LYON and Kurt Vonnegut have known each other since meeting as public relations specialists at the General Electric Co., Schenectady, New York, in the late 1940s, following their military service in the U.S. Army during World War II. They have remained friends ever since. Ollie continued his career in New York, Rome, and elsewhere as a vice president of Young and Rubicam, the New York advertising firm. He and his wife, Billie, later returned home to Lexington, Kentucky, where he served as an active member of the Board of Trustees at Midway College.

DONALD E. MORSE, Ph.D., Rockefeller Study Fellow; Soros Visiting Professorship of American Studies; Professor of English and Rhetoric, Oakland University, and Visiting Professor of English and Fulbright Professor in American Studies, Kossuth University, Debrecen, Hungary, a prolific author and editor,

Morse's works include poetry, ten volumes of criticism, and more than fifty articles. He also served as Chairman of the Board, Hungarian-American Fulbright Commission, Executive Secretary of the National College English Association, and Chair of the International Association for the Fantastic in the Arts.

MICHELLE PERSELL, Ph.D., received her degree from the University of California, Santa Barbara for her dissertation *George Gissing and the Dickensian Inheritance*. Her recent publications include "Capitalism, Charity and Judaism: The Trumvirate of Benjamin Farjeon" (forthcoming in *Victorian Literature and Cutlure*), "The Jews, *Ragtime* and the Politics of Silence" (*Literature and Psychology*, 1996), and "Dickensian Disciple: Anglo-Jewish Identity and the Christmas Tales of Benjamin Farjeon" (*Philological Quarterly*, 1994). Her current projects include a book-length project on George Gissing and the article "'How Can I Be Both That and This?': Fictions of the Self and the Trial of John Demjanjuk in Philip Roth's *Operation Shylock*."

LOREE RACKSTRAW, M.F.A., Emeritus Professor English at the University of Northen Iowa, was a student of Kurt Vonnegut when she studied in the Iowa Writers' Workshop. The former fiction editor of the *North American Review*, Rackstraw has taught fiction writing, mythology, and interdisciplinary courses in the humanities.

PETER J. REED, Ph.D., Professor of English at the University of Minnesota, wrote the first book-length treatment of Kurt Vonnegut in 1972, *Writers for the 70s: Kurt Vonnegut*. He has written biographical essays on Vonnegut and critical studies of his fiction for numerous journals and collections. With Marc Leeds he edited *The Vonnegut Chronicles: Interviews and Essays* (Greenwood, 1996), and is the author of *The Short Fiction of Kurt Vonnegut* (Greenwood, 1997). He collected the short stories in Kurt Vonnegut's *Bagombo Snuff Box* (1999), and for which he wrote the preface. Like Vonnegut, Reed is a survivor of aerial bombardment—his childhood home in London was destroyed in the Blitz.

SHARON SIEBER, Ph.D., Assistant Professor of Spanish at Idaho State University and a recent Fulbright Professor in Colombia, has published articles in *Taller de Letras*, *Selecta*, *Feministas Unidas*, and the *CEA Forum*, and is currently working on a book on Octavio Paz and "Simultaneity." Recent publications include: "Elena Garro's New Synthesis: Epic and History in *Los recuerdos del porvenir*"; "The Dream Image: Simultaneity in *Viento entero*," and "The Deconstruction of Gender as Archetype in Rosario Castellanos' *El eterno femenino*." Sieber is special editor and contributor to an issue of Idaho State University's academic journal *Rendezvous* on translation, and is translating a novel set during the time of the Spanish Civil War and its aftermath.

ERIC SIMENSON wrote the stage adaptation for and directed the production of *Slaughterhouse-Five* for the Steppenwolf Theatre in Chicago. He is the recipient of the NAACP Media Award, the Princess Grace Foundation Award, and received a Tony nomination for directing *The Song of Jacob Zulu*. He is currently working with on a trilogy of plays based on the life of Frank Lloyd Wright.

ROBERT B. WEIDE wrote and produced the screen adaptation of Kurt Vonnegut's novel *Mother Night*, starring Nick Nolte, John Goodman, Sheryl Lee, Alan Arkin, and Kirsten Dunst. After more than a decade, he is nearing completion of his authorized film biography *Kurt Vonnegut: American Made*. His next feature script is an adaptation of Vonnegut's 1959 novel, *The Sirens of Titan*. His other credits include *The Marx Brothers in a Nutshell*; *The Great Stand-ups*; *Mort Sahl: The Loyal Opposition*; *Lenny Bruce: Swear to Tell the Truth*; and *W. C. Fields Straight Up*, winner of the national Emmy award as Outstanding Information Special. Weide is president and founder of Whyaduck Productions, Inc., and from 1990–1994 served as vice president of Development for Rollins & Joffe, Inc. (producers of Woody Allen's movies). He has lectured at several colleges and universities and conducted seminars on producing, writing, comedy, and film history.

ISBN 0-313-30975-2

90000>

EAN

9 780313 309755

HARDCOVER BAR CODE